Wanting a Daughter, Needing a Son

Wanting a Daughter, Needing a Son

Abandonment, Adoption, and Orphanage Care in China

Kay Ann Johnson

Edited with an Introduction by Amy Klatzkin

YEONG & YEONG BOOK COMPANY
ST. PAUL, MINNESOTA

Yeong & Yeong Book Company
1368 Michelle Drive
St. Paul, Minnesota 55123-1459
www.yeongandyeong.com

Designed by Stephanie Billecke

Library of Congress Cataloging-in-Publication Data
Johnson, Kay Ann.
   Wanting a daughter, needing a son : abandonment, adoption, and
orphanage care in China / Kay Johnson ; edited with an introduction by
Amy Klatzkin.
      p. cm.
Includes bibliographical references and index.
   ISBN 0-9638472-7-9 (hardcover : alk. paper)
   1. Orphanages—China. 2. Adoption—China. 3. Abandoned
children—China. 4. Intercountry adoption—China. 5. Intercountry
adoption—United States. I. Title.
   HV1317.J64 2004
   362.73'0951—dc21
                                                        2003010625

Printed on acid-free paper

Manufactured in the United States of America
13   12   11   10   09   08   07   06   05   04

In memory of
D. Gale Johnson
Loving father, grandfather, teacher
July 10, 1916–April 13, 2003

Contents

Acknowledgments

I have received support for the research presented in this volume from many sources over the past twelve years. The Ford Foundation provided two generous grants for extensive collaborative research in China, and the National Endowment for the Humanities awarded two fellowship grants to allow me time off from a hectic teaching schedule to analyze and write about my research findings. I am also grateful to Hampshire College for unfailingly providing support each summer through faculty development grants to help me move forward with my work even when I was teaching full time.

My work is greatly indebted to the collaborative efforts of my fellow researchers in China, particularly Huang Banghan of Anhui Agricultural University and Wang Liyao of the Anhui Academy of Social Sciences. The most important research in this volume would have been impossible without them. Many others at Anhui Agricultural University and the Anhui Academy of Social Sciences have helped as well. My multiple connections to this network of friends and colleagues have been one of the greatest personal satisfactions that I have gained from this work. Hefei has indeed been a home away from home for me.

Among my American colleagues I am most profoundly indebted to Susan Greenhalgh, who more than ten years ago encouraged me to wade deeper into these intellectual waters. Since then she has served as a long-distance mentor in a subfield of

China studies that was new to me at the beginning of this work. As an anthropologist and China scholar, she pioneered efforts to better understand the impact of population policy on China's little girls and shared with me her writing, her critical analysis, and her unswerving commitment to furthering that inquiry. Not only has her work inspired and influenced mine in both fundamental and particular ways (as the notes in this book clearly attest), but she has also generously read and provided invaluable feedback on the early drafts of many of the articles that appear in this volume. My intellectual and personal debt to her is enormous.

In recent years, Tyrene White has shared her work in population studies and helped me develop my understanding of the political dynamics of birth-planning policies. She has become an important colleague, one who shares not only my academic interests, but also the joyous experience of adopting and raising a child from China. In addition, I am thankful to Zhang Weiguo for sharing with me his current research on adoption in rural China. His insights on the increasing value of daughters in adoption and his ongoing research in this area have given me a deeper understanding of the dynamics of rural family change and greater confidence in my own and others' findings on Chinese villagers' growing desire for daughters.

Families with Children from China (FCC), especially the New York and New England chapters, has provided moral support and access to an eager and appreciative lay audience for the academic work I do. The many opportunities I have had to write for and speak to the adoption community through FCC have been a privilege, one that has given my work far greater meaning than it would have had if it had remained confined to academic journals and conferences. I feel a personal connection to this community and a sense of obligation to share what knowledge I have with those who, like me, have undertaken the sometimes daunting task of raising a child adopted from China in North America. It is my hope that I can help provide a greater understanding of the conditions in China that gave rise to our international adoptions.

For the children who have been adopted internationally, I hope to provide some historical record of their origins and of the experience of their cohort who stayed in China. Someday, when today's children are young adults, I believe that many of them, including my own daughter, will want to learn more about where they came from and why they ended up crossing national and cultural borders to find new families. My greatest personal and professional satisfaction will come if and when they find the work presented here useful in their quest for this knowledge.

I am additionally grateful to FCC and its vast network of adoptive families in the United States and Canada who have graciously hosted and shared their adoption experiences with my Chinese colleagues in their research trips to North America. This generosity and openness have made a truly reciprocal relationship possible, providing Chinese scholars with the opportunity to understand the situation of adopted Chinese children in North America while we have been helped to learn more about our children's lives in China before they were adopted. FCC–New York generously provided financial support for this purpose as well. For all of this assistance, I am most grateful.

My family also provided support, and tolerance, for my long hours of work over the past twelve years, as I squeezed my research and scholarship into a full-time teaching schedule. Since kindergarten, my daughter has more than once identified her mother to friends as "the woman in front of the computer." Both my son and my daughter have cheerfully accompanied me to China on numerous occasions as I dragged them around to the places most important to my work, making it possible for me to have my children and my work too. When I needed to make extended research trips alone, my spouse and co-parent, Bill Grohmann, gladly took on the responsibilities of a full-time single parent for whatever period of time I needed to be away. Although I always missed my family, I never needed to worry about them. Without such support, carrying out research 10,000 miles from home would have been far more stressful.

My father played a most special role throughout these twelve years. He was there when I adopted my daughter in Wuhan in early 1991, helping me bring her to Guangzhou, Hong Kong, and home to the United States when she was small, vulnerable, and sick. He was also a most important colleague to me in recent years, as he made China the center of his academic interests and personal commitments in the final years of his professional life. An internationally renowned agricultural economist and a dedicated teacher, he shifted his research and teaching concerns to understanding the impact of post-Mao economic reforms on the lives of Chinese farmers and built a network of Chinese economics students, mostly at Beijing University, who have become like extended family in China. A loving grandfather and devoted father, he has been my fact-checker on the Chinese economy and my teacher on the relationship between population growth and economic development. His intellectual contribution to my work is palpable and incalculable. This book is dedicated to his memory. In 2002 he moved to my home in Amherst from Chicago, where he had lived and taught at the University of

Chicago for sixty years. His grandchildren, especially my daughter LiLi Helen (named after my mother), were the light of his life in his later years. Indeed, he loved children and had a special place in his heart for them. The only time I ever saw him cry openly and publicly, other than at my mother's death, was the first time he walked through a Chinese orphanage. He died on April 13, 2003, just as I was finishing this manuscript. It was exactly twelve years to the day that he escorted me to the Hong Kong airport to bring my daughter LiLi home to the United States for the first time. Over the past twelve years, he accompanied us to China on many occasions, making it possible for me to travel with young children and work at the same time. I will be eternally grateful to him for all he has given me and will always miss his gentle, dignified spirit and commitment to knowledge in the pursuit of a more humane world.

Finally, I would like to thank our publisher, Brian Boyd, who has been serving the adoption community for many years. I am grateful to him for wholeheartedly embracing the idea of publishing this collection as a resource for adoptive families with children from China and for the children themselves as they grow older. Last but definitely not least, I would like to thank my colleague, fellow adoptive parent, and editor, Amy Klatzkin. It was originally her idea to pull my academic research on abandonment, adoption, and orphanage care in China together in one place and make it more accessible to the adoption community. Her unwavering devotion to this project has made it possible. An experienced China studies editor and adoption writer, she has taught me concision in writing, a lesson I hope I shall be able to carry forward, and has worked tirelessly to turn my disparate articles into an edited whole. She has also put up with my erratic schedule and, in the last months, the emotional distress that accompanies enormous loss. I am extremely grateful to her for her friendship, her patience, and her professional talents.

K.J.

Amherst, Mass., July 2003

Introduction

By Amy Klatzkin

In all of 1988 the U.S. State Department issued 12 immigrant visas to children adopted from Chinese orphanages. By 1991 the yearly intake had risen to 61. Then came 1992, with a sudden leap to 226, then 330 in 1993, 787 in 1994, and an astonishing 2,130 in 1995. The numbers of children adopted from China increased every year in the 1990s—despite a yearlong moratorium, a complicated bureaucratic reorganization in Beijing, and some negative publicity in the West—peaking at 5,053 to the United States alone in 2000 and again in 2002.[1] Adoptions to Canada and Europe also increased rapidly during this period.

Veterans of international adoption will point out that a quick rise in numbers isn't in itself surprising. Ever since Henry Holt first brought Amerasian adoptees to the United States after the Korean war, it's not been unusual for a country to suddenly open an international adoption program—or suddenly close it. Still, there was something different about China. The rules for adoptive parents in 1992–99, for example, were highly unusual. Instead of setting a maximum age, as many countries do, China wanted parents who were older than thirty-five but still childless. Even more striking, nearly all the children available for adoption were girls. Moreover, the most common reasons for the availability of children for adoption—out-of-wedlock births to women overcome by shame or too young or too poor to raise a child on their own—did not seem to account for the large numbers of abandoned female infants. The orphanage population China revealed to parents and professionals in the world adoption community was different from anything they'd seen before.

Where did all these children come from? Why were so many of them girls? Why the unusual rules for adoptive parents? What was going on in China at that time that caused the country to open adoption to foreigners? When the children adopted from China ask why their first parents didn't keep them, what can we tell them?

The answers we give children when they are young must be fairly simple. Even the children's book that addresses them most directly—*When You Were Born in China,* by Sara Dorow—is too complicated for many young children, who are just beginning to understand what adoption itself means. Yet the detailed, unemotional, complex answers they will want when they are grown are not readily available outside university libraries, and most of the scholarship assumes a familiarly with Chinese history and culture, not to mention social science terminology, that neither parents nor adoptees may possess.

Trying to explain in a clear, concise way anything about a country as vast, dynamic, and complex as China calls for both caution and humility. Oversimplification looms on one side and mystification on the other. For an outsider to know China well requires decades of study. Yet for those touched by international adoption from China—parents, relatives, teachers, friends, adoption professionals, and especially adoptees themselves—a collection of stereotypes, assumptions, and guesses is a poor basis for understanding. They need to know what was going on and why. In compiling this book, we hope to make some of the most important scholarly research on abandonment and adoption in China accessible to the general reader, with enough background information to provide a context for the complicated picture that is beginning to emerge.

Rethinking the Conventional Wisdom

The one-child policy and a cultural preference for boys—those are the widely accepted reasons why, year after year, countless thousands of healthy infant girls entered Chinese orphanages and became available for international adoption in the 1990s and on into the new millennium. Chinese couples, the story goes, can have only one child, and they want a son. Girls are not even a "small happiness" under these conditions and must be dispensed with so the parents can try again for a boy. Unwanted female fetuses are aborted. Infant girls who aren't killed at birth are abandoned, at great risk to the birthparents, whose actions are illegal but unavoidable. Fortunately, foreigners have been allowed to adopt girls from China since the early 1990s. Unfortunately, there aren't enough foreign adoptive parents to give homes to all the abandoned girls. With little hope of adoption by Chinese families, the unwanted girls languish in wretched orphanages. According to some highly publicized accounts, the babies are routinely abused and neglected by ignorant orphanage staff and allowed to die for no reason other than their gender. Our children, some say, are lucky to be alive, let alone wanted and loved.

Like most cultural myths, this one has many variations, some more sympathetic to Chinese birthparents, caregivers, and the Chinese state, others even bleaker. And like most conventional wisdom, there are elements of truth in these myths. To be sure, the felt need for a son is embedded in culture and remains strong among many Chinese, while the government's strict population policy puts great pressure on parents to limit births, depriving some of the ability to obtain a son without resorting to illegal behavior. But this predicament does not mean that parents are literally forced to abandon a female child to fulfill the need for a son. It also does not mean that daughters are unwanted or unwelcome, as is often assumed, nor does it mean that prospective adoptive parents in China reject the abandoned girls languishing in orphanages either because they are girls or because they are abandoned. The degree to which such common assumptions are inaccurate makes an enormous difference in how we interpret our children's earliest life experiences and how those children will understand their own histories.

Questioning these assumptions leads to further questions. If there wasn't a strict one-child policy in the 1990s, why did infant abandonment increase? If Chinese want daughters and are even willing to raise other people's (even strangers') daughters, why are there so many healthy female infants in Chinese orphanages? If Chinese people have been adopting children all along, why were the orphanages overflowing? We can be sure many of our China-born children will want to know.

One Son/Two Children: Population Planning in Rural China

After two decades of the strictest birth control policies ever attempted, the fertility rate in China was down to 1.8 births per woman by 1998.[2] If that rate continues, China's population will eventually decline. But because the large cohort of females born in the 1960s to mid 1970s, when fertility rates were much higher, are not yet past child-bearing age, China's population will continue to grow for many years. This fact, coupled with the way that population planning has entrenched itself throughout the political system over the past twenty years, has slowed efforts to pull back from the harshness of the one-child policy, although such efforts are clearly under way. Above all the new birth-planning law, finally passed in 2002, brings population control under "the rule of law" rather than the rule of politics and mobilization campaigns. Efforts have also been made to professionalize the birth-planning apparatus and to place far more emphasis on reproductive health care delivery to women of child-bearing age. Despite these positive developments, the so-called one-child policy persists as official policy and continues to generate the problems discussed in this volume: female infant abandonment, the obstruction of adoption inside China, and the denial of basic citizenship rights for many "overquota" children.

Since 1979, when Deng Xiaoping instituted the one-child policy as part of his wide-ranging program for reforming post-Mao China, population control has been a central concern in every aspect of Chinese state planning. Foreigners doing business in China report the participation of population planners in decisions not only about transportation but also about energy policy and resource management. Even armchair travelers have seen photos of the ubiquitous billboards showing a father, a mother, and a daughter smiling together under the exhortation "One Child Is Good!" or the pudgy, pampered offspring called "little emperors" on whom two parents and four grandparents lavish their undivided hopes for the future.

Under the population-planning policy, all Chinese who live in cities, as well as some in densely populated rural areas or relatively wealthy suburban areas, are limited by law to one child per family, with the exception of minority peoples (a mere 8 percent of the population,[3] who are routinely permitted two or more children) and couples who are themselves only-children (who are also allowed to have two). There are a few other exceptions as well, but for the most part it's fair to say that urban Chinese can have only one child. Perhaps because most Western journalists in China (and their sources) live in cities, and because most Chinese who came to the West in the late twentieth century emigrated from urban areas, the popular media outside China routinely simplify China's array of population-planning policies to a catch-phrase: "the one-child policy." The government in Beijing uses the same phrase.

By the 1990s, however, the one-child policy did not strictly apply in most rural areas, where 75–80 percent of Chinese people live. Beginning in the mid to late 1980s (the shift did not take effect all at once), provinces were permitted to modify the population policy for rural areas in response to widespread popular resistance to the one-child restriction. Acknowledging parents' desire for a son to take care of them in their old age and carry on the family name, most provinces implemented a slightly more lenient "one-son/two child" policy for rural residents. Under this rule, if a couple's first child is a boy, they are restricted to only one child. If it's a girl, however, they are permitted to have a second child several years later. In some places parents are allowed to have two children, well spaced, regardless of the gender of the first.

Most observers inside and outside China who were paying attention to these changes expected the more flexible policy to result in fewer abandonments and less crowded orphanages. Instead, they got a surge in abandonments, and orphanages filled to bursting. It turns out that the slightly more lenient policy was enforced much more vigorously in rural areas than the previous one-child policy had been. As a result, orphanage populations skyrocketed, with predictable consequences, such as rising infant mortality rates in understaffed, ill-equipped institutions. To make matters worse, the first national adoption law, passed in 1991, made domestic adoption more difficult by requiring that adoptive parents be over thirty-five and childless. At the same time, this law also officially opened the country to international adoption to help ameliorate the overcrowding and underfunding of the orphanages (see Chap. 1). That law came into effect in 1992, the year annual U.S. adoptions from China jumped from 61 to 210.

Population Planning, Abandonment, and Adoption

Kay Johnson's groundbreaking studies, presented together for the first time in this volume, reveal a complicated picture of one aspect of Chinese society at the turn of the twenty-first century. Despite thousands of years of patriarchal tradition and present-day rates of female infant abandonment that rival patterns previously seen only during war, famine, or economic crisis, Chinese daughters today are valued more highly than ever before. It is increasingly common for people across the social spectrum, from university-educated urbanites to poor rural farmers, to want a daughter as well as a son. Not all can have both, but more than a few will try.

How can these seemingly contradictory trends—the revival of female infant abandonment in a time of relative prosperity, and new cultural trends that are encouraging people to value daughters as well as sons—be happening in the same place at the same time? Looking at abandonment together with population-planning policies and adoption practices brings each aspect into focus in a new light. In late twentieth-century China, a rapidly changing culture both hastened a positive revaluation of daughters and undercut that process with policies that revived, continued, and exacerbated one of the worst aspects of traditional patriarchal practices.

The data collected in China from adoptive parents and birthparents in the 1990s, limited though they are, appear unambiguous on several points: These days many Chinese people, even in rural areas where old traditions are assumed to linger longest, want to have a daughter. If one isn't born to them, they may well adopt one. If they can't adopt legally, they may choose to do so illegally. Parents still need a son to carry on the family name and take care of them when they are too old to work; having only daughters is unacceptable to many. Nevertheless, they rarely abandon a first-born girl.

In other words, most infant girls abandoned in China since the "one-child policy" began—and by extension most of those who now live overseas with their adoptive families—have older biological sisters living at home with their birthparents. Yet even though the fieldwork investigating reasons for abandonment shows that fewer than 10 percent of the abandoned girls were first-born children (see Chap. 4), we cannot extrapolate from the general to the specific and tell a given adoptee that she has an older sister living with her birthparents. For most children adopted from China, nothing whatever is known about their families of origin. In that context, statistical probability can suggest likelihood but cannot provide individual answers.

Twelve Years of Study

Kay Johnson's research, with important contributions from her colleagues Wang Liyao and Huang Banghan, is the most comprehensive and long-term body of work available in English on the subject of abandonment and adoption in contemporary China. Others writing about adoption from China in recent years have often cited Johnson's scholarly work, and her analytical framework has occasionally appeared in paraphrase without the attribution it deserves. She has been extraordinarily generous in sharing her findings with other scholars as well as writers and journalists. Yet until now most of her own writings have been published only in scholarly journals with limited circulation. That needed to change.

Wanting a Daughter, Needing a Son brings together more than a decade of Johnson's fieldwork on abandonment, adoption, and orphanage care in China. Four of the seven chapters first appeared as articles in academic journals, one was written for Families with Children from China, one was presented as a paper at the 2003 annual meetings of the Association of Asian Studies, and one was written specifically for this collection. The previously published articles have been substantially revised and updated for this volume while still reflecting what was known about abandonment and adoption in China at the time of the original research. Johnson has developed and refined her views as more information has come to light, and these chapters, presented in chronological order, reveal the development of her analysis.

In revising the text, we retained some overlap of content so that each chapter can stand on its own, as originally intended. The chapters themselves are like time capsules, preserved to illuminate the different periods our children came from China. Notes at the back of the book contain substantive information as well as citations, and those dated 2003 provide information not available at the time of original writing. Altogether the collection encapsulates a history of the first twelve years of international adoption from China, to aid adults' understanding today and to answer some of our children's questions tomorrow—for the China in which they were born and adopted is rapidly changing.

The book opens with an early view of the crisis in Chinese orphanages in 1991–92, as the population of foundlings surged and the government established both a national adoption law and a process for international adoption. Chapters 2 and 3 address orphanage care and infant abandonment in the first half of the decade. While strongly disagreeing with Human Rights Watch's portrayal of Chinese orphanages as little better than extermination camps for baby girls, Johnson criticized Chinese government regulations that impeded domestic adoptions and urged changes that would ease the pressure on orphanages and the children in their care. Some of those changes came to pass, although much remains to be done.

Chapter 4, written with fellow researchers Wang Liyao and Huang Banghan, looks into the causes of the revival of female infant abandonment in China and presents groundbreaking

statistical evidence that first-born daughters are rarely abandoned. The final three chapters, written in the first years of the
twenty-first century, look at the politics of international and
domestic adoption in China, the struggles of Chinese parents
who adopt children outside the welfare system, and the state of
orphanages today. In closing, Johnson shares some of her own
family's adoption story, describes dramatic changes in the social
welfare system over the twelve years of her research, and advocates further policy changes to protect children and support
adoptive families in China.

In publishing this volume, we hope to provide a vital resource
for everyone touched by adoption from China since 1991, especially for the future adults that our children will become.

A.K.

San Francisco, July 2003

CHAPTER ONE

A Chinese Orphanage, 1991–92

Saving China's Abandoned Girls

Nowhere is the tenacious Chinese preference for sons more clear than in China's orphanages. These institutions are disproportionately filled, as they were in the past, with girls whose parents are either unable or unwilling to raise them. In earlier times, the abandonment of girls was strongly associated with poverty, and, predictably, the numbers of such children grew dramatically in times of famine and economic hardship. In the 1980s and early 1990s, most areas of the countryside experienced increased prosperity, and the majority of analysts agree that even the poorer segments of the population have generally done better economically than in previous decades. Yet over these years the number of abandoned children accommodated in orphanages and similar welfare institutions appears to have increased. This growing problem stems from the government's population control policies; orphanages report that their numbers increase whenever population control efforts heat up in their area. Since official government policies have become more flexible in allowing routine exceptions to the one-child rule in most rural areas, one might have expected this and related problems to ease. That has not been the case, however.

This, at least, has been the experience of the Wuhan Orphanage in Hubei province.[1] Although it is impossible to know how widespread the problems found at the Wuhan Orphanage are today, the orphanage officials believe they are not unique. Visits to a similar orphanage in Changsha, in neighboring Hunan province, revealed similar conditions and trends, as have visits to smaller welfare houses in western and southern Hubei.[2]

Orphanages as Institutions for Saving Girls

One of the most striking things about the Wuhan orphanage is that nearly all the infants and healthy older children are girls. Many of these girls suffer "disabilities" ranging from minor birthmarks to severe retardation, though increasingly girls are being deposited there without any disabilities aside from gender. Rarely are boys found in orphanages today; those who are found there usually are severely disabled and in need of institutional care. Scattered evidence from the eighteenth, nineteenth, and early twentieth centuries suggests that these institutions were traditionally filled by girls far more than boys.[3] At this fundamental level—the level at which someone decides to keep or abandon a child—the gender bias of Chinese society is overwhelming.

Although Chinese women are by no means passive victims of their society and culture, as is increasingly emphasized in

anthropological and social historical scholarship,[4] they have had
to confront considerable obstacles in their efforts to overcome
the powerless and lowly status formally assigned to them by
dominant ideology and law. Chief among those obstacles has
been an extreme patrilineal family and kinship system, under-
girded for centuries by the political ideology and laws of a powerful central state.

Because the central state no longer provides unambiguous
support for patriarchal social organization, and because kinship no longer organizes local society as tightly as it once did,
the gender bias has been mitigated since 1949. Yet the living
traditions and values of Chinese culture continue to shape and
reflect a society that, to an extreme degree, has been organized
by and around agnatic (male) kin groups, groups that in a formal sense exclude females or at best define them as marginal
members. In a variety of ways, government policy in the
postrevolutionary era indirectly reinforced these patterns—for
example, by restricting the mobility of the rural population
and by relying on the rural family, patrilineally defined, as the
first and preferred source of welfare and old-age security. Even
today in Chinese villages, many older people, when asked
about their "children" (haizi)—e.g., How many children do
you have? What do they do? etc.—will answer as if only sons
count, failing even to mention the existence of daughters
unless specifically asked.

Similarly, when relating their family histories in a North
China village in the late 1970s and early 1980s, informants
reported a suspiciously small number of daughters and sisters.
These oral family histories, told primarily by native village men,
yielded an extremely skewed sex ratio, reflecting the highly

patrilineal definition of the family internalized by these informants. As a peasant woman in the documentary film *Small
Happiness* aptly put it nearly forty years after the revolution
arrived in her village, "Daughters are not family, they are only
relatives."[5] Indeed, despite significant changes in marriage patterns (such as the increasing prevalence of intravillage marriage), dominant norms in the countryside, where most of
China's population still resides, continue to dictate that young
women marry patrilocally, symbolically if not always literally
leaving their natal family and transferring their primary obligations to their husband's family.[6] Therefore, unlike sons, people
still speak of daughters as being "lost" at marriage or "belong-
ing to other people." These attitudes and patterns help explain
why orphanages in China have long been disproportionately
filled by girls.

Population Control and "Missing Girls"

Such attitudes are most starkly revealed in interaction with the
government's population control efforts. The collision of state-
imposed population control with China's patrilineal culture
has compounded the traditional liabilities of being born female
in China, of which one manifestation is the recent increase in
the population of abandoned girls in orphanages. In earlier
times, the starkest manifestation was seen in skewed sex ratios,
which resulted at least in part from infanticide, abandonment,
and other practices that led to higher mortality rates among
young girls.[7]

One should not, however, assume, as many Western
observers have, that infanticide or the abandonment of children

was more widespread in China historically than in other societies, including many Western societies. In Europe and
America, these practices were at times widespread and lingered
as social problems well into the twentieth century.[8] But the gender bias in these practices has been more extreme in China than
in most other places. While the evidence suggests that these
phenomena decreased significantly in China in the 1950s and
1960s, population control efforts in the 1980s revived the practice of female infanticide and abandonment and reestablished a
highly skewed sex ratio among young children.

In other ways, too, a disproportionate share of the costs
and burdens of population control has been borne by women
and girls. Women are, of course, primarily responsible for birth
control—including sterilization, with its attendant risks[9]—and
are also the primary targets of coercion when an overquota
pregnancy occurs. Such pregnancies are supposed to end in
abortion, and frequently do, regardless of the gestational
month in which they are discovered. Women are simultane-
ously under pressure from husbands and in-laws to bear sons
and are frequently blamed, abused, or sometimes abandoned
when they disappoint the family by giving birth to a girl.
Equally important is that women, given their own needs—that
is, the traditional desire to build around themselves their own
uterine family as a source of solace and influence in a patriarchal, patrilineal world[10]—are themselves likely to desire a son
and may be intensely disappointed when their one or two
allotted pregnancies fail to produce a boy. These pressures too
often militate against their desires to retain the daughter, who
otherwise would have been welcomed in these prosperous
times as part of a growing family.[11]

Given this collision between policy and culture, China has developed what is perhaps the most skewed sex ratio in the world today among young children. Survey data indicate that in 1987, 1989, and 1990 there were between 110 to 113 boys for every 100 girls under the age of one. The biologically determined sex ratio at birth is around 105 boys for every 100 girls. Significantly, the ratios in the 1953 and 1964 Chinese census data approximate this normal ratio for newborn infants (children under one year).[12] But after 1980, with the implementation of the "one-child" policy, the data have shown an increasingly skewed ratio. By 1990, there were one million fewer girls reported born per year compared with normal sex ratios, according to the 1990 national census.[13]

What is happening to these girls?[14] Some unknown percentage of them are victims of infanticide or die from neglect before they are registered.[15] But most of the missing girls probably suffer a fate far less tragic, although one that disadvantages them in many ways. Many girls are not legally registered and are "hidden," either literally or through informal adoptions and fostering. These strategies enable their parents to continue trying to produce a son and to escape a fine for an overquota birth, a fine they would probably be willing to pay if they had produced a boy. Although only about 10,000 to 15,000 domestic adoptions were officially registered each year from 1980 through 1991, sample survey data indicate that the real figure was much higher, perhaps over 500,000 in the late 1980s, if private and unregistered adoptions are included.[16] The evidence also suggests that the numbers of such adoptions have increased significantly in recent years and that an increasingly large majority of these informal, unreported adoptions are girls. While some of these girls may make it into the census data, many do not.[17] An even larger number fail to appear in the official household registration records, which are reported to be seriously and increasingly inaccurate.[18]

While in China's legal and historical records, official adoptions have been associated primarily with the adoption of boys for the purpose of obtaining an heir,[19] customary adoption practices have more often involved infant girls.[20] One of the primary reasons for adopting an infant girl in the past was to obtain a *tongyangxi,* a future daughter-in-law and wife for an infant son. Through this method, not only did families avoid the often ruinously expensive ritual costs associated with a "normal" marriage, including a bride price, but they were also able to raise their own daughter-in-law to assure her loyalty and integration into the patrilineal family. Sometimes childless couples would also adopt *tongyangxi* in the belief that adopting a daughter would help "lead in" a son, that is, enhance the adoptive mother's chance of giving birth to a boy. In some parts of China, particularly in the south and southeast, this practice of adopting an infant to raise as a future daughter-in-law was common in the nineteenth century.[21]

While it is unlikely that this practice has totally disappeared, informed observers agree that it is no longer common. Orphanages today try to scrutinize the motives for adoption and would not knowingly serve as an accomplice in this now illegal practice, a practice that was detrimental not only to the child's status but to her very chances of survival in childhood.[22] Staff at the Wuhan Orphanage report that in the 1980s and early 1990s their postadoption investigations had found no evidence of child brides-to-be, although admittedly such evidence would be difficult to detect in the first few years after adoption.

Today the reasons for adopting are more likely to be related to a desire to enlarge one's family in the face of stringent birth restrictions and to the expected caretaker role that a child, even a daughter, undertakes for parents when they get older. Informal adoptions may also be a way of shielding the daughters of one's relatives or friends from population control authorities.

Large numbers of girls are also believed to be living secretly with their parents in their natal villages without benefit of registration, while local cadres pretend not to notice or are misled as to the child's true identity.[23] Children born when the parents were working outside their place of residence may be identified by their parents as "adopted" when they are brought back home to live, as one construction worker readily admitted to a reporter. The "floating population" grew to over fifty million in the early 1990s, so the opportunities for such deception increased. That hidden births are a widespread problem is indicated by periodic government campaigns to register these unregistered (or "black") children prior to census gathering. Sometimes these efforts are accompanied by promises of amnesty for the offenders, but such promises do not seem to carry much credibility. Most people expect to be punished if caught. In 1988 the Public Security Ministry estimated that there were about one million unregistered children.[24]

Finally, an increasing number of unwanted or overquota girls are simply abandoned.[25] While abandonment amounts to infanticide in some cases, in others the intention is for the child to be found and taken care of by others. An unknown percentage of these children end up in the network of orphanages and welfare institutions run by the bureaus of civil affairs and local governments at various levels.

This is the context within which orphanages found themselves operating in the early 1990s. In 1991, some official publications reported 11,000 abandoned and orphaned children in China being cared for in 60 orphanages and 800 "social welfare houses,"[26] but the real numbers are no doubt much higher. In 1991 the Ministry of Civil Affairs reported that there were 140,000 of these orphaned and abandoned children, and according to the *Beijing Review* there were "tens of thousands" of abandoned children being cared for in over 5,000 child welfare homes.[27] One of these establishments is the Wuhan Orphanage, run by the Wuhan municipal government.

The Wuhan Orphanage

The Wuhan Orphanage is located on Garden Hill, Wuchang, and is housed in the buildings of what was originally an Italian Catholic mission built in the late nineteenth century. An American Franciscan bishop later took the site over to house abandoned babies who were received by Saint Joseph Clinic next door (now the Wuhan Hospital for Traditional Chinese Medicine), a clinic the bishop established in 1924. In 1928 the orphanage opened as the Wuchang Foundling Hospital to receive orphans and abandoned babies directly.

Before 1949 it was one of the largest of several orphanages in the area. It took in from two hundred to eight hundred children each year and in most years reportedly suffered horrendously high mortality rates of over 90 percent. The new Communist government publicized these mortality rates as proof of the foreign-run orphanage's brutality and neglect.[28] But in fact such high death rates were common at other orphanages in China at the time, whether foreign- or Chinese-run; extremely high mortality, ranging from 70 to over 90 percent, was also characteristic of orphanages in Europe and America in the eighteenth and nineteenth centuries.[29] After Liberation, in June 1951, the orphanage was taken over by the Chinese government and has been supported by the government ever since.

Although the current orphanage traces its origins to a foreign mission, local records indicate that there is a long tradition in the Wuhan area (Wuchang-Hanyang-Hankou) of providing this kind of social service. A large orphanage was established in Wuchang with donations from local officials in 1731, and two smaller ones were established in nearby Hanyang in the same decade, a period of relative prosperity and political stability. In the nineteenth century, two were built in Hankou, one by the local community and one by the government. Ho Ping-ti also cites evidence that there was a large, well-funded orphanage established in the nineteenth century by local gentry in nearby Xiaogan, Hubei, that was credited with saving the lives of "more than ten thousand baby girls" within the first three years of its founding.[30]

This history also supports the contention of several knowledgeable people interviewed in Wuhan that there is a long corollary tradition in this area of "throwing away babies." The director of the Wuhan Orphanage reiterated on several occasions that Hubei and Hunan were areas where the "custom of throwing away [girl] babies" was particularly pronounced, compared to many other parts of China.[31] Certainly there is evidence that the practice of taking *tongyangxi,* while far less common than in the southeastern regions of China, was widespread in this area, and the existence of orphanages may have helped provide a supply of girls for that purpose.[32] However, the presence of several orphanages may or may not have been at all peculiar to this area; there is evidence of many such welfare institutions in China in the eighteenth century and earlier.[33] Though many of them disappeared after the Qing dynasty collapsed, by that time growing numbers of orphanages in China were run by foreign missionaries.[34]

Little systematic research has been done on the existence of such institutions or on the problem of abandonment, so we can do no more than speculate. It is clear, however, that the culture and conditions in the Wuhan/Hubei area have long conspired to create a pool of abandoned baby girls; these conditions have also led to efforts to ameliorate the resulting suffering. Thus the current orphanage represents a long tradition of efforts to save the lives of girls whose existence has been made precarious by a severely patrilineal kinship system and culture.

Under the Communist government up until the 1980s absolute intakes at the Wuhan Orphanage fluctuated (Table 1.1). The two periods of peak intake during those three decades were the mid to late 1950s (the years of rapid collectivization) and the early 1960s (the period of severe famine that followed the Great Leap Forward). In the latter period, the number of abandoned children was so high—almost 4,000— that the city of Wuhan had to set up a dozen temporary orphanages to handle them. Significantly, during this period the intake of nondisabled abandoned children accounted for more than 50 percent of all intakes, as parents found themselves unable to find food for their children. Once the famine eased, at least some parents reclaimed their children. In normal times,

Table 1.1 Annual Intake at the Wuhan Orphanage

Year	No. of children received	Year	No. of children received	Year	No. of children received
1950	139	1965	109	1979	150
1951	57	1966	56	1980	161
1952	37	1967	49	1981	144
1953	72	1968	52	1982	252
1954	82	1969	47	1983	261
1955	149	1970	42	1984	246
1956	305	1971	60	1985	187
1957	177	1972	67	1986	–
1958	166	1973	77	1987	–
1959*	120	1974	68	1988	300
1960*	125	1975	86	1989	–
1961*	67	1976	89	1990	590
1962	127	1977	102	1991	895
1963	54	1978	96	1992	1,200+
1964	126				

*During these years of the Great Leap Famine, twelve other temporary orphanages were opened, housing 3,929.

the orphanage reports that only a handful of children are reclaimed each year, usually around 1 or 2 percent; the number reclaimed from the 1960–62 period was just over 6 percent.

A period of persistently low intakes ensued. Orphanage documents show that the intake of children for the entire period of 1966–75 hovered around only 50 to 80 a year. This trend suggests a significant easing of the problem of abandonment. It contrasts with the period 1946–50, when the orphanage was taking in around 200 babies a year at a time when the population of Wuhan was small and there were several other orphanages still operating in the area. (All the orphanages in the municipal area were consolidated under the Wuhan Orphanage in 1951.)

By the 1980s, the picture of a declining number of abandoned children had changed decisively. The late 1970s saw the numbers gradually climb back over 100 per year and continue to grow throughout the 1980s. In 1982–83, when a national population control campaign swept many parts of the country, numbers jumped to over 250; in the mid 1980s intakes fell again somewhat, as population control pressure eased in China. But they began to climb again in 1988, when the figure reached 300, and between 1988 and 1992 the numbers escalated sharply, roughly doubling every two years and reaching around 1,200 in 1992.

The sudden jump in intake in 1991 shown in Table 1.1 was partly a consequence of television publicity that the orphanage attracted on International Women's Day (March 8). This inadvertent contribution to the escalation in numbers was strongly felt only a few days after the broadcast, when the orphanage found five babies on its doorstep in one twenty-four-hour period. For years the orphanage had tried to keep its existence quiet if not secret. Indeed, the intentionally ambiguous sign over the entrance read "Wuhan Kindergarten" (Yu youyuan). City and orphanage officials believed the number of abandoned babies would skyrocket if parents knew of a safe place to leave an infant where it would be well cared for and later adopted by others. The orphanage already felt strained beyond its limits.

For the most part, orphanage officials attribute the increases of recent years to tighter implementation of population control in the surrounding area, which has about five million urban and one million rural residents. This link was particularly evident in late 1991. Orphanage officials heard that the local rural areas were in the midst of a "mobilization campaign" to sterilize all women who had had two children. In those months, the orphanage received up to ten children a day, with an unusually large number of older girls (between the ages of two and five) abandoned during this period.

These were truly the saddest cases for the orphanage, for these children were old enough to miss their parents and their homes and to show the emotional scars of abandonment. The director mentioned a miserable five-year-old girl who arrived at the orphanage with a poem written by her parents in her pocket. It lamented the fact that they were giving up their child, bitterly blaming the government's population control policies for forcing them into this act. The parents hoped that someday they could come back and retrieve their daughter, although, as noted, few parents ever do return to claim a child.

In 1990 the number of abandoned children brought to the orphanage was over 590, exceeding the worst previous year, with the exception of the "three bad years." In 1991 the numbers continued to escalate, with 895 children brought in by year's end. From January 1 to mid April 1992, the numbers escalated even further; during this period 290 new children were brought in, which was nearly 100 more than for the same period in 1991. By year's end, over 1,000 were expected.

Provinces vary somewhat in the number of children they allow in rural areas. Hubei has been a "one-son-or-two-child" province since March 1988; that is, if a couple's first child is a girl, they may try again for a boy.[35] A few provinces, such as Guangdong and Yunnan, now allow rural couples to have two children regardless of sex, while only a few rural areas, primarily the wealthy areas of Jiangsu and Sichuan, still maintain a strict one-child policy for rural as well as urban areas.[36] Exceptions to the one-child rule in rural areas were introduced in the mid to late 1980s in response to widespread resistance to the one-child policy.[37] It was hoped that a slightly more flexible and lenient approach would make the policy more palatable and reduce the negative consequences of infanticide and abandonment.[38]

Yet the experience of the Wuhan Orphanage leads one to be cautious about predicting the effect of population control efforts just from looking at a policy on paper. Although an ostensibly more lenient policy, the "one-son/two-child" policy brought in its wake *higher* rates of abandonment because local areas in Hubei and elsewhere came under pressure to implement the revised policy more thoroughly, which in practice often meant more coercively. In the Chinese policy debates, this adjustment has been referred to as "opening a small hole in order to close a large hole."[39] In Hubei the escalation of abandonment coincided, in 1988, with the introduction of the one-son/two-child policy.

Implementation efforts vary enormously from province to province and area to area, making generalizations difficult. But in the early 1990s there were indications on a national level of efforts to implement the existing policies more thoroughly. Some planners argued, in addition, that the policies should be made more restrictive once again, allowing fewer exceptions to the one-child rule, although this position seems to have lost out in upper policy-making circles in favor of the "small hole" approach.[40] Furthermore, while the one-son/two-child policy may well reduce the risk to first-born daughters, it clearly shifts the risk to second- and later-born ones. While their numbers will be fewer, the risk has been greatly heightened by high-pressure campaigns to sterilize women after the birth of a second child. The Wuhan Orphanage sees only the tip of the iceberg, but the trend it sees is indicative.

According to orphanage records, the gender bias that is obvious today has been fairly consistent over the past forty years (Table 1.2).[41] Figures indicate that through the 1970s

Table 1.2 Percentage of Girls in the Wuhan Orphanage

Year	% Girls	Year	% Girls
1951	89.2	1984	83.0
1958	99.0	1985	76.0
1960	88.2	1988	
1980	75.0	1989	
1981	81.0	1990	90+
1982	80.0	1991	
1983	85.0	1992	

from 88 to 98 percent of the abandoned babies taken in by the orphanage each year were girls. In the first half of the 1980s, the percentages dropped slightly, ranging from 75 to 85 percent.[42] Exact percentages are not available for any year after 1985, and after 1988 the exact figures were declared secret by the government because of growing sensitivity about the implications. But in visits to the Wuhan Orphanage in 1991, orphanage staff said that the percentage of girls had been significantly above 90 in recent years and that girls currently accounted for nearly 99 percent of the intake.

It is also notable that as the numbers of abandoned children climbed, first in the wake of the Great Leap Forward and then again in the 1980s, the percentage of healthy children being abandoned rose significantly (Table 1.3). In the 1950s and the 1970s, 96 percent or more of the children were classified as "disabled" (although this category is broadly defined to include many minor problems such prominent birthmarks or largely cosmetic problems such as malformed outer ears or harelips).

Table 1.3 Percentage of "Handicapped" in the Wuhan Orphanage

Year	% Handicapped	Year	% Handicapped
1956	96.4	1980	46.5
1959	41.3	1981	48.6
1962	56.0	1982	35.7
1966		1983	36.4
1972		1984	48.8
1973	98.0	1985	56.7
1974		1992	20.0

The only exception to this trend was the period of famine in the early 1960s when, as in the 1980s, nondisabled children were about as numerous as the disabled. In the early 1980s, though, the percentage of disabled children in the orphanage fell from over 95 percent to less than 50 percent. In 1982–83, when a high-pressure population control campaign swept the country, the figure dropped to only about 35 percent. By 1992, a staff member estimated that fewer than 20 percent of the babies had any known disability.

Thus, as a result of the population control policies of the 1980s, the majority of children taken in by the orphanage in the early 1990s are healthy; they are abandoned by their parents only because they are female, and probably second daughters in most cases. Conversely, the figures suggest that prior to the late 1970s and the implementation of strict population controls, healthy daughters were rarely abandoned except during famine.

Most of the babies abandoned in the streets of Wuhan and the surrounding areas are thought to come from poor rural areas. It is extremely difficult for an urban resident to abandon a child without being detected and punished, given the neighborhood and work unit networks of surveillance and registration. Some of the abandoned children are believed to be infants born in "guerrilla pregnancies," where a pregnant woman leaves her own village and goes to live with friends or relatives in or near the city to give birth. If the child is a boy, she takes him back to the village and registers him; if it is a girl, especially if disabled, she abandons her and returns to the village with yet another chance to try to give birth to a son.[43] Rural parents may believe, correctly, that in or near the city the child will have a better chance of being found quickly and cared for. A small but increasing number of children are abandoned directly in front of the orphanage, indicating that precise knowledge of the existence of the orphanage is spreading.

Conditions at the Wuhan Orphanage, 1991–92

In the spring of 1991, when I made several visits to the orphanage, most of the children were being housed in three large rooms on the second floor of a large, clean, but draughty late-nineteenth-century building. One of the rooms contained about fifteen children aged two to five, most of whom had no visible disabilities. Most were watching a children's program on a large TV in the center of the room, which contained some children's furniture but no toys. Others were playing together, but one two-year-old stood alone in a corner gazing down at nothing in particular. We were told she had only recently arrived and remained sad and withdrawn from the others. Another large room contained five or six severely mentally and physically disabled older children unable to walk or care for themselves. A few were sitting propped up in chairs, while several others lay immobile in beds. The orphanage had no special equipment or rehabilitative facilities for these children.

The largest room was for infants: more than thirty cribs lined the walls of a long, high-ceilinged room with large, high windows on one side. A double row of cribs occupied the center of the room; a small stove kept the whole room slightly warmed, the temperature outside being around 8° C (45° F) and the weather rainy. Some cribs contained two babies, each wrapped at the opposite end of a single large, thick, brightly printed cotton-padded blanket.

The exact number of infants in the orphanage varied from week to week and month to month. During the winter and spring of 1991, the number of infants in the orphanage at any one time ranged from 25 to around 60, usually filling one room. By spring of 1992 about 120 infants occupied three large rooms. By August, when 160–180 babies were being housed, all available space was filled with cribs, including a large first-floor room that had served as the administrative offices. The desks had been moved into the hallways, which also contained cribs at times. Throughout 1992, an additional 10 to 20 infants were in foster homes outside the orphanage; most of these infants were waiting for foreign adoptions, and their relatively expensive foster care would be paid for by their new parents.

The orphanage does its best to give its infants an identity by naming them, and until the recent deluge it did so with care. This is particularly noteworthy given that in the past girls' names were often generic (e.g., Xiao Mei, Little Sister; or Zhaodi, Calling Brother), in contrast to the highly individualized names for boys, and married women may be known to other villagers only by a relational term (for example, so-and-so's mother).[44] Yet each of the children is named when she comes into the Wuhan Orphanage. All those who arrive within the same month are given the same surname (for example, all arriving in January 1991 were surnamed Tang),[45] and each child is given an individual name that seems to suit her in some way. If the child stays in the orphanage for a period, she acquires a nickname. Caregivers refer to children, even newly arrived infants, by their individual names or nicknames.

Only on rare occasions does a healthy boy arrive. During my visits in March and April 1991, only one infant boy was brought in. He was perhaps the child of an unwed mother, one worker speculated, trying to figure out what circumstances would lead someone to abandon a healthy boy. He was clearly a precious commodity, even to those who worked in the orphanage. He was located directly next to the only stove in the long, high-ceilinged room. The waiting list for adopting boys is long, and many peasants wait in nearby hotels in case one turns up. Thus he was adopted almost immediately on his arrival and was merely waiting for the paperwork to be completed. When a healthy infant boy was brought to the orphanage a year later, in June 1992, the staff immediately took the child and hid him to prevent the orphanage from being deluged with requests to adopt the boy should word of his arrival leak out.

Even moderately disabled or critically ill boys may be adopted quickly too. Occasionally, sick babies abandoned in the hospital are brought to the orphanage. Three such babies were boys who were thought to be "at death's door," that is, beyond treatment. In each case, the vice-director of the orphanage was able within hours to locate would-be parents on their waiting list who came immediately to adopt the babies and take their new sons for intensive medical care. In all three cases, the dying boys survived. Had these children been girls, they may have died, as the orphanage cannot so readily find adoptive parents willing to invest in the medical care necessary to try to save a critically ill infant girl when there are so many healthy infants available. This is, in effect, what happened at the orphanage to numerous infant girls who were simply too weak or underweight to survive despite the orphanage's efforts to care for them as best they could with their limited resources. The overall mortality rate there in the early 1990s was between 40 and 50 percent; one person in the orphanage claimed that about 20 percent of the healthy infants died during a period of extreme heat in the summer of 1992. Thus a frighteningly high number of the predominantly female infants died.

I heard repeatedly that people increasingly prefer daughters and are happy to adopt the girls. Daughters, it is often said, care much more for their parents when they grow up and are more thoughtful than sons. Numerous people spontaneously repeated this opinion to me in Wuhan and elsewhere, including a woman customs officer at the border. Nevertheless, such emotional preferences have yet to fully challenge the patrilineal realities of family life that favor sons throughout Chinese society, especially in the countryside, where social security was virtually nonexistent in the early 1990s. For tens of thousands of girls, these continuing realities became life threatening in the context of population control efforts.

Many of the babies in the large, drafty room looked underweight or premature. Many of the infants were coughing. Half a dozen had their temples and the top of their heads shaved, indicating a recent trip to the nearby hospital for the treatment of pneumonia or bronchitis. At the hospital, infants were given intravenous injections of antibiotics in the veins at the side of the head for a week or more. While the orphanage was unable to afford the kind of medical care necessary to save the most critically ill children, it was obvious that many of the babies were being sent for medical care. The orphanage's inadequate budget forced the staff, in effect, to practice triage.

The two attendants assigned to the room did their best to rush bottles to crying infants, standing and holding the bottles as the babies drank or propping the bottles up in the crib when possible. There were obviously not enough attendants, and it was not clear that weak and underweight babies could get enough nourishment in this way to survive. While the orphanage was able to supply food and warm clothing, it was not well equipped to take care of this number of infants for any length of time. There were not enough staff even to hold the babies briefly while bottle-feeding them, let alone provide any special handling for sick or weak babies, even though such handling would have improved the infants' chances of survival. The increase in numbers of abandoned children clearly taxed the orphanage's ability to care for its wards.

Abandonment and Adoption

Up until 1991, the orphanage did not have great difficulty finding adoptive homes for healthy children, even though they usually had only girls to offer. Although most people clearly prefer sons over daughters, daughters are by no means considered to be without value, even in rural areas. Any child is likely to be highly valued by a childless couple. To be childless in Chinese culture is a socially unacceptable condition and considered a severe deprivation—if not, as in the past, a moral failing. With little chance of adopting a son, many childless couples are eager to adopt a daughter. Aside from the emotional satisfaction of raising a child, a daughter is, in traditional terms, a means for a sonless couple to obtain a son-in-law in the future and thereby, perhaps, even a male heir in the next generation. Also, as noted earlier, the belief may still linger that adopting a daughter will "lead in" a son for a childless couple.[46] Daughters, as only children, are also increasingly expected as adults to fulfill more fully the role of caretaker to their own parents and not just to in-laws.

Indeed there is growing evidence that the desire for daughters has increased, and the ideal family in rural areas is more often seen as one that has a child of each sex, especially among those whose first child is a son.[47] Many who have already given birth to their "quota" of children are happy to enlarge their one- or two-child family by adding an adopted daughter. Although according to government adoption regulations at the time, only childless couples were allowed to adopt, postadoption investigations by the Wuhan Orphanage found that quite a few adopting families already had a child, often a son, and adopted because they wanted a daughter. Thus, for a variety of reasons, the orphanage was able to place most of its healthy infants fairly quickly, although older children might take a bit longer, partly because many parents want to hide the fact of adoption from the child.

Fang Qiu, "The One Who Was Sold"

A few of the healthy infants at the Wuhan Orphanage, however, had been living in the large understaffed room for months. One of them was Fang Qiu, an eight-month-old girl whom police had seized from a man who had bought her for 400 yuan from another man who claimed to be her father. These circumstances led orphanage officials to keep the baby while they conducted an investigation and while an orphanage worker was dispatched to the district from which the child allegedly came. The fear was that the man who sold her might have actually kidnapped her and that her real parents might be looking for her.

When I saw her, she was quietly lying awake on her back in her little crib. Compared to the other babies, she looked large and plump with big red cheeks. Although she seemed unusually passive for an eight-month old, she looked healthy and smiled readily at anyone who looked at her. Like many of the other babies, however, her head was partially shaved, indicating that she too had recently been to the hospital for treatment of pneumonia or some other infection. Infections spread readily within the single understaffed room, where most babies had to lie in their cribs all day. Calcium and vitamin A deficiencies were apparently common among the babies in the winter months owing to the lack of sunshine and deficiencies of vitamins A and D in the milk-and-rice formula used to feed the babies. These deficiencies increased their susceptibility to illness, according to a pediatrician who used to work in the nearby hospital. The main problem with the care provided by the orphanage, she felt, was the lack of staff to handle the babies and take them outside in the sunshine each day. Inactivity and lack of stimulation compounded the dietary deficiencies.

Fang Qiu had been in the orphanage for six months, but it was hoped she would soon be leaving. The investigation had ended without locating any clues about her parents. The local public security office had been less than enthusiastic in their efforts to help, believing that the child was most likely abandoned or given away by her own parents and that it was a waste of effort to try to locate the family. So Fang Qiu was to be adopted fairly soon, perhaps by a Canadian couple who were waiting for a referral. While everyone was sorry she had had to wait in the orphanage so long, she was fortunate to have come through the wait with her health and sweet disposition intact.

Imperfect Children: The Case of Yuan Hui

While most healthy infants have until recently been adopted fairly quickly, children who are disabled in any way have little chance of being adopted. This was not always the case. Orphanage documents indicate that in the 1960s and 1970s, when the vast majority of the children in the orphanage were disabled in some way and the demand for adoption far exceeded the number of children being abandoned, even disabled children were often adopted. During most years, around 75 percent of adoptive parents were peasants, many of them from outside the province. In 1983 the orphanage sent a team to investigate previous out-of-province adoptions, mostly clustered in a few counties in Hebei, Shanxi, and Henan.[48] Of the sixty-five adoptions randomly chosen for investigation in these areas, forty-one had involved adoptions of children with disabilities, albeit mostly minor ones.[49] Some of these disabled children no doubt included the few boys who arrived at the orphanage each year. But since the vast majority of even the disabled children at the orphanage have been girls, most of these forty-one adoptions must have been girls as well.

Yet when I visited the orphanage in 1991, the officials said that today even girls with minor disabilities are unlikely to be adopted, although boys with anything but severe disabilities are still likely to find homes. Since couples adopting in the early 1990s were supposed to be childless and were allowed to adopt only one child, the vast majority of adoptive parents wanted their one child to be perfect. Current eugenics campaigns stressing the need for "fewer but better" children may also contribute to negative attitudes about the disabled. With so many healthy children available, girls with disabilities or cosmetic imperfections often do not get adopted. Thus, the population policies that have caused an increase in the abandonment of healthy girls have also indirectly produced a greater likelihood of an institutionalized life for girls who are born imperfect in some way.

One such child was Yuan Hui, an adorable fifteen-month-old girl whom I met one day when we were asked if we could drive two of the orphanage workers and the child to a nearby hospital. Yuan Hui had developed a cough, and they wanted a doctor to check her out. The girl was bundled in a warm padded jacket and padded pants and, aside from her apparent cold, seemed to be a healthy and animated young toddler. I was therefore surprised to learn that she had lived in the orphanage since she was born. The workers explained that she was "disabled," showing me her hands, each of which had two or three fingers that were deformed and too small. Also, all five toes on her left foot were missing. Otherwise the child was normal, and her cognitive and motor skills were developing at a normal rate, although she was a bit slow and awkward in learning to walk. The decision to abandon this slightly disabled child had been made immediately after her birth; the police had found her abandoned on the street when only a few days old. No one had been found to adopt her, and there was little hope that anyone would ever be found domestically, since there was always an abundance of healthy, completely normal infants available as well as a few older healthy girls. Yuan Hui seemed destined to pass her childhood in an institution. At seven or eight she would move to a facility with a school where she would live until eighteen, at which time the school would assign her a job for the disabled.

If Yuan Hui, a lively child with only minor physical problems, cannot be placed, more seriously disabled children have no chance. For this reason, the orphanage has often been willing to spend a great deal of its scarce resources to correct minor or cosmetic problems. An infant with a harelip had recently arrived, and the orphanage immediately consulted a physician about correcting the problem. After surgery, they explained, she could be adopted; without it, they would be unable to find her a family.

In the United States, adoption agencies find that those willing to adopt children with special needs are often those who have other children, either adopted or biological. In the case of Yuan Hui, one of the orphanage workers became strongly attached to her and wanted to adopt her, but the worker could not obtain permission because she already had two older children.

At first I thought this policy an irrational extension of the population control regulations. While the effect of the adoption regulations has indeed been inadvertently cruel in many cases, I later learned that its origin was not related to population control policies, although those policies became a crucial part of the rationale for maintaining the policy and codifying it into law in 1991. Orphanage documents indicate that the 1991 legal requirement that couples be childless and infertile dates back to the 1950s. The reasoning at that time was that if there were any biological children in the family, the adopted child would be likely to suffer discrimination. Implicit in this concern is the fear that people who already have children may have ulterior motives for adopting a girl, such as the desire for a servant, a laborer, or, as in the past in some areas, a future daughter-in-law (*tongyangxi*).

These were once all considered legitimate reasons for wanting to "adopt" a girl. An orphanage was a logical place to go to obtain a *tongyangxi* or a servant.[50] As noted earlier, orphanage officials today consider these purposes inhumane as well as illegal and try hard to guard against them in screening applicants for adoption. Even when an applicant is childless, they try to scrutinize motives carefully, at least until the recent increase in numbers made this precaution impossible. They told the story of a retired disabled soldier from Wuhan who was decorated and had a substantial retirement salary. He was over fifty and wanted to adopt a daughter to take care of him, as he had lost the ability to care for himself. While orphanage officials recognize that social security in old age is a common and legitimate reason for wanting to have children, they found this man's motives blatantly exploitative. They turned down his application, telling him that they would not give away children to be raised as servants.

Despite the original policy's legitimate concern for children's welfare, with the number of abandoned children rapidly exceeding that of available adoptive families, continued insistence that couples document their childlessness, not just that they have appropriate motives, meant that even nondisabled children remained in the orphanage for a longer time, thereby endangering their health and depriving them of the kind of attention necessary for young children to thrive.

A new national adoption law, passed in December 1991 and implemented in April 1992, codified the requirement that adopters be childless and solidified restrictions on those who could legally adopt healthy children. But the law attempted to remedy the difficulty of finding adoptive homes for disabled children by dropping the requirement that a couple be childless if they adopt a disabled child. Because this clause significantly enlarged the pool of prospective adoptive parents for these children, while making the adoption of healthy children difficult, it proved useful in finding homes for some mildly or moderately disabled children. It immediately allowed the placing of disabled children in a growing number of foreign adoptions, which were subject to the same regulations as domestic adoptions.[51] It also helped place several girls with minor disabilities in Chinese families.

Orphanage staff did not personally disapprove of parents with children adopting another child, even through deception, and they may have welcomed this practice as a means to find more adoptive homes. But they did worry about their increasing inability to screen or supervise adoptions. Reinforcing those concerns were the frequent reports that have appeared in the Chinese press in recent years about an illegal and often forcible traffic in women and children. The purpose of the trade is often left unstated and unclear, but is sometimes said to supply brides to men who cannot otherwise attract wives, such as those who live in poor and remote areas. The children involved are presumably sold as *tongyangxi* or for other unspecified illicit purposes.[52]

Sometimes infant girls are taken forcibly from their mothers by a spouse or in-law to gain another chance to produce a boy. Some of the personal pain and turmoil involved in this practice was revealed one day when, in the orphanage courtyard, I saw a young woman sobbing and pleading for help. The woman had recently disappointed her husband by giving birth to a girl. After an angry fight, her husband took the baby away and returned without her, refusing to tell his wife what he had done with the child. The woman had spent several days frantically looking for her infant before learning from the police about the orphanage. Much to the woman's relief, the infant had indeed been brought to the orphanage a few days earlier. On producing the birth registration and filing a report, the woman would be able to leave with her daughter.

The vice-director recently caught another father trying to leave his three- or four-year-old daughter at the doorstep of the orphanage. Hearing a child crying loudly on the street early one morning, she looked outside the courtyard gate and saw a man walking away from a weeping child. When the child called the man "daddy," the staff member ran after him and scolded him for abandoning his child. In the end, she got him to take the child away with him. She later heard that the child was again seen alone and crying in a nearby neighborhood, but the police were unable to locate her. The staff member worried that she had made a mistake in trying to persuade the father to keep his daughter, yet felt she had no choice but to try to prevent him from abandoning his child, especially in the light of the increasingly crowded conditions in the orphanage at that time.

The orphanage was not the only institution feeling an increased burden from the pressures of population control policies and the increasing abandonment of girls in the early 1990s. In 1992, the Wuhan Children's Hospital transferred to the orphanage more than ten sick babies who had been abandoned in the hospital by birthparents. The hospital claimed that the children were well and no longer needed to be hospitalized.

Were the children still in need of hospital care, presumably the hospital would have been obliged to keep them until they were fit to be discharged, even though there was no one to pay the bills. Since their parents had disappeared, it was now the responsibility of the orphanage to accept and care for them. In nearly all cases, the children proved to be extremely ill and died.[53] The orphanage director protested repeatedly to the Civil Affairs Bureau, which has jurisdiction over the orphanage, but to no avail, since the hospital is under the Health Bureau and cannot be disciplined in any way by the Civil Affairs Bureau. Orphanage workers were understandably distressed by the hospital's seemingly deceitful and self-serving behavior, but in the absence of outside government funding to defray the extra medical costs of care for these abandoned children, it is not surprising that this shifting of responsibility occurred. The budgets of state welfare and social service institutions have been particularly strapped as Beijing tightens its fiscal belt. As already noted, the orphanage itself was forced to practice a form of triage because of an inadequate budget. There is no doubt that some of the severely ill children in the orphanage died because the cost of saving them would be too great, as indicated by the case of the three boys discussed above who were saved only because adoptive parents were available to pay extraordinary fees for intensive medical care. On one visit, we asked about one of the very sick infants lying in a crib in the large room. We were told that the doctors had sent the child back to them to die because she was "too ill to save."

In the early 1990s, the orphanage received only 60 yuan (less than US$8) per month per child. This amount had not changed for many years despite the rising costs to feed and clothe each child. From this 60 yuan, the orphanage also paid for the hospital and medical bills of children who become sick. As we have seen, many babies arrive in a weakened state and greatly need medical care. Medical treatment charged to the orphanage can be expensive even for routine illnesses, and these costs had risen in recent years. In 1991 a standard ten-day in-patient treatment for pneumonia cost 800 to 1,000 yuan (around $100–125). With so many babies requiring treatment for pneumonia and other ailments, the pressure against "wasting" scarce resources on a child who might not survive or whose bills would be prohibitively expensive was great and growing.

Turning to Foreign Adoptions

Clearly the orphanage needed more funds as well as more adoptive parents. Fortunately, beginning in the early 1990s it was allowed to raise funds and find homes for some of the children through foreign adoptions. This new source of income became possible when in April 1992 the central government issued the adoption law. This was the first adoption law the Chinese government had ever issued, aside from a single clause in the marriage law. Although the process for domestic adoption became more centralized and bureaucratic, the new law made it easier than before to arrange foreign adoptions.[54] First, the government issued guidelines under this law for local notarial offices to approve foreign adoptions and to supply the legal documents required by most other countries. Most important, the law also removed the previous de facto practice of limiting foreign adoptions to people of Chinese ancestry and those who had worked in China or had special ties to China.

Although the Wuhan Orphanage had started arranging foreign adoptions a few years earlier, it only processed two or three a year. In 1992, after the passage of the adoption law, it quickly processed thirty-five to forty foreign adoptions, charging a fee of US$3,000 for each. (In the early 1990s, domestic adoptions cost between 200 and 800 yuan, roughly US$25–100.) The orphanage kept a significant portion of this money. In the first years of international adoption, it used the fees to expand and renovate the old buildings to accommodate more children and staff, to install air conditioners in the infant rooms, to pay for some of the expensive medical care, and to keep a larger number of children in foster care.[55]

The desire to use foreign adoptions to gain needed funds to run the orphanages and to obtain scarce foreign exchange was great, tempting orphanages to push up the numbers of foreign adoptions by whatever means. There was also the possibility of serious corruption, which creates vested interests at various levels of the local government bureaucracies that oversee the adoption process. Thus, after the adoption law was implemented in April 1992, the China Adoption Center was set up in Beijing to oversee international adoptions. In this way, Beijing hoped to keep a close eye on the growing foreign adoption business and keep a lid on corruption. At the same time, the authorities in Beijing seemed eager to increase foreign adoptions in an orderly way as a means to fund state welfare institutions and to alleviate one of the dire consequences of their population policies—abandonment of female children. Beijing's willingness to facilitate such adoptions also reflected the new mood of openness and reform.

Solutions

Whatever the future holds for the prospects of foreign adoptions, it is obvious that, even at best, such developments do not address the social crisis created for China's girls by government population control policies.

It is surprising that so little critical comment has been offered by various women's groups and magazines in China about the way women and girls disproportionately bear the consequences of the population control policies and about the severity of those consequences.[56] This reticence does not seem simply a matter of fear of censorship; since the 1980s, women's magazines and the Women's Federation have raised critical voices about many issues.[57] The silence may instead reflect most urban people's uncritical acceptance of the necessity of population control policies and the high-pressure tactics that support them, even if they do not like them. Many of these people, like the prominent pro-democracy authors of the well-known television documentary *River Elegy* (*He shang*), blame peasants for the severity of the population problem and believe that uneducated peasants have been responsible for lowering the quality of the population by having too many children. It is precisely the most powerless and isolated groups in society who are most negatively affected by the coercive population control policies and whose lives are put at greatest risk—that is, rural women and girls.

The government has shown some signs of concern over the skewed sex ratio,[58] and it has periodically condemned practices such as infanticide and abandonment. The current mood of openness and willingness to facilitate foreign adoptions in itself indicates a greater willingness to allow others a glimpse of this growing social problem, which might in turn prompt greater domestic attention. But blaming backward "feudal" thought and the ignorance of "backward" peasants, as those both inside and outside the government so often do, sidesteps the responsibility that the government's own policies must bear as the primary catalyst for this new wave of abandonment, infanticide, and "missing girls."

Of course, peasant attitudes and the social patterns that bolster them are the proximate cause of these problems. But this study of the Wuhan area suggests that abandonment, or the custom of "throwing away babies," which has long plagued this area, dropped significantly among the local peasantry prior to the late 1970s; for years this "custom" had virtually vanished with regard to healthy daughters. But the duress created by draconian, coercive measures undertaken to implement the population control policies has revived practices that were dying. What is at stake for peasants today, above all else, is not a set of abstract attitudes that lead them to adore boys and disdain girls, but a concrete traditional survival strategy, demanded by the patrilineal, patrilocal culture of rural Chinese society, of relying on sons for security in old age. This strategy is not easily changed by an act of individual will, but must be eroded on a widespread social basis by socioeconomic change and government policy. Daughters still "belong to other people" in many rural communities; it is daughters-in-law (other people's daughters) and the sons who bring them into the family whom one can and must depend on. This is not, as one Chinese friend remarked to me, a personal "opinion" or an "attitude" but a "fact" that individual parents of daughters must confront and that they can change only with great difficulty, if at all.

While most urban residents, through state sector employment, have long enjoyed government pensions on retirement, the government has yet to provide any credible alternative in the countryside. With the return to family farms in China in the 1980s, even the meager charity once provided by collectives disappeared in many areas. One of the most important things the state could do to alleviate the severe consequences of their population control policies would be to institute a national pension plan for the countryside. If the government had pursued this goal with the vigor and single-mindedness it has employed in its population control efforts since the early 1980s, the ensuing problems of infanticide, abandonment, and "missing girls" would be far less severe. A pension would not be a fully adequate substitute for the status and solace that an adult child can bring by caring for an aging parent, but it would help substitute for the financial security provided by a son.

A national pension plan, while an extremely formidable task, is not beyond the current financial means of the government, although it may be beyond its political will and priorities. The pattern of state expenditures in China has long discriminated against the countryside while being relatively generous in subsidizing the urban population directly and indirectly (as in the Stalinist-Maoist practice of paying artificially low state prices for agriculture so that urban residents could have cheap food). For example, providing all peasants over age sixty-five with 50 yuan a month, which was close to the 1991 national per capita rural income, would have cost less than the monthly food price subsidy given in 1991 to all urban residents, most of whose income far exceeded rural income.[59] In the early 1990s, the government was in the process of eliminating this urban food subsidy, but various other hidden subsidies remain. One can imagine few investments more beneficial to the long-term health and stability of China than to find ways to establish a pension plan for peasants and others not covered by existing plans. An increasing number of experts inside and outside China have urged the government to move in this direction, and the leadership at various levels has been actively examining various possibilities for providing greater old-age security for the countryside.[60]

In the meantime, if the government continues to press its ambitious population control policies, as it almost certainly will, the key to alleviating the immediate crisis lies with more direct measures to ameliorate the consequences. At a bare minimum, the government has a responsibility to provide much more generous funding to the welfare institutions and hospitals that care for abandoned children, and a far more effective network of relief must be set up in the countryside.[61] Some orphanage officials guessed that a majority of the abandoned babies die before they are recovered, especially those abandoned in the countryside.[62] As noted, even the babies picked up in the city are often extremely weak by the time they reach the orphanage. Among those lucky enough to be brought to the Wuhan Orphanage in the early 1990s, only slightly more than half would survive. The welfare houses located in smaller cities and towns were apt to have even higher mortality rates. Officials at one near Shijiazhuang, Hebei province, disclosed that they had a death rate of 90 percent among their predominantly female foundlings. Those death rates are particularly staggering given that outside the orphanages, infant mortality and survival rates among young children were extremely good for a country at

China's economic level.[63] Low infant mortality is one of the great accomplishments of the People's Republic of China.

Experience in other countries indicates that moving away from orphanage care toward a supervised network of foster home care can greatly reduce mortality rates, although this method of care can be much more expensive and cumbersome to run well.[64] Releasing orphanages from the necessity of upholding the single-child family norms of state population control policies would also quickly enlarge the pool of adoptive parents and would help move children into adoptive homes much more readily. This would save many lives.

Given the severe consequences, the waves of high-pressure mobilization campaigns, which often include coerced sterilization of women who have borne two children, seem particularly unconscionable and counterproductive. These campaigns cost the lives of untold numbers of infant girls and pressure beleaguered parents to abandon older children they would otherwise be happy to raise. The government must find ways of implementing policy that are more temperate and less coercive, even if that means letting more people slip by the regulations.

To abandon high-pressure methods is not tantamount to abandoning all effective population control efforts, although Chinese policy makers and many Western observers often seem to assume so.[65] A more humane, noncoercive policy may mean a larger Chinese population, but it does not necessarily mean uncontrolled and disastrous population growth. At least a few observers in the field have offered alternatives that would be less coercive than current policies.[66] A well-funded family planning program that allows for peasants' felt need to have at least one son and that emphasizes education, health care, and improved quality and delivery of contraception may be less "effective" in the short run, but more sustainable in the long run and certainly less damaging to the social and moral fabric of Chinese society.[67]

Moreover, careful study has led at least some experts in the population field to argue that the benefits gained from reducing population growth are not as great as usually assumed and are not significant enough to warrant coercion.[68] When such coercion threatens or ends the lives of hundreds of thousands of children each year, a more careful look at less deadly alternatives and less coercive methods is surely required of all those responsible for devising, implementing, and evaluating these policies.

CHAPTER TWO

Orphanage Care in China, 1989–95

A Response to Human Rights Watch

The 1995 report on Chinese orphanages by Human Rights Watch (HRW) received widespread publicity and strikingly little criticism, except from a predictably defensive and closed Chinese government and from adoption agencies, which were understandably fearful that China's international adoption program would slow down or close as a result of this bad publicity. Adoptive parents who have visited orphanages and seen things that contradict the HRW report have been given little credence and dismissed as naive.

I am an adoptive parent, but I am also an academic who has studied China for more than two decades. I have been studying the problem of infant abandonment and orphanages in China for several years. I am no apologist for the Chinese government; my previous publishing record makes that clear. (For example, I was one of four foreign researchers participating in a village study that has been reviewed as the "bleakest" and most critical village study to have been published on post-1949 China.) Given my knowledge and continuing research on this topic, I do not find the basic assertion of the HRW report convincing—that there is a state policy of extermination and intentional abuse of abandoned children in Chinese state-run welfare institutions.

HRW bases its assertion on two pieces of evidence. First, it has evidence of abuse in one such institution—the Shanghai Children's Welfare Institute—from the late 1980s until 1993, when the institution underwent a significant overhaul, which HRW dismisses as "cosmetic." Second, HRW cites statistics from the Chinese Civil Affairs authorities for several provinces in 1989–90 indicating that mortality rates in welfare institutions that care for abandoned children were between 50 and 80 percent.

Without much further evidence, HRW puts these two pieces of shocking information together in a tight causal relationship and concludes that they are proof of "widespread atrocities" and a national policy, carried out in hundreds of local institutions across China, to reduce the population of abandoned infants by the "routine murder of children through deliberate starvation."

My research leads me to reject this sweeping thesis. Of course I have not investigated the hundreds of institutions that care for the escalating population of abandoned, primarily female, infants in China. Neither has HRW. The only evidence they bring to light is about Shanghai. I have no independent knowledge of the Shanghai orphanage, which may indeed have seen terrible abuses, just as some mental institutions in my own state of Massachusetts did in the 1970s. But I have learned a

great deal about several other major Chinese child welfare institutions and several smaller ones in different locations in China.
Nothing I have seen in their records, in my visits, or in extensive interviews has led me to believe that they have practiced the
policy alleged by HRW.

I learned about the escalating problem of abandonment and
of the tragically high mortality rates among abandoned children
living in orphanages five years ago when I made repeated visits
to a large state orphanage in central China. I found the staff and
management of the orphanage to be surprisingly open, given
my intrusive presence and endless, pointed questions. I was
allowed free roam of the place, without any concern about
unannounced visits. My questions, including those about the
growing numbers of infants and the mortality rate, were
answered frankly and, as I have since ascertained through
numerous other sources and limited-circulation documents,
accurately in every instance. I was upset and initially surprised,
indeed shocked, by what I learned of this new and quickly
growing problem. But the staff, though sometimes reticent,
never attempted to hide information or give me a misleading
impression of conditions at the institution.

The explanation for the high mortality rates involved many
factors, most beyond the control of the orphanage staff. First, a
high percentage of infants were extremely ill on arrival. I saw
evidence of this phenomenon on several visits, as new children
arrived. A large proportion suffered from congenital disabilities,
many of which were life threatening or terminal.

The act of abandonment was itself life threatening, and many
infants (such as my own daughter) who were born without disabilities were brought to the brink of death from malnutrition,

exposure, and illness before they reached the orphanage. The human infant is a fragile being under the best of circumstances and does not tolerate well even a short period of deprivation, which is tragically part of almost all acts of abandonment in China.

While birthparents may not intend it, or allow themselves to contemplate the fact, abandonment is all too often tantamount to infanticide. Furthermore, many children are abandoned precisely because they are extremely ill. When dying children were left in hospitals by parents who ran away to avoid bills they might be unable to afford, the hospital authorities routinely brought the terminally ill children to the orphanage to die. In effect the orphanage served as a hospice. It was the orphanage that was left to deal with the tragic problems that no one else would shoulder, neither birthparents nor other institutions. In most cases these tragic problems represent the negative consequences of population policies, policies that have been internationally supported and praised for their "success," even as China has been periodically condemned for their inevitable, horrible consequences. A double bind if there ever was one.

In the early 1990s the orphanages I learned about were inundated with escalating numbers of infants for whom staff and resources were sorely inadequate. HRW scoffs at these reasons for high mortality in Shanghai and all of China. HRW is wrong. Where I investigated, there were neither funds nor staff to provide the intensive medical treatment and individual round-the-clock care that many infants required. There simply were not funds to provide extraordinary medical treatment to children who were unlikely to survive. But expensive medical care *was* provided for those most likely to benefit from it.

Had there been a policy in 1991, as HRW asserts, to limit the population in this particular orphanage, a short delay in taking my daughter (and a dozen others like her whom I saw in early 1991) to the hospital for an intensive and expensive two-week treatment for pneumonia would have resulted in her rapid death. At the time her medical records show that she was a severely malnourished, underweight one-month-old who could all too easily have expired from even a minor infection. Only quick treatment saved her.

I also saw two infants with harelips who had just returned from a medical evaluation and who were scheduled for surgery to correct the problem, making it possible for the orphanage to find adoptive homes for them. Obviously, the orphanage staff had to decide carefully how to use scarce funds, and they chose with an eye to getting the most benefit for the children they felt they could help. These were tough choices I would never have wanted to make.

When I first visited this orphanage and a few others, there were virtually no international adoptions from China, and there were no "showcases" for foreign consumption. While this was one of the largest and possibly one of the best-run orphanages in China, its main business was to save as many children as it could within its resources and arrange for domestic adoptions. It had in fact always been able to find domestic adoptions for the healthy infants it received and for those it could restore to health. It arranges hundreds of domestic adoptions each year. This orphanage had in the early 1960s established nationwide networks for recruiting adoptive parents, despite the restrictive qualifications (i.e., that adoptive parents be childless and over age thirty-five).

Other large orphanages I investigated also emphasized recruiting domestic adoptive parents and were quite successful in doing so, a fact that HRW chooses to downplay. It was only in the early 1990s that the escalating numbers began to strain this orphanage's ability to find Chinese parents for its healthy infants and toddlers and that the longstanding "childless" restriction became a problem for them.

At this point international adoptions began to open up, bringing a new source of prospective parents as well as an important new source of funds to this and other orphanages. As a result, physical conditions and staffing have improved greatly. Since 1993 this orphanage and others have also benefited from a campaign, endorsed by Party leader Jiang Zemin (himself adopted as a child), to "aid and support orphans." This initiative has brought new domestic donations and, most important, medical volunteers from the local hospitals that used to charge the orphanage high prices for medical care. Improvements are strikingly evident here, as in a dozen or more other institutions.

HRW sneers at these improvements as "cosmetic." In fact they are precisely the kinds of improvements we would hope for; they provide clear evidence that fees gathered through foreign adoptions are being put to good use. Nonetheless these changes have not solved the basic problem for Chinese orphanages— escalating numbers of abandoned children because of strict implementation of population control policies and the de facto use of orphanages by birthparents and other institutions as hospices and repositories for disabled and "unadoptable" children.

There is at least one point on which HRW and I agree. Easing domestic adoption regulations would quickly help reduce the numbers of children in orphanages. China has long traditions of adoption, and today many couples who have had one or two sons, or older parents whose biological children have grown, strongly desire to have a daughter. Contrary to widespread belief outside China, contemporary Chinese popular culture increasingly values daughters as a source of emotional support and closeness for parents.

Unfortunately, the HRW report does nothing to help those in China who agree that domestic adoption laws should be changed, a position that is suggested in numerous popular magazines that did not need HRW's sensationalized report to "educate" them. Furthermore, the report might have jeopardized the international adoption program, which has done so much to help orphanage directors meet the recent crisis.[1]

I strongly believe that HRW has pointed its guns in the wrong direction, calling for a witch hunt among civil affairs and orphanage staff to blame them, along with an alleged national policy of extermination, for the high mortality rates among abandoned children. When I left the orphanage discussed above, I felt extremely critical of the conditions and policies that had created the crisis and the high death rates—the inadequate resources, the understaffing, the lack of help from other institutions, and above all the severe campaigns aimed at limiting China's growing population.

I have also been critical of American adoptive parents who, all too frequently, have seemed unwilling to take any risks in adopting children with even minor, correctible disabilities, children who are so much more difficult to place in China, where adoptive parents do not have the kind of income or medical insurance most American parents have.

Changing the domestic adoption regulations will not help those children. But the orphanage staff and the civil affairs bureaucracy in places I have investigated have not been responsible for creating these problems. Although I do not doubt that some orphanage workers perpetrate abuse in this undersupervised system, those that I have met were hard working, conscientious, and surprisingly open people who occasionally, in secret and private moments, showed the emotional toll their jobs took on them. I left with admiration for them and a desire to see their work more fully supported.

HRW does not provide that support; indeed it slanders and hurts them as a group. I only hope the Chinese authorities will not react with defensiveness and churlishness to this attack. They would be wise to let the unjustified generalizations of HRW go by while dealing in earnest with the real problems presented by abandonment, adoption, and orphanage care in China.[2]

CHAPTER THREE

The Revival of Infant Abandonment in China, 1989–95

One of the least investigated consequences of birth-planning policies in China is the abandonment of infants. Chinese officials, as well as the population involved, have shrouded this practice in secrecy, reflecting shame and political embarrassment. As a result, "hard data" on abandonment are extremely difficult to obtain. Because of the lack of systematic data, and perhaps because of the political sensitivity of the topic, demographers and other scholars have also avoided the subject, including those who have investigated the problem of China's "missing girls."[1] Studies of the missing girls have explored causes other than abandonment; yet abandonment, while not tantamount to infanticide, often leads to death as well as statistical "disappearance."

Some investigators have dismissed abandonment as a practice that could help explain the problem of the "missing girls." Zeng Yi and colleagues assert that while some parents may abandon a female child, they do so in a place where the child is easily found and then taken to a local civil affairs department, where she will be well cared for.[2] They imply that the children who undergo this experience are both few in number and at no significant risk.

While phenomena such as abandonment and infanticide may account for only a minority of the rapidly increasing numbers of "missing girls"—growing in the 1990s by over one million missing female births per year, according to some estimates[3]—there is mounting evidence that the problem of female infant abandonment is severe in some regions of the country and that many tens of thousands, perhaps hundreds of thousands, of children are abandoned each year. Evidence also suggests that mortality rates among foundlings may be extremely high. The problem clearly deserves more attention from scholars and policymakers alike.

Statistics that directly address the problem of abandonment and the related issue of infanticide are predictably few. Top birth-planning officials have compelling reasons to obscure the problem. Understandably, they do not want to acknowledge the extent to which infant girls have become victims of their policies, and they no doubt fear the criticism that might be raised against their policies if the extent of this and related problems was fully revealed. While the civil affairs bureaucracy has been somewhat more willing than those working within the birth-planning apparatus to discuss abandonment,[4] in the mid-1980s the Ministry of Civil Affairs notified orphanage officials that records detailing the growth and composition of their foundling population should be kept secret.[5]

Nevertheless, some public discussion of the plight of "orphans"—a term that implicitly, if not always explicitly, includes foundlings—has emerged. The decision several years ago to permit international adoptions of Chinese foundlings signaled a willingness to allow the problem to be glimpsed outside China. In August 1995 a civil affairs official granted a videotaped interview to a CBS film crew taping a segment on Chinese orphanages for a network news show in the United States.[6] The official candidly admitted that there were problems of overcrowding and underfunding in China's orphanages, even as he defended his government against accusations raised by a controversial documentary on conditions in Chinese orphanages aired on Britain's Channel Four in June 1995.[7] Since the early 1990s, domestic readers have also been able to learn more about this problem through local newspapers and magazines, at least in anecdotal form, and there have been frequent public solicitations for aid and donations to help orphanages. This willingness to allow mention of the problem began at a time when Beijing was increasingly urging local civil affairs authorities to find new ways of raising their own funds.[8]

This chapter will examine the problem of abandonment, focusing primarily on Hunan (a province with a population of 65 million in 1994), about which some unusually candid official investigative information was published.[9] The statistical data available on this problem in Hunan are far from adequate to reach firm conclusions, but when augmented with other relevant information and documentary evidence, they provide insight into the problem of abandonment. Interviews conducted in four areas of China between 1991 and 1995, including the author's earlier research in neighboring Hubei province, will be used to supplement the discussion of the Hunan materials.[10]

A Regional "Tradition" of "Throwing Away Babies"?

When visiting an orphanage in Hubei province in early 1991, I was told by a municipal official that there was a long "tradition" of "throwing away" very young children in this part of the country. As a result, people from northern China sometimes come to this south-central region to adopt children. Similarly, officials in the Ministry of Civil Affairs in Beijing have told potential adopting couples that while "most" of the children available for adoption in the north are disabled, many healthy abandoned infants are available in parts of the south. Whether these broad generalizations would hold up to careful comparative investigation and whether they reflect long historical differences is not certain. Scattered statistics from other places suggest that the escalating rates of abandonment experienced in areas of Hunan and Hubei in the late 1980s and early 1990s may not have been as marked everywhere in the country. For example, statistics from major orphanages in Shanghai and Tianjin suggest some increase at the beginning of birth-planning campaigns around 1980 but do not show substantial increases in the late 1980s.[11]

Whether or not parts of the south are particularly marked by customs that promote the abandonment of unwanted, primarily female, children,[12] there is considerable evidence from local histories that female infant abandonment, and perhaps infanticide, were long-standing phenomena in the south-central provinces of Hubei and Hunan prior to 1949. The compilers of a Hunan provincial history published in 1988 note that prior to 1949 abandonment was widespread there and that it involved almost entirely girls.[13] In Hunan, as in many other parts of China, girls occupy a marginal place in a patrilineal kinship and family system that puts them at far greater risk than boys of being abandoned.[14] Conversely, the central importance and cultural value of sons in family and kinship lines make it highly unlikely that a boy would be abandoned except under dire circumstances.

According to the aforementioned provincial history, widespread infant abandonment and infanticide led to the criminalization of these acts by the late seventeenth century and to the creation of a provincewide network of foundling homes.[15] By 1849, there were sixty-eight county-run establishments to care for foundlings.[16] In 1934, a provincial official told a national meeting of charity organizations that the largest of these institutions, the Foundling Institute of the Provincial City (Changsha) Salvation Center, had "saved the lives of several hundreds of thousands" of baby girls in its 220-year history.[17] These organized efforts to ameliorate the problem of female abandonment and infanticide persisted through the late 1930s, after which the entire network apparently collapsed in the wake of the Japanese invasion.

Birth-Planning Campaigns and Abandonment in the 1980s

The compilers of the 1988 Hunan provincial history note briefly that abandonment and infanticide declined significantly from the 1950s through the early 1970s.[18] In the late 1970s, however, with the implementation of restrictive birth planning, the problem reappeared. In remote mountain areas, a minority of peasants, still influenced by "remnant feudal thoughts" of valuing males and disparaging females and wanting male heirs to continue the ancestral line, abandoned or even killed their infant daughters. The authors cite Loudi city as an example. There, from 1979–81 the civil affairs department received fifty foundlings, forty-nine of whom were girls. The authors conclude with a plea to pay more attention to the problem and to punish the perpetrators of these crimes.

While abandonment began to increase in Hunan in the late 1970s, the situation appears to have worsened considerably by the late 1980s. In 1987, a report by the Yueyang City Civil Affairs Office, printed with editorial approval in the national publication of the Ministry of Civil Affairs, discussed the need to strengthen efforts to oppose the practice while taking steps to improve the welfare system's ability to care for the increasing number of abandoned infants.[19] In 1991 the Hunan provincial government launched a special investigation into the problem of abandonment in Hunan, the report of which was also published.[20]

According to the 1991 investigation, abandonment increased greatly in the late 1980s, alongside the growing problems of private adoption and of "secretly giving children to others to raise" as a means of getting around birth-planning restrictions. More than sixteen thousand abandoned children were brought to civil affairs departments in the province between 1986 and 1990. The vast majority of these children came from rural areas, 92 percent were girls, and most were very young, sometimes only a few days old. At one presumably typical welfare home cited as an example, 55 percent of the foundlings taken in between 1988 and 1990 were under one year old.

The report also notes that 25 percent of the abandoned children were "disabled" (*canji*) in some way. While the investigators treat this figure as if it were large, it is actually low compared with abandonment elsewhere and in previous decades, indicating that substantial numbers of healthy children were being abandoned. As noted above, it is commonly reported that most children in orphanages in the north are disabled.[21] The records of the Wuhan Foundling Hospital, a large municipal orphanage in neighboring Hubei, indicate that over 90 percent of the abandoned children received in the 1950s, 1960s (with the exception of the famine years of 1959–61), and the early 1970s were classified as "disabled."[22] Only with the advent of birth-planning campaigns did peasants in the Wuhan area of Hubei province resort to abandoning large numbers of healthy daughters. While the pattern may be different in Hunan, there too the rise in numbers of abandoned children probably reflects an increase in the percentage of healthy female children abandoned in the wake of population control efforts.

In 1990, the last year covered by the investigation, the numbers of abandoned children in Hunan were much higher than in preceding years. As an example, the investigative report cites Hengyang city, where the number of abandoned children found in 1988 was 233, rising to 352 in 1989 and 854 in 1990. This was the trend throughout the province and in neighboring Hubei during the same period.[23] In the late 1980s much of this south-central area seems to have experienced an escalation of birth-planning efforts, even though the policy had changed from a strict one-child rule to one that allowed rural residents to have a second child if the first was a girl. Thus by the late 1980s the formal policy in both Hunan and Hubei became "one son or two children." But as early as 1987, Hunan embarked on stricter administrative controls to pressure local cadres to attain better compliance with the policy.[24] Under these controls, cadres in areas that failed to meet their birth-planning targets would be ineligible for promotions or bonuses, and their units would be disqualified from becoming "advanced units" in agricultural production, a title that usually entails privileges and advantageous connections. As a result of these measures, the number of birth control operations (e.g., IUD insertions, sterilizations, abortions) increased after 1986, an indication to provincial authorities that birth-planning work was improving. Unfortunately, this "improvement" brought with it a wave of infant abandonment.

Elsewhere in China, a similar tightening in policy implementation was reported in the late 1980s. In Shaanxi province, Susan Greenhalgh found a distinct change from an informal, locally negotiated policy that allowed peasant families leeway to obtain a minimally desirable outcome in the number and gender of their children (two children, including at least one son) to a strictly enforced one-son/two-child policy implemented from the top.[25] This change in the area Greenhalgh studied occurred around 1988, and it had devastating consequences for infant girls. In the period 1988–93, reported sex ratios at birth—male births per 100 female births—increased sharply. Although Greenhalgh found no direct evidence of abandonment, and local cadres denied any knowledge of the practice, she also found no explanation of what was happening to the girls who should have appeared as live births if a biologically normal sex ratio at birth prevailed. In her three-village sample, the sex ratio of newborns fluctuated from 114 in 1979–83 to

98 in the locally lenient period 1984–87, with a high of 145 in the 1988–93 period of strict policy enforcement. Thus, whatever happened to the female infants—whether they were hidden, secretly given away in adoption, aborted after fetal sex determination by ultrasound, abandoned, or killed—increasing numbers of infant girls were missing from these villages.[26]

The investigative report of Hunan's Civil Affairs Bureau makes explicit the connection between abandonment and birth-planning campaigns. It even regards the province's welfare centers as barometers of birth-planning work in particular areas: when birth-planning work is "grasped tightly," more foundlings are received in local welfare facilities; when the campaigns wane, the numbers sharply decline. For example, in November 1990, when Shaoyang district vigorously developed a new birth-planning campaign, the municipal government received as many as sixteen foundlings in a single day. Although some of the increase in abandonment was attributed to the "chaotic" sexual mores of the so-called floating population—especially village youth who go to work temporarily in the city and end up having unwanted children out of wedlock—most was attributed to birth planning.

Ultimately, of course, this state of affairs was blamed not on central policies and their implementation but on the "feudal attitudes" of peasants who continue to hold the ideology of "raise a son to secure one's old age" and "raise a son to continue the ancestral line." It was said that in some areas in recent years the power of these "feudal remnants" had become stronger. According to the report, it was fashionable in some villages to secretly establish genealogical charts, set up lineage organizations, and elect lineage leaders. In such places those without sons suffer ridicule and discrimination, such as being slighted or passed over in allocating household plots or building new houses. It is difficult to know how widespread such revivals of lineage organizations and corporate ancestor worship are, or indeed if they are truly "revivals" at all, but others have also reported them in Hunan and elsewhere in China.[27] Certainly the cultural and religious requirements of patrilineal forms of kinship remain an important factor in the continuing desire for sons, and it is unlikely that this desire disappeared during the collective era. But social security needs must loom especially large in the countryside, where the vast majority of peasants have never enjoyed an adequate, guaranteed old-age pension. Even the minimum welfare provisions for the sonless elderly provided by many collectives disappeared in the 1980s.[28]

The layers of religious, cultural, and sometimes political significance of male offspring, combined with a need for basic social security, create formidable pressures—indeed, for many an absolute need—to have at least one son regardless of state birth-planning policies. These pressures place many girls, especially second-born daughters, in jeopardy, however more desired girls have become.[29] Now that the state has forced peasants to conceptualize their fertility in strictly limited numerate terms, the "traditional" desire for sons has for some become a near obsession.[30]

Cadres and Courts: Caught in the Middle

The Hunan Civil Affairs report gives glimpses of how local power holders aid and abet abandonment in the cultural and political context of the late 1980s. Cadres, charged with implementing unpopular and difficult policies, inevitably experience conflicting pressures from, on the one hand, fellow villagers who want more children than a strict reading of state policy allows and, on the other hand, the increasingly vigorous but locally variable demands from higher authorities for implementation of these policies. Strictly enforcing the policy breeds anger among peasants forced to forego what they strongly desire, and this reaction can make daily life difficult for local leaders.[31] Appearing to be too lax in enforcing the policy, however, brings reprimands and penalties from superiors.

One way of blunting these conflicting pressures and minimizing intrusions into the courtyards and bedrooms of neighbors is to enforce birth-planning targets by monitoring the size of a family rather than monitoring pregnancies and births. With a one-son/two-child policy, parents whose first child is a daughter are entitled to a "second-child permission certificate." According to the Hunan report, some parents take this certificate as a license to try an unlimited number of times to produce a son. Local cadres abet this behavior by not inquiring into the outcome of particular pregnancies and births, but merely requiring that the couple end up with the authorized number of children. When asked, peasants may claim that the pregnancy ended in miscarriage or stillbirth or that a young daughter suddenly became ill and died, and cadres make no further inquiries. According to the report, many of these daughters in fact end up as foundlings; others may be taken elsewhere to be raised surreptitiously by adoptive parents, at least temporarily. A few may even be victims of outright infanticide. The report blames local cadres for allowing this behavior to flourish and suggests that birth-planning officials must carefully monitor pregnancies and births, not only final outcomes. Turning a blind eye to abandonment, it seems, is a cadre strategy for coping with conflicting pressures and providing an escape valve for the most desperately motivated villagers.

The report also blames local cadres for directly participating in "throwing away" children by gathering up abandoned infants in their area and secretly transporting them elsewhere, such as to the gate of a municipal welfare center. The report refers to this practice as "organized abandonment" and expresses alarm at evidence of its increase. Cadres are also criticized for turning their backs when residents engage in "traveling abandonment"—that is, boarding a train or bus to transport a girl child to distant railway stations or other public places to abandon her. Presumably cadres do not want foundlings to be discovered in their jurisdiction because the presence of abandoned children would indicate that local birth-planning work had not been properly monitored. Cadres apparently also do not want the cost of caring for foundlings to come out of their own meager funds.

Thus different agents of the local bureaucracy argue among themselves about who should be responsible for managing and paying for this problem. The pattern at the county level, according to the report, was "Push away [the problem], send away [the foundlings], don't do anything [to address the practice]." As an example, the report describes a Shaodong county meeting of birth-planning cadres, civil affairs cadres, and Women's Federation cadres to discuss the foundling problem. Local civil affairs personnel argued that civil affairs departments are charged with caring for orphans and disabled children, not foundlings. The problem of abandonment, they argued, is part of the work of birth planning; hence the responsibility for foundlings properly belongs to birth-planning personnel. They should know who is most at risk for this behavior, and they have funds raised from birth-planning fines. In response, birth-planning personnel claimed that their work was difficult enough without taking on this task and that they did not have the responsibility or means to rear children. Civil affairs receives relief funds from the government to care for children, and thus they should take on the new foundlings. Apparently the meeting concluded without resolution, and upper administrative levels failed to resolve the dispute.

Finally, the provincial civil affairs report criticizes authorities at various levels for failing to enforce the law by investigating and punishing those who abandon children or those who aid and abet them. The report claims that as of 1991 there had not been a single successful prosecution and sentencing for the crime of abandonment. Even in areas where local civil affairs officials energetically investigated and collected evidence against abandoners, courts either failed to impose strict sentences or allowed their enforcement to be indefinitely delayed.

Presumably, authorities in a variety of units lack the political will to prosecute those who resort to abandonment to overcome birth-planning restrictions. Local cadres are often loath to uncover cases of abandonment lest they themselves be blamed for foundlings in their jurisdiction. Cadres and courts also reflect some sympathy for the plight of those who are desperate enough to turn to a practice clearly associated with great personal pain and shrouded in shameful collective silence.

The evident relationship between the act of abandonment and the high-priority policies of a central government that tolerates little criticism of its directives contributes to the silence and the difficulty leaders at various levels experience in pursuing the problem. In the mid 1980s, as I noted earlier, upper-level

government officials made the increasing problem of abandonment a state secret and informed local welfare officials that the
records concerning the numbers and composition of foundlings
in their institutions were to be kept closed. A problem officially
made secret, especially one surrounded by shame, is difficult to
call attention to and tackle effectively, no matter how well inten-
tioned local cadres may be. Such government-enforced public
silence may also contribute indirectly to abandonment, for it
keeps the public, including those who may be considering abandoning a child, from knowing about the inadequate facilities for
foundling care and the high risks of illness and death that an
abandoned child faces.

Welfare Centers and Provisions for Foundling Care

While local cadres argue among themselves about who is responsible for caring for foundlings, at most levels the responsibility falls
to the civil affairs bureaucracy, which runs the government welfare centers (*fuliyuan*). Yet civil affairs departments, reputed to be
the poorest of all the bureaucratic arms of the state, were ill pre-
pared to handle the sudden increase in abandonments in Hunan,
according to the 1991 provincial report. They had been allocated
no special funds for foundlings, and the number of welfare centers was sorely inadequate for the task. Most centers were run-
down and poorly equipped, with inadequate medical supplies. In
the entire province in 1991, some fifty welfare centers served fourteen districts and ninety-eight counties—fewer, it seems, than in
1849, when there were reportedly sixty-eight county-level facilities for foundlings. Of the fifty in 1991, only about ten had the
minimal equipment necessary to care for foundlings. Counties

without a welfare center had to find individual caretakers willing to provide foster care and pay 70–150 yuan a month for each child (or about US$16–35 at 1990 exchange rates).[32]

In fact, foster care may be much better for infants than institutional care and often results in lower mortality rates. But it is clear that local areas did not have the funds to pay for foster care for large numbers of foundlings or the ability to supervise whatever care they managed to arrange. Many local areas ended up exhausting their natural-disaster relief funds to pay for the care of foundlings in their jurisdiction. The 1991 report gives Yueyang city and Meiluo county as examples of areas that had been forced to use such funds in 1990, spending 230,000 and 70,000 yuan respectively. These problems no doubt contributed to "organized abandonment" and cadres' complicity in transporting foundlings to other areas.

Compounding civil affairs departments' difficulties in providing minimally adequate care for foundlings, the welfare centers themselves had trouble obtaining *hukou,* or official residential registration, for their foundlings from public security officials. Public security and other authorities strictly control the number of people allowed to change their registration from rural to urban areas because, among other things, the urban registration carries with it entitlements such as monthly cost-of-living subsidies, subsidized housing, and, until recently, access to grain at a subsidized price. Some parts of the bureaucracy treat the foundling issue as an aspect of the much-touted problem of the floating population, which raises the specter of massive transfers of rural residents into more privileged urban areas. These cadres assume that foundlings are the offspring of peasants not entitled to urban residency in the then-current quasi-caste system. Hence many public security bureaus were reluctant to issue residence certificates for foundlings living in welfare centers, which are usually located in towns or municipalities. In this way, migration control policies created additional obstacles for victims of population control, even though they were not intended to do so. Despite a 1986 provincial order entitling "genuine foundlings" to proper registration, welfare establishments were often unable to obtain hukou for foundlings in their care. A welfare center in Yueyang was said to have obtained registration for only twenty of forty-seven foundlings. Since the unregistered foundlings could not get subsidized grain, coal, cloth, or the monthly subsidy, the center had to pay more for their upkeep, further straining its inadequate budget.

Obstacles to Adoption

A final set of problems noted in the civil affairs report involved the obstacles to permanent adoption, one of the means by which civil affairs departments arrange care for foundlings.[33] The report complained that the adoption process is poorly coordinated, involving certification from public security authorities, birth-planning committees, and civil affairs departments. There are so many obstacles, the report claims, that some adoptive parents have reluctantly returned babies to welfare centers because they were unable to obtain all the certifications required for a legal adoption.

Although the report does not specify the difficulties, many arise from concurrent birth-planning efforts to stop illegal or informal adoptions and to prevent people from using adoption to remove daughters from the household and then try again for a son. Unless the child is an orphan (i.e., both parents are dead, in which case friends or relatives could adopt without restrictions), adoption regulations in the 1990s usually required adoptive couples to be childless, infertile, and above thirty-five years of age.[34] Yet in an atmosphere of strict birth planning, some couples regarded adopting a daughter from an orphanage as a desirable way to enlarge a small family, especially if they had no daughters and were not allowed to have any more births. While welfare officials sometimes overlooked the restrictions or knowingly accepted falsified certification in order to find homes for foundlings, the bureaucratic obstacles prevented many prospective adoptive couples from adopting a daughter. In some cases, if birth-planning officials discovered that a couple with a biological child had adopted another child, whether from a state welfare center or through some other channel, they could punish the parents as if the child were an overquota birth; in some cases, they might even take the adopted child away.[35]

In other words, the state's birth-planning policies and goals not only create foundlings, but also obstruct local officials' efforts to find permanent homes for them. State policies and established practices to control migration from the countryside may further impoverish those foundlings who are consigned to care in inadequately funded welfare centers. While the Hunan report does not criticize central policies and practices for causing these problems, the evidence points strongly in that direction.

Birth Planning and the Protection of Children's Rights: The Case of Xiong Qi

Multilayered political obstacles to the treatment, prosecution, and prevention of abandonment as seen in Hunan have also hindered women's-rights activists. Women's Federation cadres and welfare workers who took up the cause of abandoned girls have stated that it is extremely difficult to fight openly against the practice because of the lack of official support at various levels.[36] Drawing attention to abandonment is seen as an implicit criticism of birth-planning policies, and birth-planning officials complain that such efforts make their work more difficult. Thus, in a 1993 article about efforts to implement the omnibus Law Protecting Women's Rights and Interests, female infant abandonment was mentioned as an issue where contradictions with state policy made implementation impossible. Those involved with protecting women's rights had been told "not to interfere with these cases too much."[37]

In 1993, women activists in Beijing raised the issue of how to protect the "interests of the child" in cases of abandonment. The context was a well-publicized case of a small girl named Xiong Qi who was found, poorly dressed, rummaging through garbage for food in a neighborhood in Beijing.[38] This case did not explicitly implicate birth planning; rather, it highlighted the social problems created by the rural-to-urban migrant population and their alleged contribution to declining morals and the abandonment problem. But the case shows how the interests of abandoned girls get lost in a host of other considerations and why such cases rarely lead to prosecution or punishment of the perpetrators.

Those investigating Xiong Qi's situation learned that the mother, a rural woman who had married a mentally disabled Beijing resident (presumably to get a Beijing registration) had disappeared, leaving the young girl in the care of her incapacitated father and a great grandfather who also was not up to the task. The father's parents, retired Beijing workers, refused responsibility for Xiong Qi's care. After locating the mother and grandparents, the police and the courts told them that the law required them to care for the child. The courts further demanded that they reimburse the state for the cost of her temporary care at the Beijing Children's Welfare Center, where she lived for a year. But the mother would neither pay nor take back the child unless the grandparents provided the money; the grandparents refused, arguing that caring for a mentally disabled son was burden enough. The courts then threatened both parties with legal punishment, including jail, if they did not agree to take Xiong Qi back and rear her.

This case drew the attention of Xie Lihua, the founder and editor of *Rural Women Knowing All*, a small magazine published for and about rural women. Because Xiong Qi was the daughter of a rural woman, Xie decided that the magazine should officially represent the child's interests, interests that Xie felt the court and police were ignoring. On behalf of the magazine, Xie sued the court to prevent the return of Xiong Qi to her mother or grandparents and requested that the magazine be allowed to seek an adoption for the girl. Far from imposing guardianship on Xiong Qi's unwilling parents and grandparents, Xie argued, the court should completely sever their rights of guardianship over the child. They should then be fined and jailed for their criminal behavior. They were clearly unfit to rear a child and would only inflict further suffering on her. The court, which seemed interested only in ridding the state of the burden of paying for this child's care, should instead protect Xiong Qi's right to a decent home and to guardians who cared about her. Because of the attitude of the court, Xie continued, not only are the rights and interests of abandoned children neglected, but also those who commit the crime of abandonment go unpunished even when caught, aside from being forced to take back their child.

After the court refused to accept Xie's suit, the magazine sponsored a public meeting of experts to discuss the case. At the meeting the director of the Beijing Children's Welfare Center, Bian Youyi, defended the court's ruling, saying that if the court severed the guardianship rights of parents to protect the best interests of their abandoned child, the number of abandonments would skyrocket. The problem was already serious; the Beijing orphanage had more than 600 children, although it was equipped for 500 at most. Ninety percent of these children were foundlings. The state simply could not invite yet a greater burden and hence had no choice but to try to prevent abandonment by upholding the legal obligation of parents to care for their children. Even the publicity surrounding this case had led to a wave of abandonment at the orphanage's doorstep. A member of the Academy of Social Sciences concurred, arguing that if the guardianship rights of parents who abandoned their daughters were legally revoked, "China would not have an orphanage large enough to hold the foundlings."[39]

New Attention to Welfare Centers and the Plight of Orphans

Around 1993 public attention to the problem of "orphans" and disabled institutionalized children increased, and obliquely the existence of a sizable population of foundlings was acknowledged. This change was spearheaded by the reform-minded vice-minister of civil affairs, Yan Mingfu, and endorsed in early

1994 by President Jiang Zemin (himself adopted as a child) and other top leaders.[40] Among other steps, efforts were made to raise sizable charitable donations from Hong Kong and Taiwan to help fund orphanages and institutions that care for disabled children. Private foreign donations were favorably publicized.[41] There was also a campaign in many cities to promote public concern for orphans and disabled children and to solicit charitable donations from the public at large.[42] Orphanages in several major cities reported a significant increase in community support and involvement, including in some cases the provision of sorely needed free medical services from local hospitals.[43] In this new atmosphere of acknowledging the existence and the plight of Chinese orphanages and their wards, people were asked to donate money, do volunteer work, invite children living in welfare centers to celebrate holidays in their homes, and adopt eligible orphans and disabled children.[44] For the most part, these initiatives continued and even accelerated throughout the 1990s.

Through most of the 1990s, however, these efforts did not signal a formal easing of the restrictions on adopting healthy foundlings,[45] and the publicized examples of adoption involved only disabled foundlings and orphans. Despite top-level support to improve conditions for "orphans," this major obstacle to bettering the care of foundlings was not addressed for years out of concern that changes would impinge on higher-priority family-planning efforts to bolster the "one-child policy" by strictly limiting adoption to childless couples.

The opening of international adoption in the 1990s also helped several major orphanages, such as those in Changsha, Hangzhou, Hefei, Nanjing, and Wuhan, to acquire a new source of funds. While fees were relatively low by international standards, orphanages, or the local civil affairs welfare departments that run them, collect the lion's share, and these added substantially to their budget. A number of large orphanages were able to improve their facilities and medical care significantly during the 1990s thanks to the funds brought in by international adoption. Beijing has made an effort to spread these adoptions around, but it is unlikely that the poorer welfare centers outside major cities have yet benefited as much from these developments. The campaigns to solicit public involvement and foreign donations also targeted major cities.

Consequently, while the conditions of care have improved in some places, a great deal remains to be done, and the needs of many welfare centers are urgent. Mortality rates in the welfare centers that house foundlings are rarely revealed publicly—even in limited-circulation reports that are otherwise candid, such as the Hunan documents discussed above. But scattered statistics from civil affairs documents, as well as interviews with knowledgeable officials at different bureaucratic levels and in different regions, indicate that mortality rates among infants exceeded 40 percent in some of the major state-run orphanages in the mid 1990s.[46] In an on-camera interview with an American news crew, the director of the Tianjin Child Welfare Center—a relatively well funded and reputedly well managed orphanage caring for a high percentage of disabled children—reported that 25 percent of the children brought in during the winter of 1994–95 died despite efforts to save them.[47] Visits and interviews at several smaller, more remote, or more poorly equipped welfare centers revealed mortality rates as high as 80 percent.[48] Children who do not make it into the state welfare system may fare even worse.[49]

We don't know nearly enough to assess how much of this excessive mortality results from deficient orphanage conditions. A sensationalized, crudely researched television documentary on Chinese orphanages, aired in 1994 by Channel Four in Britain, charged that high mortality rates among foundlings were primarily the result of inadequate care and negligence within the orphanages.[50] While poor conditions in welfare centers no doubt contribute to high mortality rates, even a well-equipped and devoted orphanage staff would face a daunting task. A high percentage of children brought to welfare centers are in critical condition when they arrive, suffering from exposure, dehydration, malnutrition, and other preexisting conditions that may make it difficult to save them within the means of an average Chinese medical facility.[51] It is likely that many abandoned infants die before they are recovered or are not recovered at all, especially those abandoned in rural areas.[52]

Abandonment in China, as in other countries that have witnessed this social phenomenon, is a serious problem with life-threatening consequences. The institutions charged with dealing with this problem are too few and have been inadequately funded. As was true for foundlings in Europe in the nineteenth and early twentieth centuries,[53] the mortality rate for foundlings in China in the 1990s far exceeds that for children in the general population. And, as we have seen, Chinese foundlings are disproportionately girls.

Abandonment and the "Missing Girls"

From publicly available information, it is impossible to estimate the total number of children abandoned each year in

China. Yet it seems likely that abandonment contributes notably to the annual million-plus "missing" female births.[54] In 1991 an official in the Ministry of Civil Affairs reported that there were 140,000 "orphans" in China without mentioning what percentage were foundlings.[55] A 1994 article in a Chinese publication estimates that there were 100,000 homeless (primarily abandoned) children in China, only 20 percent of whom had found their way into the state orphanage system,[56] while articles in civil affairs publications around the same time often cited a figure of 160,000 abandoned children.[57] These estimates probably erred on the low side, but even if they were roughly accurate, they do not tell us the dimensions of the problem, for we know nothing of the "turnover rate" that results from mortality or adoption.[58] We know that some adoptions are done legally through welfare centers, but many more take place outside legal channels and hence go unregistered.[59] If there are 100,000 abandoned children at any one time in China, several hundreds of thousands may be abandoned each year, some of whom die, some of whom are adopted, and many of whom never get recorded in population registers. Abandonment may indeed be sufficiently widespread to contribute to the problem of "missing girls."

Even a government determined to uncover the true dimensions of the problem would have difficulty doing so. There is ample reason, as I have noted, for local cadres to hide the problem, and many foundlings never reach the attention of civil affairs or public security authorities. But whatever the real numbers may be, they add up to a huge toll of human suffering and discrimination that will leave scars not only on the surviving children, but also on those who must live with their deeds in shameful silence. As reflected in child abandonment, the price of birth planning in China has indeed been high.

Conclusion

Most solutions to the problem of infant abandonment involve either punishing parents more severely or enforcing birth planning even more strictly. A worker at one welfare center in Hunan reported that the numbers of abandoned children started to decrease at her center in the summer of 1992 for the first time in many years because, she believed, birth-planning efforts in the area had been heavy-handed for some time.[60] With large numbers of women now sterilized, there were fewer women able to produce "illegal" children. She also thought that people were no longer able to get away with giving birth, abandoning the child if a girl, and giving birth again, because the authorities were monitoring births carefully. I cannot ascertain whether the slight decline she reported in her area continued or whether it was representative of Hunan generally. Evidence suggests that abandonment has remained high in the Hunan-Hubei area. But her reasoning reflects birth-planning authorities' view of how to deal with the problem: on the one hand, implement greater surveillance and more thorough birth-planning efforts; on the other, force unwilling parents to rear their daughters and forego the chance to have a son. Even those who emphasize the "interests of the child" primarily recommend punishing parents for their lack of morality and respect for the law.

Yet it is difficult to imagine ratcheting up birth-planning efforts any further. The campaigns in many rural areas in the early 1990s were precisely what caused the waves of child

abandonment in the first place. It is also hard to imagine moti-
vating courts and local cadres to participate in a massive crackdown on parents when these forces have proved so weak in the
face of the contradictions revealed by such efforts. (For example,
there is the contradiction of forcing parents to take back a child
while sending one or both of them to jail as punishment for
their crime.) For local cadres, caught between state and society,
abandonment has mediated the conflicting pressures created by
birth-planning policies. Yet few voices challenge the policies or
the coercive campaigns used to implement them, campaigns that
push ordinary people to inflict great pain on themselves and on
the helpless children who are the primary victims of this population war. Nor is the need to address some of the underlying
social problems that give rise to desperate acts of abandonment
often raised in these discussions, such as providing for basic
social security needs in the countryside (although the central
government clearly understands that social security is an important policy issue).

Until these fundamental issues are addressed more ade-
quately, or until birth-planning campaigns are relaxed and
reoriented away from coercion, the most one can realistically
hope for is to ameliorate the conditions of the foundlings by
providing better care and more rapid adoption. Changing
domestic adoption regulations to allow couples with one or
more children to adopt foundlings while actively promoting
national adoption networks for local welfare centers could
quickly help civil affairs departments find new parents for
foundlings.[61] Increasing adoptions would reduce crowding in
welfare centers and help lower the high mortality rates that
obtain when young children are kept in institutional settings,

especially when those institutions are inadequately funded. Of course, more money for foster care and welfare centers that take in foundlings is needed as well.[62]

For the most part we can only speculate on the experience of parents who feel driven to abandon their babies. Sometimes an abandoned child has a note tucked in her clothes. One found on a toddler abandoned in an area affected by a high-pressure birth-planning campaign in early 1991 excoriated the government for the extreme pressure that led the parents to give up their beloved daughter, whom they hoped to recover some day. Another note accompanying an infant abandoned in Hunan read: "This baby girl was born on — 1992 at 5:30 A.M. and is now 100 days old. . . . She is in good health and has never suffered any illness. Because of the current political situation and heavy pressures that are too difficult to explain, we, who were her parents for these first days, cannot continue taking care of her. We can only hope that in this world there is a kind-hearted person who will care for her. Thank you. In regret and shame, your father and mother."[63]

CHAPTER FOUR

Infant Abandonment and Adoption in China, 1996–2000

By Kay Johnson, with Huang Banghan and Wang Liyao

Infant abandonment in China has revived in the past fifteen years after decades of abatement following the establishment of the People's Republic. In the late 1980s and early 1990s a number of orphanages, especially in the south and central regions of the country, witnessed significant increases in their populations, causing severe overcrowding and high mortality rates.[1] These increases coincided with the government's efforts to implement birth-planning policies more strictly.[2] While many Chinese orphanages have greatly improved since the early 1990s, thanks to increased support from the state, from charitable organizations inside and outside China, and from international adoptions, they are still far from adequate places to raise young children.[3]

In the past some orphanages were able to arrange domestic adoptions for many of the predominantly female children in their care. Published records from one large orphanage in central China indicated that in the 1960s and 1970s, when the orphanage population was relatively small and contained a high percentage of children with disabilities, they were able to find homes for nearly all healthy infants and even for some moderately disabled children, using a recruitment network that reached into several other provinces.[4] In the early 1990s, however, as the number of children in their care grew, timely adoption placements became increasingly difficult, even with the advent of international adoptions.[5] Moreover, many orphanages were never effective in arranging domestic adoptions, and for them the increase in abandonment led quickly to severely overcrowded conditions with insufficient staff and funds.

Scholars who have written about orphanages and adoption in recent years have assumed that domestic adoption of foundlings is uncommon in China today owing to cultural and social attitudes that devalue daughters and shun adoption outside the bloodline.[6] In addition, in late 1991, in a move that directly limited the pool of potential domestic adopters, the State Council passed an adoption law that restricted the adoption of healthy foundlings to those who were both childless and over thirty-five years old. This law, effective April 1992, reiterated, augmented, and codified local regulations used in the 1980s to bolster birth-planning efforts and the one-child norm. Even before the law was officially passed, when many of its restrictive provisions existed more flexibly as guidelines or regulations, some welfare officials complained that the bureaucratic obstacles to domestic adoption discouraged potential adoptive parents. At the same time, the new law permitted international adoptions by childless people over age thirty-five, thus enlarging the potential pool of adoptive parents outside China. In 1999 this law was amended to allow Chinese and foreign parents over age thirty, with or without birthchildren, to adopt from orphanages; however, adoptions outside the orphanages still require that parents be childless. These changes, which are only now beginning to take effect, will be discussed at the end of this chapter.

Because the issue of adoption is crucial to the fate of tens of thousands of foundlings in China today, we wanted to know whether there was a "culture" in China that allowed for the adoption of foundling girls. We were also interested in learning about the impact on domestic adoption practices of the 1991 adoption law and the previous regulations on which it was based. Did this law deter prospective parents? Were people willing to adopt children unrelated by blood and of unknown parentage? If so, were they willing to adopt daughters, given the well-known preference for sons? Were childless couples the only ones likely to be willing to adopt abandoned girls? Or did the adoption law unnecessarily deprive foundlings of prospective adoptive homes in China?

Although pre-1949 practices have been the subject of anthropological and historical study, there has been little systematic study of adoption practices in China since 1949. In the early 1990s, the topic of adoption reemerged in the work of a few demographers seeking clues to the fate of the so-called missing girls, that is, the shortfall in recorded female births compared to biologically normal ratios of female-to-male births.[7] The shortfall began to grow in the 1980s, creating an increasingly skewed reported sex ratio among young children. What was happening to infant girls? Were they being killed, aborted, or simply hidden from the record? It appeared from an analysis of sample surveys that "informal" and unregistered adoptions accounted for many of these "missing girls."

But were the parents in these "informal adoptions" merely friends and relatives "hiding" girls from the authorities? Were the placements temporary? How was abandonment related to the missing girls and to adoption? Chinese demographers have asserted that abandonment is not an important contributor to the missing girls because abandoned girls end up in government-run welfare centers that care for them and presumably record them.[8] Yet such assertions seem based on little knowledge either of the difficult conditions and high mortality rates in the orphanages or of the extent of abandonment and the state's recovery of abandoned children.

No one, including the Chinese government, truly knows how many children are abandoned each year. Various government officials and civil affairs publications in the 1990s estimated between 100,000 and 160,000 orphans, which would include abandoned children.[9] Such figures are likely to be conservative. Furthermore, as at least one article in a Chinese publication acknowledged, only about 20 percent of these abandoned or homeless children end up in state care.[10] If that is true, then what happens to the other 80 percent?

It was clear from the outset of our study that three phenomena affecting young girls increased from the mid 1980s on: skewed reported sex ratios, some sort of "informal" adoption involving girls, and female child abandonment. I hoped to learn more about each of these developments and the interrelationship between them. My underlying concern was to learn more about the implications for the well-being of young girls today and to understand what needs to change to improve their situation.

Methodology

From late 1995 to 2000, questionnaires gathered information from nearly 800 adoptive families and 250 abandoning families. This chapter analyzes in detail the data gathered from 771 families who had adopted children and 247 families who had abandoned children. In-depth interviews were conducted with more than 60 of the adoptive families, some of whom were visited several times during the period of study. Approximately 85 percent of the abandoning families and 75 percent of the adoptive families were drawn from twenty counties in one south-central province in China. The rest came from scattered locations in north, central, and south China. More than 95 percent of the abandoning families and about 85 percent of the adoptive families lived in rural villages or towns. We located the families using informal networks and word of mouth. The adoptions spanned the period from the 1950s to the present, but most (over 90 percent) occurred in the 1980s and 1990s. All but 10 of the 247 cases of abandonment analyzed here also occurred in the 1980s and 1990s.

We gathered further information on adoption and abandonment from welfare centers and interviews with local officials, including police, hospital staff, county and township governments, and civil affairs departments. In addition, we collected materials from government publications, newspapers, magazines, and journals.

Abandonment

The abandonment of female children has a long history in China. While not necessarily the same as infanticide, abandonment was often seen as a form of it. Reference to the social practice of infanticide in China can be found as early as the Han dynasty.[11] Although abandonment was no more widespread in China than in many other places,[12] it was notable for a strong gender bias: in China, all evidence indicates that infanticide and abandonment disproportionately affected females.

The practice varied regionally and over time. It is known to have waxed and waned according to economic conditions, worsening in times of famine and hardship. There is evidence that the practice was particularly widespread in areas along the Yangzi River and in the south and southeast.[13] In many of these areas, foundling homes sprang up in the seventeenth, eighteenth, and nineteenth centuries.[14]

After 1949, evidence suggests that the incidence of infanticide declined with the return of political stability, social order, and the gradual improvement of economic conditions. Efforts to raise the status of women and socioeconomic changes related to women's labor also may have had salutary effects.[15] Similarly, abandonment seems to have declined in all but the famine years of 1959–61, when it increased markedly in many places.[16]

Yet despite widespread improvements in rural living standards, birth-planning efforts in the 1980s appeared to revive the twin problems of infanticide and abandonment, and particularly the latter. In the early 1980s the government launched its first major campaigns to implement a one-child policy to reduce population growth, taking these campaigns into rural areas where they met stiff resistance. In response, government implementation efforts eased somewhat for a brief time. As a small concession to peasant resistance, many provincial governments in the late 1980s codified a "one-son-or-two-child" policy for rural areas. Under this policy a couple is allowed a second child only if the first is a girl. In a few areas, policies allowed two children, several years apart, regardless of gender. But along with this policy concession, provincial governments reinvigorated efforts to implement birth-planning policy, an approach known as "opening a small hole to close a large hole."

In the countryside, enforcement can involve monitoring households' reproductive behavior, "persuasion" (at times including direct coercion), stiff escalating fines, and sterilization for "overquota births." The vigor with which the policy is enforced has varied over time and place, but in general enforcement has been more vigorous and persistent since the late 1980s.[17] In the middle and lower Yangzi area and elsewhere, the problem of abandonment became acute in the late 1980s and early 1990s as well-organized birth-planning efforts went into high gear.[18]

Families Who Abandon Children

While the circumstantial evidence linking abandonment with birth planning is strong, until recently we lacked direct evidence of who abandons children and why. For obvious reasons, birthparents who abandon children have not been easy to find. Even court cases that seek to uncover culprits and motives have been exceedingly few.[19]

In our fieldwork we were able to gather information directly from 247 abandoning families whose experiences spanned the 1980s and 1990s. All the birthparents of abandoned children were married except for three cases involving children born to unwed mothers. We used a short standardized questionnaire that elicited general information about the composition of the family and the circumstances of the abandonment. We also conducted open-ended in-depth interviews with a small number of abandoning parents. While this sample was not random, it provides some clues about who abandons children, what kinds of children they abandon, why they do it, how they do it, and with what consequences for themselves.

Orphanage and civil affairs officials believe that the vast majority of abandoned children, even those abandoned in cities, are from rural areas or from the "floating population" of rural residents working "outside" their home villages. The vast majority (88 percent) of our cases of abandoning families were from rural villages and designated "agriculture" as their occupational category and type of household registration (known as *hukou*).[20] Only 3 percent of the abandoning families came from cities and 8 percent from county towns; about one-third of the latter also had agricultural *hukou*. While our measures of economic conditions were imprecise, most families seemed average for their area; in our sample, abandonment in the 1980s and 1990s was not related to relative impoverishment. Abandoning parents also had an average education for their age and region that consisted of primary school or junior middle school. Some parents, mostly older women, specified that they were illiterate, as older rural women often are in these areas. At the time of abandoning a child, parents were in their middle to late childbearing years, ranging from mid to late twenties to late thirties.

Gender and Abandonment: Who Is Abandoned and Why?

The evidence from orphanages suggests that the overwhelming majority of abandoned children are girls. Many orphanages also report receiving a high percentage of disabled children.[21] The preference for boys has long been rooted in Chinese society.

Sons are necessary to continue the patrilineal family line and all that it stands for in the family-centered culture and religious life of rural China. Most important, sons are permanent members of their father's family and are still the major source of support for elderly parents because rural China, outside of a few wealthy suburban areas, lacks a social security system. Daughters "marry away" and join their husband's family, where they are obligated to support his parents. The main problem with daughters is that they "belong to other people."

Because China ostensibly has a one-child policy, it is sometimes assumed that parents abandon their first child if it is a girl because they want their only child to be a boy. In fact, relatively few rural areas have a simple one-child policy.[22] Most of the rural areas from which we gathered information had the more common one-son/two-child policy. Those who live in cities, major towns, or county seats and have an urban *hukou,* including all employees of the state (such as employees of government offices, state-owned factories, and state-run schools), fall under a one-child policy.[23] Wealthy suburban areas of major cities also often have a one-child rule. The policy in place in a given area and the way it has been implemented shape the patterns of abandonment that we found.

In our sample of abandoning families, the most important determinants of who was abandoned were gender, birth order, and the gender composition of siblings. Not surprisingly, almost 90 percent (221) of the children who were abandoned were girls. But unlike the population reported in many orphanages, 86 percent of the abandoned children were healthy and without any known disability at the time of abandonment.

Yet it appears that not all girls are at increased risk. Birth order and the presence or absence of a brother were crucial in determining which girls were abandoned (Table 4.1). Of 205 abandoned girls for whom we have information on birth order and siblings, 179 (87 percent) had no brothers. Of these, 73 were second daughters, 64 were third daughters, 27 were fourth daughters, and 3 were fifth daughters. Only 12 were first daughters without brothers (only children), and in 7 of these cases extenuating circumstances led to the abandonment: 4 of the first daughters were disabled; 2 were abandoned because their father died and mother remarried; and 1 was abandoned because her birthparents were not married. Of the remaining 5, 2 were born to some of the few parents in our sample who fell under the one-child rule, one to a state-employed teacher with an urban *hukou* and the other to a resident of a wealthy suburban area of a major city. One of the disabled first-born daughters was also born to an urban resident.

In all cases of abandonment where there were no sons in the family (aside from the one child born out of wedlock), the

Table 4.1 Abandoned Daughters, by Gender of Siblings

Reported abandonments	No.	Percentage
Only child (first daughter)	12	5.8%
Brother(s) only	4	2.0%
Brother(s) and sister(s)	22	10.7%
One sister, no brothers	73	35.6%
Two sisters, no brothers	64	31.2%
Three sisters, no brothers	27	13.2%
Four sisters, no brothers	3	1.5%

SAMPLE SIZE: 205 abandoned daughters.

primary reason for abandoning a daughter was the desire to have a son by preserving the chance for another pregnancy in the context of the current birth-planning restrictions. Sometimes people also mentioned the fear of being fined for an overquota birth, either the one in question or the hoped-for next attempt to have a son. However, the avoidance of a steep economic penalty was given as the sole reason for abandoning a child only when sons were already present and the abandoned child was a second or third overquota child.

Of the twenty-six abandoned girls who had brothers, all but four also had older sisters, making a total of only sixteen abandoned girls in the entire sample who had no sisters. It was indeed rare for the only girl born into a family to be abandoned, regardless of birth order and sibling composition. In one of the four cases in which an only daughter with a brother was abandoned, the girl was disabled. In two other cases, the families said they were avoiding high fines from birth-planning cadres; one of these birthparents, who already had two sons, said he had also been threatened with losing his job in a local factory unless this second overquota child "disappeared." In the fourth case, the family already had two boys and said simply that they "didn't like girls."

Such extreme sentiments were rare. In most cases where a girl with a brother was abandoned, she was a second or third daughter with one or two older brothers. These cases of large two-gender sibling groups were more likely to have occurred in the 1970s or early 1980s; only three involving healthy girls occurred in the 1990s. "Economic hardship" and "too many children" were the most common reasons cited for these earlier cases of abandonment; such reasons were never cited in more recent cases.

There were only 26 abandoned boys in our sample of 247 abandoning families. The most striking feature of this group is that fully 60 percent (16 boys) were disabled or severely ill, in contrast to only around 8 percent of the abandoned girls. Three of these boys were known to have subsequently died. Of the 10 healthy boys in the sample, 2 were born to unwed mothers, and 2 were abandoned after the father died and the mother could not bring the child into a second marriage.

Interestingly, two cases of abandonment of healthy boys mirrored the typical case of female abandonment: the abandoned boy was identified as a third son with no sisters, and the birthparents said they abandoned him because they "had too many sons" and were hoping for a daughter. Had the child been a girl, they would have paid the fine and kept her. Although these cases are few, they indicate that strict birth-planning policies may make gender a liability even for healthy infant boys under certain circumstances.

Wanting a Daughter, Needing a Son

As we have seen, the typical profile of an abandoned child is a healthy newborn girl who has one or more older sisters and no brothers. She is abandoned because her birthparents already have daughters and want a son. These birthparents routinely say they did not want to abandon the child, but that given their desire for a son, birth-planning policies left them "no choice." In many cases, the birthparents were avoiding future fines by abandoning a second daughter to try again for a son; the birth of the second daughter herself would not cause her parents to be fined. Perhaps more important, they are avoiding pressures to abort the next pregnancy if they get caught, for in many areas overquota pregnancies, if discovered, will be targeted for abortion.

When birthparents abandon a third or higher-parity daughter, they usually expect to be fined for a future birth but feel they cannot afford the escalating costs for each overquota child; fines, which may equal a year's income even for the first overquota child, rise sharply with each birth. Most important, in some areas in the 1990s and later, people who are caught giving birth overquota several times are required to undergo sterilization. Thus while families who "go overquota" may expect to pay fines for one overquota child, which they hope will be a son, they often cannot afford to pay fines for two or three, especially since the fines escalate for higher-parity births. Once marked as an overquota family, they may experience such heavy pressure and scrutiny that it becomes impossible to go forward with another pregnancy, depending on the birth-planning atmosphere in their local area at that time.[24] Hence they see no choice but to get rid of the overquota girl.

In short, girls are not readily abandoned. Although many people abandon female infants in their quest to have a son, most do so only after they have reached or exceeded the limits imposed on them by birth planning. It is notable how many of the abandoned girls in our sample are higher parity and overquota. Even in the 1990s, when birth planning was relatively strictly enforced, people often managed to have one or more overquota children—either by "hiding" them or by paying fines—before turning to abandonment.

Moreover, few married couples abandon first-born daughters even when sons are present and the daughters are overquota. While doing this research we met several people whose first children were boys who then proceeded with overquota births because they wanted to have a daughter. In the 1990s, most people paid fines for these girls. This is consistent with another finding of our research that will be discussed later: most people want to have a daughter in addition to a son. While few will abandon a son to have a daughter, some will proceed with overquota pregnancies and accept fines in their quest for a daughter, while others will adopt a girl after giving birth to one or more sons, an act that may also result in a hefty fine, as we will see below. In the 1990s, most parents who abandoned daughters had had multiple births without producing a son.

This profile suggests two seemingly contradictory patterns of behavior: birth-planning restrictions eventually lead some people to abandon "excess" daughters in their quest for a son; but at the same time, most people want to have and keep at least one daughter.

How and Where Children Are Abandoned

The manner in which children are abandoned suggests that a continuum of care and planning is involved, ranging from those who simply leave a child in a convenient place where the abandoning party will not get caught to those who surreptitiously attempt to orchestrate a specific "adoption plan."

It is believed that parents sometimes travel long distances to abandon a child, riding on trains or buses to take the child to a crowded public place. Orphanages in major municipal areas report that children are often found in railway or bus stations. Officials believe that children abandoned in the city usually have been transported from rural areas. Some documentary evidence also suggests this kind of "traveling abandonment."[25]

Distant crowded places offer anonymity and the assurance that the child will be found quickly. This method of abandonment also removes the "problem" from local cadres' jurisdiction and thus reduces or eliminates their motivation to investigate and punish a case of abandonment.

But in the sample we gathered, many children were abandoned in areas not far from the birthparents' home. On rare occasions birthparents specified that they abandoned the child in their own village, but more often they went to another area in the same township or county or one nearby. Children are left on frequently trodden paths leading to fields, on roads connecting villages, on bridges, at the entrance to government or hospital buildings, and not infrequently at people's doorsteps. About 20 percent of abandoning parents said they placed their child at someone's doorstep. These abandoning parents stated that the targeted families were chosen because they seemed likely candidates for adoptive parents. As we will see when we look at adoptive parents, the doorsteps of childless couples and of families with sons but no daughters are favored places for abandonment. Whether a child was left on a doorstep or on a public road, about half of the birthparents claim to know what happened to the child. Some watched to be sure the child was picked up. When children are abandoned locally, word of mouth also provides a means of discovering what happened. Many birthparents expected that the child would be adopted directly by a local family. Yet other birthparents report they have no knowledge of what happened to the child and do not even know whether the child is alive.

Evidence that some cases of abandonment are carefully planned with an eye to finding a new home for the child, thus blurring the distinction between abandonment and arranging an adoption, will be discussed further when we review our research on adoption, for that is where we learned most about this behavior.

Consequences of Abandonment for Birthparents

Abandonment is clearly specified as a crime in the Marriage Law of 1950 and 1980 and in the omnibus Law Protecting Women's Rights and Interests passed in 1992. But as legal scholar Li Xiaorong points out, there are few special provisions for the prosecution of this escalating crime, and most commentators agree that there have been few prosecutions.[26]

In our sample, most people who abandoned children were not punished, even though most were unable to keep the act a secret. Out of 247 abandoning families, only 58 (about 25 percent) reported being discovered by the authorities and punished. In many of these cases, the birthparents said that neighbors had reported what they did to the authorities. Punishments consisted of fines that in 17 cases were coupled with sterilization for the birthmother. In some places the risks of being caught and punished seemed to be much higher than in others. As with birth planning in general, some counties and townships exerted far stricter control than others. But despite pockets of strict enforcement and punishment by birth-planning authorities, it was clear in the areas where we gathered information that abandonment was often a successful method of concealing live births, avoiding punishment for overquota births, and thus preserving the opportunity for another pregnancy.

When birthparents were caught and punished, fines ranged from several hundred yuan to several thousand. In the

1990s fines ranged from 2,000 to 5,000 yuan, similar to the fines for having an overquota child. These punishments were in fact considered birth-planning punishments, meted out for attempting to get away with overquota births; in no case was abandonment treated as either a criminal or a civil offense, for endangering or violating the rights of the child, or as a violation of the Marriage Law, which also prohibits abandonment. In only two cases were the courts involved at all. In one, the punishment was not specified. In the other, the courts punished the family with "education" and sent a local television crew to the house to videotape the guilty parties so that they could be publicly exposed and criticized. We also heard of another case, not in our sample, in which a woman who had abandoned children three times was tried by the courts and imprisoned briefly. In all other cases the punishment was administered by birth-planning authorities, not the courts. In the government's concern over abandonment, what has been at stake is not the interests or legal rights of children but the state's firm grip on birth planning and population control.

Although most birthparents escape legal consequences and birth-planning punishments for abandonment, some nonetheless suffer emotional consequences. Some birthmothers said they felt the loss of the child for many years, although most claimed to have gotten over it in time. In one in-depth interview, a birthmother claimed at the outset, in a matter-of-fact manner, that after almost ten years "time had healed" her wounds. Yet despite her words and initial demeanor, the interview ended when she became overwhelmed by tears and had to walk away, saying she never again wanted to think about this matter. In another interview, a birthmother wept silently before we even began to speak; several years after abandoning her second daughter, she remained uncertain whether she would ever again proceed with another pregnancy even though she held a certificate of permission to give birth again and was under great pressure from her husband and in-laws. She vowed that if she did decide to become pregnant, she would never again abandon one of her babies regardless of gender. The questionnaires alone, however, elicited little of the underlying pain and emotion that certainly existed in many of the cases.

Public opinion about abandonment seems mixed. Most people do not condone abandonment, and many strongly disapprove, regarding those who commit this act as immoral or cold-hearted at best. Some birthparents reported that their neighbors had turned them in to the authorities. But many people also express "understanding" for the motivation of those who feel compelled to abandon a child, and many do not wish to meddle or judge those who commit this act. Thus public opinion in villages appears to provide some leeway for this behavior. We also heard of cases in which lower-level officials knew of an abandonment but did not pursue the matter; cadres seemed more likely to look the other way when the abandoned overquota child did not end up in their jurisdiction. But even if cadres wished to find abandoners, it would be a difficult task without popular support for the endeavor, especially if the child came from outside the cadres' jurisdiction, as is often the case. Few local cadres are likely to pursue the search unless they are under great pressure from above.[27] Abandonment has become a de facto escape valve for the most desperate sonless families determined to circumvent harsh birth-planning regulations.

Adoption

While birthparents often escape punishment for abandonment, what happens to the children who fall victim to this practice? As stated earlier, our interest in adoption arose in part out of a concern for the fate of abandoned children who needed adoptive homes. As social scientists, we also had a larger theoretical interest in how adoption customs had changed after decades of political upheaval, rapid economic development, and now severe legal restrictions imposed by the state on fertility and family size. In a society with strong patriarchal, patrilineal traditions and a long-standing preference for sons, can contemporary popular culture accommodate the adoption of foundlings as daughters? Or does Chinese society today resemble Korean society in this respect, unable to provide sufficient numbers of adoptive homes for homeless children because of negative attitudes toward adoption outside of close bloodlines? If traditional practices relating to the adoption of girls (as servants or "little daughters-in-law," as we will discuss below) are no longer prevalent, are there new reasons to adopt girls? Even if there is a cultural capacity for adoption, are people willing or able to adopt children given the regulatory and legal restrictions on adoption that have developed to bolster birth planning? Are these legal restrictions widely enforced? Has the desire for a daughter grown strong enough in contemporary Chinese society to lead people to risk defying such restrictions?

Government Regulation of Adoption

By the mid 1980s adoption had become a matter of population control, and as such it came under increasing governmental regulation, first as part of birth planning and later as part of civil law. As stated earlier, the 1991 adoption law mirrored and reinforced the one-child policy, stipulating that healthy children—whether foundlings or children put up for adoption by their birthparents—could be adopted only by parents who were childless and over thirty-five years old.[28] Disabled children and true orphans—defined as children whose parents have died[29]—were exempt from these restrictions.

In fact, similar provisions sometimes existed as orphanage guidelines for adoption in earlier decades as well (see Chap. 1). But the purpose of these guidelines in earlier years was to prevent people from adopting girls to become servants or wives for sons in the adopting family; reformers insisted that the girls be adopted to become daughters. By the 1980s, when such regulations were being enforced by both birth-planning cadres and civil affairs units handling adoptions, the traditional practice that gave rise to such guidelines—the adoption of girls as "little daughters-in-law"—no longer existed to any significant extent. In the 1980s and 1990s such provisions were enforced to buttress population control efforts, not to protect the interests of the adopted children.

At least partly as a result of legal restrictions, the number of officially recorded adoptions has been fairly low since the passage of the 1991 adoption law. In 1992, civil affairs recorded only about 2,900 registered adoptions.[30] For the mid 1990s, no officially published figures are available, but civil affairs officials claimed that only about 6,000 to 8,000 legal domestic adoptions were registered each year.[31] Other official sources claimed somewhat higher figures of up to 20,000 per year during this period, perhaps including an estimate of unregistered adoptions done through private contract.[32]

For a population the size of China's, especially one with various traditions of adoption, even the higher figure is a relatively low rate. In the United States, with one-quarter the population and much weaker traditions of adoption prior to the twentieth century, there are about 120,000 legally processed adoptions each year, although statistics on U.S. adoptions are also scattered, local, and incomplete.[33] Chinese officials readily admit that many adoptions are not registered. Among other things, families arrange adoptions through private contracts, following the long-standing custom. As long as these contracts do not violate the provisions of the adoption law, it appears that they are not technically illegal, at least according to some ministry officials. Yet there is no specific apparatus to supervise these adoptions. In practice, the matter is generally left to birth-planning cadres to police as an extension of their birth-planning work. As stated earlier, some demographers estimate that more than six hundred thousand "informal" unregistered adoptions occurred every year in the late 1980s, far more than the number officially registered. Such adoptions are one of the places where "missing girls" are thought to go.[34]

The 1991 adoption law was meant to plug up this means of escaping from birth planning, that is, to prevent birthparents from arranging adoptions for "excess" daughters so they could try again for a son. Thus, despite increasing abandonment and overcrowding in sorely underfunded orphanages plagued by high mortality rates, China's first adoption law directly served birth planning and population control, not children's welfare. This use of adoption policy seems without precedent in the world, even in other poor countries struggling to reduce population growth through government programs.[35] In fact, because of overcrowding in Chinese orphanages, the 1991 law was revised in 1999 to drop the childless restriction for those adopting foundlings living in orphanages and to lower the minimum age of adoptive parents to thirty for all adoptions. However, these revisions took effect after most of the present study was completed. Their possible impact on adoption practices will be discussed at the end of this chapter.

With both theoretical and practical policy issues in mind, we gathered information from 771 adoptive families from late 1995 until early 2000. This sample is both too small and too biased to provide clear longitudinal information, and it only hints at the extent of adoption today. But the patterns and attitudes we uncovered provide some basis for understanding contemporary adoption practices. By comparing these practices both with what is known about adoption in the past and with more recent studies, we can gain some ideas about the direction of change in recent decades.

A Brief History of Adoption in China

A rudimentary knowledge of Confucianism and Chinese society might lead one to assume that adoption, especially adoption outside of close bloodlines, is likely to be unusual and largely proscribed by custom in China because of the presumed Confucian emphasis on blood ties. Traditional Chinese law prohibited adoption across surname lines, and normative texts argue against adoption. But in practice, adoption has a long and varied tradition in China and has been quite common for hundreds of years (although some scholars suggest that it declined in the mid twentieth century).[36] A number of strains in Confucianism and in popular culture support adoptive ties outside as well as inside bloodlines and encourage the adoption of both boys and girls to build family and kinship.

Ann Waltner concludes her study of adoption and kinship in Ming and Qing China by arguing that "law and other normative texts, viewing the family as a patrilineal and patriarchal institution with a primary obligation to continue ancestral sacrifices, prohibited adoption across surname lines. . . . But adoption across surname lines was nonetheless relatively prevalent. And furthermore, the practice was accompanied by an ideological structure that described and justified adoption across surname lines. This competing ideology, encapsulated in the term *ming-ling tzu,* suggests that the lines dividing outsider from insider, stranger from kinsman could in fact be crossed."[37]

The literal meaning of *ming-ling tzu* (pinyin: *mingling zi*) is "mulberry insect children," but the term is used to refer to adopted children, in particular children adopted outside a close circle of patrilineal relatives. This usage derived from the belief that a certain type of wasp took the young of the mulberry insect and transformed them into young wasps, making them "its own" children. According to folk belief, the wasp raps and taps outside its nest, in which it has put the mulberry insect's young, and prays, "Be like me, be like me." After a while, young wasps emerge. Thus, one who becomes the child of someone other than his or her birthparents is known as a *mingling zi.*[38]

The metaphor is remarkable in its near total denial of the significance of heredity in shaping the child, emphasizing the wholesale transformation of the biological offspring of one set of parents into the likeness of their adoptive parents by virtue of being raised by them. Almost no trace of biological origins remains. The Confucian emphasis on upbringing and cultivation as the key to character provides further support for ties built on nurture and social relationships rather than biology and heredity.

Not only does popular ideology sanction adopting outside the bloodline, but in practice anthropologists, observing customs in the nineteenth and twentieth centuries, also often found a preference for adopting strangers rather than relatives. Adopting the children of strangers, perhaps through intermediaries, helped protect adoptive ties from future interference from birthparents or other biological relatives and made it less likely the child would try to return to his or her birthfamily.[39]

Gender and Adoption

Similarly, while most formal adoptions gleaned from historical documents and court records involve the adoption of a male heir—the only type of adoption sanctioned by law—popular adoption practices often involved females.[40] As Waltner observes, female adoptions were not likely to be part of the historical record, in either genealogies or court records, because within the prevailing patrilineal kinship system their adoption did not bear on lineage matters or involve issues of property and inheritance.[41] At the same time, girls were more likely than boys to be available for adoption because they were more expendable from the birthfamilies' point of view. Furthermore, the ambiguous position of females, especially children, in the formal kinship structure and bloodlines made girls more readily exchangeable and hence more "adoptable" as daughters whether they came from sources inside or outside the bloodline. Our research suggests that this traditional view may continue to make the adoption of daughters of unknown parentage a relatively easy and acceptable matter for adoptive parents in contemporary China.

Anthropologists studying adoption in prerevolutionary China found that the most common form of female adoption was taking in an infant girl to raise as a future daughter-in-law for the parents and wife for a son; a girl in such an adoption was known as a "little daughter-in-law," or *tongyangxi*.[42] Childless couples also adopted girls in the hope that doing so would "lead in" a son. If the hoped-for son did not materialize, the couple at least had a daughter who might serve as a caretaker and as a possible means to obtain a son-in-law uxorilocally, that is, to find a man who would marry into his wife's family and allow his son to become his father-in-law's heir. Although this type of marriage was considered a lowly arrangement for a man, poor men might be willing to marry in this way for economic reasons.

In some communities in the nineteenth and early twentieth centuries, these practices were so widespread that the majority of girls were adopted and few people raised their own birthdaughters.[43] In other areas, these practices affected only a small minority, but their existence showed the flexibility of traditional practices and the ways families could use adoption to compensate for inadequate outcomes of biological reproduction. They also provided a precedent for the adoption of girls. Another tradition that resembled adoption involved buying girls as household servants. Although these girls were not considered daughters, they were often treated as household members and, like daughters, had marriages arranged for them by the household head.

Does the adoption of girls today follow any of these traditional patterns? While the practice of taking in a *tongyangxi* was made illegal in the twentieth century, as was buying children as servants, reports of various traditional practices—ranging from arranged marriages to trafficking in women and girls as wives, servants, and prostitutes—suggest that some adoption traditions may have either persisted or been revived. Recent fieldwork, however, has not come across these practices. If they have in fact faded away in most areas of the mainland, as they have in Taiwan, then what purpose does the adoption of girls serve today?

Given that we have little knowledge of contemporary adoption practices and little prior fieldwork to draw on, even more fundamental questions arise. What proportion of adoptions involve girls rather than boys? Susan Greenhalgh found in her study of three Shaanxi villages that adoptions, involving about 4–5 percent of the children, affected both genders in equal numbers prior to the 1970s but only girls after the implementation of strict birth planning.[44] Using survey data from the late 1980s, Sten Johansson and his colleagues also found that a disproportionate and growing number of informal adoptions in China involved girls.[45]

But it was unclear whether Johansson's informal adoptions were true adoptions or simply a means of temporarily hiding girls from the authorities. Would we find a similar gender imbalance in adoptions? What kinds of people adopt today? Are most adoptions arranged between relatives, or do many involve strangers? How many involve abandoned children? What reasons do people give for adopting children? Do the reasons differ according to the gender of the adopted child? How have adoptive parents been affected by birth-planning regulations and, in the 1990s, by the restrictive adoption law?

There are also many questions about the status of adoptees in contemporary society. In the past, adopted children, whether boys or girls, occupied a lower social status in their families and communities than other children. Adopted sons might be pushed out or discriminated against in inheritance if a birth-son came along after the adoption.[46] "Little daughters-in-law" were said to occupy the lowest status in the family, far below that of a birthdaughter or a daughter-in-law who married into the family as an adult. Arthur Wolf and Chieh-shan Huang found that adopted daughters had significantly higher mortality rates as infants and children than daughters raised by their birthparents, who generally fared about as well as sons.[47]

What status do adoptive children have in the family today? How are they viewed compared with birthchildren? Do they suffer discrimination within their adoptive families or from the community? Do they suffer from political or legal discrimination? Our small, nonrandom sample does not allow us to answer these questions with any certainty, but our fieldwork suggests some patterns of adoption and attitudes toward adoptees in contemporary China. These patterns in turn point to areas of change as well as continuity.

Who Is Adopted?

The 771 adoptions analyzed in Table 4.2 span from the late 1940s to the mid 1990s. Just over 80 percent took place after 1985, and almost 60 percent in the years 1990 to 1999. The vast majority of the adoptions were of children unrelated to the adoptive parents by any kinship ties; only 8 percent involved relatives.

Like Greenhalgh and Johansson, we found that the majority of adoptions (598) involved girls and that the proportion of girls increased over time. We also found a high proportion of abandoned children among those adopted. Fifty-six percent of all adopted children were foundlings, with the proportion of abandoned children increasing over time. Over 60 percent of the adopted girls were abandoned, and nearly all were under one year of age. There were also a small number of abandoned boys (58) in this sample. While only 2 out of 598 adopted abandoned girls were disabled, 7 of the 58 boys had disabilities, and 2 others were very sick when adopted. In most cases, these abandoned children were found by the adoptive parents themselves or by their friends or relatives. In only 15 cases were welfare centers involved in locating children.

Many of the remaining adoptions involved orphans, especially in the case of boys. Forty-four (38 percent) of the 115 nonabandoned boys became available for adoption because one parent (7) or both parents (37) had died. A smaller proportion (17 percent) of the 228 nonabandoned girls were orphans (39) when adopted. Male and female orphans were often adopted by relatives.

According to the adoptive parents, many birthparents arranged adoptions for girls for the same reasons other birth-

Table 4.2 Patterns of Adoption, Pre-1970 to 1999

Reported Cases	No. of Adoptions	Females	Abandoned Children
Pre-1970	19	62%	15%
1970–79	37	57%	30%
1980–84	85	78%	39%
1985–89	185	79%	42%
1990–94	274	77%	56%
1995–99	171	88%	58%
Overall	771	78% avg.	56% avg.

parents abandoned girls: these daughters had one or more sisters and no brothers in their birthfamilies, and their birthparents wanted a boy. Sometimes such adoptions (about 20 percent of the girls and 15 percent of the boys) were arranged between relatives. In several cases, a maternal aunt became the adoptive mother, while the birthmother became the maternal aunt. But only 18 percent of adoptions of nonabandoned children involved relatives; in the majority of cases an unrelated adoptive family was found through friends or relatives. In one case, which illustrates the fine line between arranging an adoption of an "excess" daughter and abandoning her, a "friend of a friend" came to an infertile couple with their third birthdaughter and pleaded that if the couple did not adopt the child, they would have to abandon her.

Adopted girls were on average younger than adopted boys at the time of adoption. Most girls, whether abandoned or not, were adopted within their first year except in the case of orphans. Boys tended to be adopted at an older age partly because more of them were orphans. Only a few boys were available for adoption as infants, and most of those were abandoned. Like abandoned girls, most adopted abandoned boys (fifty-one out of fifty-eight) were under six months old, but seven were between three and seven years old.

These patterns of adoption reflect the higher value that birthfamilies place on sons than on daughters. Overquota or "excess" sons are usually kept in the family, even though many families with one son would prefer to have a daughter than a second or third son. Boys available for adoption are more likely to be orphaned, born out of wedlock (fourteen), or relinquished by divorced parents (ten) because usually only catastrophic conditions lead families to part with boys. Boys are still seen as necessary for old-age security and for continuing the family line. More families abandon or, when feasible, seek adoptions for "excess" daughters because of the greater overall desire for sons.

Who Adopts and Why?

All the adoptive parents in our sample were married couples except for twenty-five single men and seven single women (about 4 percent of the sample). Unlike the residential distribution of abandoning families, which was more rural than the general population, the distribution of our adoptive family sample roughly fit the distribution of the area we studied. About 65 percent lived in villages, 20 percent in county-level towns, and 15 percent in cities. Around 75 percent of the sample stated that they had agricultural *hukou*. For the most part, incomes of adoptive parents were average or slightly above average for the areas where they lived, with a few well above average and a few significantly below. Adoptive parents tended to be better educated than abandoning parents primarily because more of them came from towns and cities, where residents generally enjoy better educational opportunities and higher incomes.

Approximately half of the adoptive parents in our sample (404, or 52 percent) were childless at the time of adoption (Table 4.3). Childless couples turned to adoption because they believed they were infertile. Most of the couples in this category were in their twenties. The thirty-two single parents who adopted were all childless, and all but three were over thirty-five. Childlessness is widely seen as an unacceptable and unhappy state and adoption as the logical way to overcome it.

For most married people, especially in rural areas, age thirty-five is simply too old to wait to become a parent.

Most of the childless families adopted girls simply because girls were readily available for adoption and boys were not. However, many claimed that the gender of the child did not matter, and only a few pointed out that they would have preferred a boy had one been available. The specific reasons childless couples gave for adopting tended to differ depending on whether they had adopted a boy or a girl. Functional and economic reasons were usually given for adopting a boy: "raising a son for care in old age" was most common, followed by "strengthening the family economy" and "continuing the family line." With girls, emotional reasons were more common, such as to "increase the joy of life," although care in old age was also mentioned. Many childless couples identified special characteristics that they appreciated in girls: they were more filial, closer to their parents, and more obedient than boys. Adoptive parents' attitudes also reflected the increasing economic value

Table 4.3 Family Composition at Time of Adoption

	Adopting girls	Adopting boys	TOTAL
Childless	292	112	404
Sons only	257	6	263
Daughters only	11	38	49
Sons and daughters	37	16	53
Unknown	1	1	2
TOTAL	598	173	771

of daughters today.[48] While boys may be preferred for some purposes, a daughter, who is much easier to obtain through adoption, can also bring happiness and "make a family" for a childless couple in China today.

Adopting the "Missing Gender": "Completing a Family" Through Adoption

Officials and scholars have reported that "only parents unable to bear a biological child will seek to adopt" in China today because of small-family norms, birth-planning policy, and attitudes toward adoption.[49] Yet almost half of our cases involved adoptive parents who had children at the time of adoption. Our data suggest that when families with children adopt, it is often to attain a child of the "missing gender." The desire to have a son is well known, and adoption might fulfill that need if a sonless family is lucky enough to find a healthy boy available for adoption. But the desire for a daughter also shapes the way many people imagine and build their families, by birth or through adoption. For most Chinese people today, the ideal family includes a daughter as well as a son.[50]

Thus those who only have sons may seek to make their family "complete" by adopting a daughter. As Table 4.3 shows, about one-third (263) of the adoptive parents analyzed here already had one or more sons but no daughters at the time of adoption; nearly all of those families (257) adopted girls. Almost all of those adopting girls said that they adopted in large part because they specifically wanted a daughter. "A son and a daughter make a family complete" was a common expression among these adoptive parents. Daughters were also said to be "close" to their parents and to be particularly caring and loyal.

In cases where the girl was abandoned, "sympathy for the child" was frequently an additional reason for adopting, but it was rarely a primary or sufficient reason; these girls were adopted because of their gender, not in spite of it. Of the 263 families with sons but no daughters, only 6 adopted a boy; in one of those families the birthson was mentally disabled and the family wanted a healthy son. Conversely, only 11 families with daughters but no sons adopted another daughter, and only 37 families with children of both sexes adopted girls. In other words, only 8 percent of families adopting girls already had a girl, and only 13 percent of families adopting boys already had a boy.

Similarly, most people who adopted boys had no sons. Adoptive parents who had only daughters said they wanted a boy to care for them in old age, to strengthen the family economy, and to continue the family line. Most cases involving an adoption when the same-sex child was already present in the family (70 cases) were explained by extenuating circumstances, such as the death of relatives or the inability of the adopting family to find other adoptive parents for a child they "sympathized" with. Few people claimed they adopted simply because they wanted a larger family. No one who adopted wanted a family of more than two children except for reasons of gender balance. Thus by far the most common reason for people with birthchildren to adopt was to bring a child of the "missing" gender into their family.

The Adoption of Abandoned Children

In our interviews and survey data on adoptive parents, the percentage of foundlings among adoptees was high (close to 60 percent) and increased over time. Although the vast majority of these children were girls, people expressed no reluctance to adopt because of gender. As we pointed out, many of those who adopted foundlings specifically wanted to adopt a girl and would not have been interested in adopting a boy because they already had a son. Ironically, these adopted girls, though once abandoned, probably were more "wanted" in their adoptive homes than were many second- or third-born daughters being raised by birthparents who had hoped for a son instead.

Furthermore, people expressed few qualms about adopting children of unknown parentage as long as they were basically healthy, that is, without congenital disabilities. It was assumed that if such children were raised as "their own" children, they would become like "their own" children. One adoptive mother smiled as she spoke of how her neighbors thought that her secretly adopted foundling daughter looked just like her and the younger of her two sons. She said they all share the same personality and mannerisms. According to her, children become like the people who raise them, even in their physical appearance. Her words brought to mind the *mingling zi* metaphor—the female wasp rapping and tapping on her nest of mulberry-insect babies, praying, "Be like me, be like me," then after a while looking into the nest and finding wasps like herself.

In some cases abandoning parents apparently believed that a particular family would be interested in adopting a child. In 86 of the 370 cases (about 23 percent) of adoptions of abandoned girls, the child was found outside the door of the family who adopted her. In all but one of these cases, the family was either childless or daughterless. The pattern was less pronounced with boys, but still present. In 6 of the 58 adoptions of abandoned boys, the boys were found on the doorstep by parents who adopted them, only one of whom already had a son. Although adoptive families rarely knew who the child's birthparents were, some birthparents clearly knew something about the adoptive parents.

This pattern suggests that many abandoning families are trying surreptitiously to arrange an adoption for their "excess" daughters. Given predictable patterns of gender preference, it is fairly easy for abandoning parents to guess who might be interested in adopting a girl. Clearly, many birthparents expected that their child would be adopted directly by a local family, and some learned precisely which family had the child. In one case remorseful birthparents who knew where their birthdaughter was living attempted to recover her a year after the abandonment. The adoptive parents were extremely displeased at the intrusion and successfully rebuffed repeated attempts by the birthparents. Although we heard of only three such cases from our sample of adoptive parents, the patterns of abandonment we uncovered make it possible for birthparents and adoptive parents to become embroiled in battles over children like those that have emerged occasionally in the United States. In rural China, however, it appears that the cards are stacked firmly against the birthparents. Courts cannot be called on to intervene on their behalf. Not only was their act illegal and a blatant attempt to circumvent birth planning, but it seems that most people in the community would sympathize with the adoptive parents and support their "right" to keep the child. As many people told us, "raising a child carries more weight than birthing a child."[51]

Consequences of Adopting Abandoned Children

The thin line that sometimes exists between abandoning and "adopting out" a child to try again for a son helps explain why birth-planning officials sometimes crack down on adoption, even though it seems irrational for the government to take away an adopted child only to place it, at government expense, in an underfunded welfare center. Even areas without facilities to care for homeless children may experience such crackdowns. Levying stiff fines for "overquota" adoptions is meant to discourage people from using adoption as a way to get around birth-planning restrictions by circulating "excess daughters" from those who have too many to those who have none. In fact, the adoption of healthy nonorphaned children was the purview of birth-planning cadres long before the adoption law of 1991.

Still, many who already had one or two children were willing to risk the fines and other penalties to adopt foundlings. As we will see, even after the revised adoption law of 1999 such adoptions were usually subject to penalties because most took place outside of orphanages. Of the 771 adoptions analyzed here, 677 involved healthy nonorphaned children, and only 58 involved parents who were childless and over thirty-five years old, half of whom were single (29).[52] About half the healthy nonorphaned children were adopted by childless couples, most of whom were below the required age; indeed, most were below age thirty. About 5 percent of these underage couples was fined, and all fines occurred in the second half of the 1990s. Even in the 1990s, after the first adoption law had been passed, violating the age restriction did not usually bring fines, although many underage parents said they could not register their adoption or obtain a proper household registration at the time of adoption because they were under the legal age. By contrast, 37 percent of the adoptive families with birthchildren were fined. In addition, ten adoptive mothers with birthchildren were sterilized, two lost jobs, and another lost a promotion as part of the "cost" that birth-planning authorities imposed on them for adopting in violation of adoption and population control policies. In effect, nonorphaned adopted children—especially those who were abandoned and homeless—were treated as "overquota births" if the adoptive parents had another child. Adoptive parents were fined and punished as if they had violated birth planning by giving birth to the child.

In our sample, fines ranged from several hundred to more than ten thousand yuan. In the 1980s, when incomes were lower, fines were often in the lower range, but as early as the mid 1980s, fines of 2,000 to 3,000 yuan were sometimes levied for an "overquota" adoption. In the mid 1980s such a fine would have been daunting indeed. Even today, when incomes are much higher, this fine might be equivalent to a year's earnings for a lower-income rural family in the areas we investigated.[53] In the 1990s, fines in a few cases in our sample were as high as 10,000 to 15,000 yuan. In recent years newspaper articles have reported fines in urban areas as high as 30,000 yuan for "overquota adoptions," a truly unmanageable fine even for most urban residents.[54] In several cases in our sample, people successfully avoided fines that were obviously beyond their means by arguing with cadres and steadfastly refusing to give up the child.

Fortunately for the children and their adoptive parents, in about 60 percent of the cases that violated the adoption restrictions concerning childlessness, local cadres either did not know of the adoptions or looked the other way. Many adoptive parents understandably avoided registering their adoptions or seeking residential registration (*hukou*) for the children to avoid the penalties or the risk of losing the child. As a result, many of the adopted children, whether or not they were abandoned, became part of the "missing girls." The disadvantages that government policy imposes on these children will be discussed later.

Status of Adoptees in the Family

The purpose of adoption in contemporary Chinese society is to bring children, both boys and girls, into the family "as if" they were birthchildren. In the sample of 771 adoptive families analyzed here, we found only 5 cases of the traditional practice of adopting a "little daughter-in-law" (*tongyangxi*), all but one of which occurred before the 1990s. In all of these cases the adoptive parents clearly indicated that the adopted girl was not the same as a birthchild, nor did she enjoy equal status with birthchildren in the family. In sharp contrast to most of the other cases of adoption, the adoptive parents of *tongyangxi* did not educate the adopted girl. Significantly, all five attempts either failed to produce the hoped-for marriage or were considered likely to fail. Our research confirms the decline and near— if not yet total—disappearance of this old custom.

Aside from these five cases, only a few adoptive parents felt that their adopted child was not "like a birthchild." These parents had adopted the orphans or hardship cases of their relatives out of a sense of obligation and continued to regard the child as a niece or nephew rather than "just like a son or daughter." But in the vast majority of cases, adopted children today—like the *mingling zi*—are supposed to be transformed into the likeness of birthchildren of the adoptive parents by virtue of being raised by them. Parents routinely insist that their adopted children enjoy the same status, rights, and above all love that a birthchild would.

But not all Chinese adoptive parents seem secure about the transformative power of adopting and raising a child. Parents often resort to secrecy to reinforce the similarity between adoptive and biologic ties with their children. The reasons for maintaining secrecy vary. In some cases the parents worry that knowledge of the adoption would lessen the child's loyalty and love for the adoptive parents; in other cases they worry that the child would feel confused and insecure, especially if "too young to understand." With abandoned children, some worry that the children's self-esteem would suffer from the knowledge that they had been "thrown away" by the birthparents or that others in the community would look down on them. For others secrecy is important not because of the child's feelings, but to hide the "shameful" fact of their own infertility.

Slightly more than half (55 percent) of the adoptions in our sample, including all those involving relatives, were "open" from the start—that is, not kept secret from the child or others (though perhaps kept secret from the government). When abandoned children are adopted, or when adoptions are arranged between unrelated persons, the adoption might be kept secret from the child, although usually at least some (and often many) people in the community and extended family know the truth. Many parents in our sample (around 20 percent) prefer not to tell the children when they are young, but plan to tell them when they reach a certain age (e.g., "when they are old enough to understand" or when they finish school).

Many expect that their child will eventually find out "naturally," from others, especially in rural areas, where everyone knows everyone else's business. While some adoptive parents fear this moment of truth, many expressed confidence that their adopted children would always consider those who raised them to be their "real" parents, especially in cases of abandonment.

A minority of parents (around 25 percent) planned to keep the truth from the child forever, even when others already knew that the child had been adopted. Urban parents were more likely to maintain secrecy than rural parents (40 percent in cities, 31 percent in towns, and 22 percent in villages). We were told that urban adoptive parents sometimes went so far as to seek job assignments in another city so they could live in an area where no one knew about their adoption. While hiding pregnancies and children from officials is generally much easier in the countryside, hiding such personal matters from friends, coworkers, and neighbors seems easier in urban communities. Nonetheless, even though it seemed impossible to keep the truth entirely secret in villages, one woman nearly accomplished that by bringing home an abandoned baby and telling both neighbors and birth-planning cadres that she had hidden an overquota pregnancy and given birth at a relative's home. She thereby accepted a hefty 2,000 yuan birth-planning fine (which probably would have been levied for the adoption anyway) in exchange for registering the baby as a birthchild.

Since part of the reason for wanting secrecy was to deny the adoptive parents' infertility, childless adopting couples were most likely to hide the truth to avoid the "shame" of infertility. This desire for secrecy was also more likely when the child was a boy, reflecting the greater importance of a boy's permanent connection to the parents' family and his role in perpetuating a patrilineal bloodline. In several ways, girls seemed better suited to adoptive ties. As the aunt of an adopted child explained, "Girls leave the family and belong to others when they get married anyway, so it doesn't matter" if she is adopted or not, or if people know that she is adopted. The woman's comment was not intended to reflect negatively on the child; on the contrary, her point was that her adopted niece was just as much a part of the family as her birthdaughter and her other nieces. What mattered here was gender and the more ambiguous connection that females have to patrilineal families in traditional Chinese culture. For some, this greater ambiguity makes it easier to adopt a daughter and treat her exactly like a birthdaughter; the important ties in both cases are interpersonal ones based on emotions and shared experience, not formal blood ties with their formal obligations.

Nearly all parents insisted that their feelings for the adopted child were as strong as those for a birthchild and that their sense of obligation was at least as great. Whether or not this was true in every case, the prevalence of this assertion demonstrated that in contemporary Chinese popular culture, adoption is supposed to entail deep affection and commitment. Rearing an adopted child is said to create the same love, closeness, and sense of obligation as biological ties. In extended interviews, parents expressed these feelings with great sincerity, and the limited interactions we witnessed between children and parents confirmed this impression. Many parents even claimed that they loved their adopted child more than their birthchildren—perhaps because of gender, given that girls are expected to provide an emotionally closer and more caring interpersonal relationship than boys. Also many adoptive parents said that the abandoned child evoked special sympathy and caring because she had suffered at the hands of her birthparents. Some adoptive parents wanted to "compensate" for this early misfortune suffered by a helpless infant.

The low status and fragility of adoptive ties that seemed to characterize adoption practices in the past appeared in a small number of cases we learned about. Clearly some people in China still consider adoption greatly inferior to biologic ties. We heard second hand of a few cases in which couples had returned an adopted daughter to her birthparents after giving birth to another child. Villagers told us that in one such case an infertile couple had adopted a girl to "lead in" a birthchild, specifically a boy; once the son was born, the adoptive parents had no further use for the girl. However, we did not hear of many such cases, and no one in our sample reported such behavior. Whether this pattern occurs frequently today is hard to say; given our methodology, we might not hear of adoptions that were terminated.

In our study, in almost all cases where childless adoptive parents later gave birth, the adopted child (usually a girl) was considered as important as the birthchild. Given the widespread ideal of a family with one boy and one girl, one might expect that the birth of a son after the adoption of a daughter would be welcomed as "making a family complete." For example, one adoptive mother who later gave birth to a son thought her situation was perfect: by first adopting a girl and then, after many years of infertility, giving birth to a son, she ended up with a "complete" family without even incurring birth-planning fines!

In fact, the most fragile adoptions in our sample involved adopted boys who were followed by a birthson, including one of the rare cases where adoptive parents frankly expressed "regret" for adopting. Again, the special role of sons not merely as caretakers but also as carriers of a patrilineal bloodline seemed to make adoption more problematic for boys than for girls.

Some adoptive relationships seemed less secure and less honored than others, but in our sample there were only three cases in which adopted children were returned to their birthfamilies. All three "adoptions" were used merely to hide a child from birthplanning authorities and were never intended to be permanent. These arrangements usually involved relatives living in other villages. We had wondered if the "informal" adoptions cited by demographers were this fluid type of temporary foster care. While there may have been many such arrangements in the areas we investigated, people did not generally consider these informal "foster" arrangements to be "adoptions." Most adoptions were "informal" only in that they took place outside formal government channels for adoption. Adoptive parents expected that their rights and duties as parents were complete and permanent, even when children were told about the adoption and knew the birthparents. Some ambiguity might arise when adoptive parents were close relatives of birthparents, but even here the lines were kept clear and permanent. Although these were "open adoptions," they were real adoptions nonetheless.

Negative Consequences of State Laws and Policies for Abandoned Adopted Children

While it is difficult to gauge the extent of discriminatory social attitudes toward adopted children in their families and communities, state adoption policies and the patterns of adoption they have created over the past two decades result in clear disadvantages for many adopted foundlings. As we have discussed, the 1991 adoption law overtly discriminated against healthy nonorphaned foundlings (compared with orphans and disabled foundlings) by insisting that prospective adoptive parents be childless and over thirty-five. Prior to 1999, the law severely restricted the pool of adoptive parents legally available to rear healthy foundlings, making it more difficult to find homes for them. While many foundlings did get families, these adoptions often violated the law, creating a class of adoptees—called "illegal" or "black" children—who lack full legal status. The 1999 revisions ameliorate these obstacles for children in orphanages, but, as we will discuss later, they are too limited to help most abandoned children.

It is not surprising, given the patterns of adoption we found, that few of the adoptions in our sample were properly registered with the government at the time of adoption, although some registered or attained *hukou* through various means later, sometimes much later.[55] Many adoptive parents simply refused to register adoptions. Traditional customs in this area made adoption a "private" matter that rarely involved the government or courts. But the most obvious reason for avoiding government procedures, including child welfare centers, is that most adoptions did not fulfill the requirements of policy and law at the time. Given that most of these people found their children outside government channels, often without the prior intent to adopt, also meant they had no reason to go to state welfare institutions.

In our sample of 771 adoptive families, only 15 adopted from an orphanage or welfare center. Of these, 2 couples adopted children who had not been registered or "signed in" at the welfare center, so the babies could be removed by a third party (a local official in this case) and the normal procedures bypassed. Both couples were childless but still in their twenties, well below the legal age limit. One of the other 15 cases, involving the adoption of a boy by a couple who had a birthdaughter, took place in 1990, before the adoption law was promulgated, when regulations were often more flexibly applied. In this case local birth-planning regulations (although not adoption regulations) entitled the family to have a second child because the first was a girl. In the other 12 cases, the adopters met the age requirement and were childless.

By contrast, records we obtained from welfare centers documenting over 100 adoptions indicated that, on paper at least, all the adopting parents met the legal requirements at the time (i.e., they were childless and over thirty-five). A few were single men; most were couples between thirty-five and forty. The children they adopted were all healthy foundlings. Parents who, like the majority of those in our survey, did not meet the legal restrictions would not be permitted to adopt from welfare centers.

Birth-planning policies and practices exacerbated the situation for foundlings adopted outside the law and government channels by treating them as "overquota" children. Birth-planning policies often discriminated against overquota children by depriving them of full legal status, a proper household registration in their place of residence, and various benefits and entitlements given to other children. Furthermore, because of the fines and penalties associated with illegally adopted and overquota children, many parents "hid" them, thereby relegating them to the category of "illegal" or "black" children. Finally, the restrictive adoption law, like birth-planning itself, actually increased the risk of abandonment because some birthparents who could not openly arrange an adoption abandoned the child instead.

The inability to obtain a proper household registration can have serious consequences for the child. It often makes school enrollment difficult or more costly, and it means the child will not be eligible for land allotments or other benefits that accrue to those with proper household registration in their place of residence, especially in towns or cities. It also may mean that these children will be passed over by the government's program for childhood inoculations so that basic health care suffers.

In fact, whether or not a child can get a *hukou,* and with what consequences, varies greatly, depending on local practice. In major urban areas, having a *hukou* is especially important. Without one, obtaining a formal education may be impossible. It is particularly difficult for urban adoptive parents to obtain this legal status for their adopted children. In some cases, even adoptive parents who registered adoptions, sometimes paying fines to do so, reported that authorities made it difficult for them to obtain a household registration for the adopted child.

Yet in some of our cases, children whose adoptions did not fit the legal requirements nonetheless got properly registered. In most cases outside of urban areas, parents were allowed to register the child after paying a fine, although sometimes the household registration cost an additional large sum, and parents might still be required to pay extra fees to send the child to school. Some parents were eventually able to buy a household registration in another place or in their own place without paying a birth-planning fine or even notifying local cadres of the adoption. "Purchasing a *hukou*" has become relatively easy in many places, at least for those with the means, although purchased *hukou* are not always accepted as equivalent to regular *hukou.* The going price for an urban/county town household registration in the areas we investigated was between 3,000 and 5,000 yuan. In some places, children without household registration can attend school without additional fees and get inoculations at local clinics. Nonetheless, the discrimination "hidden children" face is serious and widespread enough to constitute a new social problem, creating a class of mostly female children who lack the full protection of the law and equal access to basic social entitlements.

Even adoptions that fit all the legal requirements might run into trouble from officials. Several adoptive parents in this category complained that they had tried unsuccessfully for several years to obtain *hukou* for their children. Government publications document such discrimination against adopted and abandoned children. Hunan welfare officials, for example, complained of the difficulty they had in obtaining registration for the abandoned children living in their own orphanage, thus denying the children, and indirectly the orphanage, access to certain benefits to which they should have been entitled (see Chap. 3). Even though "truly abandoned children" are entitled to proper registration and benefits, the state's adoption law explicitly discriminates against foundlings in the higher service of population control policy. Thus it is a matter of policy to penalize children for the reproductive behavior of their birthparents.[56]

Discrimination against hidden, overquota, or informally adopted children runs counter to China's own Law Protecting Maternal and Child Health, passed in 1992.[57] It also flies in the face of other government goals, such as improving both rural education and the "quality of the population." Furthermore, it is a serious form of gender discrimination because the vast majority of children in these categories are girls.

Several adoptive parents expressed anger at these discriminatory policies and practices, especially the adoption restrictions, and pointed out that it was both cruel and irrational for the government to punish those who find and care for foundlings, especially since the alternative requires the government to pay for the child's care in local facilities that are often extremely poor, if they exist at all. The result might be death for a weak and needy child, as one adoptive parent pointed out. This relatively poor parent had already spent hundreds of yuan and made several visits to the hospital to save an adopted child. A poor welfare center could scarcely have afforded the individual attention and money this child required in her first few months of life.

Most adoptive parents who got caught and were fined managed to pay the fine and, as with overquota births, sometimes even accepted sterilization. One of the most extreme punishments we heard of for adopting a foundling was imposed on a retired couple with two adult children. They found an infant girl, nursed her back to health, and then decided to rear her after failing to find another home for her. Not only did they become deeply attached to the child, but they also feared the child would suffer if they turned her over to welfare officials who were ill-equipped to care for infants. When local officials discovered what the couple had done, they fined them 10,000 yuan and insisted that the husband, nearing age sixty, be sterilized.

In our sample, no one had an adopted child taken from them, even in the few cases where very poor parents refused to pay the fine demanded by local officials.[58] In these cases, the officials retreated after heated argument, apparently recognizing that their demands were unreasonable. However, we know from discussions with welfare officials and adoptive parents not in our sample that some children are abandoned twice because of these adoption penalties, first by their birthparents and then by adoptive parents who get caught and find themselves pressured to give up the child when confronted with fines and with the displeasure of birth-planning cadres in their area. Articles in newspapers, reports from welfare officials, and other documentary evidence also suggest that some people who have adopted foundlings have had the child taken from them when they refused or were unable to pay the fines.[59] Other adoptive parents reluctantly bring children they had hoped to raise to welfare centers for these reasons. Once in a welfare center, the child may wait years for a new family or perhaps never be adopted. For all too many abandoned children, adoption regulations put them in double jeopardy.

In one area of adoption policy in the 1990s, the government tried to compensate for the narrow pool of potential parents in China that its laws had created for the tens of thousands (out of hundreds of thousands) of children abandoned each year who end up in government welfare institutions. International adoption, which the government opened up in the early 1990s, allowed qualified foreigners to adopt Chinese foundlings under the provisions of the 1991 adoption law. By mid 2000, over 25,000 foundlings had been placed in adoptive homes abroad, mostly in the United States and Canada. This program has proceeded even though it could cause China embarrassment by making the foundling problem obvious to the outside world and risks exposing the government to criticism from supernationalists within China and Western human rights activists outside China for "selling" Chinese babies. In fact the program has been relatively free from corruption, and the money paid has supplied orphanages with funds to improve the conditions of the foundlings who remain in state care.

Still, international adoption can provide a solution for only a small fraction of the hundreds of thousands of abandoned children in China. It might even inadvertently undermine the motivation of local orphanage and welfare officials to promote domestic adoptions, as discussed below. Many more homeless children could be accommodated if adoption policies were revised to allow more Chinese families to adopt legally and openly without penalty, regardless of whether the children are living inside or outside orphanages.

Conclusion: Population Control, Abandonment, and Adoption

The connection between population policies and abandonment is clear. It can be seen in the reports of government officials who find welfare centers taking in larger numbers of abandoned babies whenever there are crackdowns in birth-planning enforcement.[60] And in our research it can be seen in the reasons given by nearly all parents who abandoned children after the early 1980s.

What happens to all these abandoned children? Many observers believe that the number of children reported by the government to be in child welfare centers and other welfare organizations (of which there were 45,000–50,000 in 2000–2001)[61] is far too small to account for most abandoned children. In the mid 1990s one Chinese writer estimated that only about 20 percent of the abandoned children made it into the welfare system.[62] Even this guess seems to underestimate the abandonment problem and the percentage that evades government attention. Critics such as Human Rights Watch have asserted that most of the "missing" abandoned children die in the welfare centers or by the roads and in the fields where they are left unrecovered. These critics claim that there are few domestic adoptions of foundlings in China; as Human Rights Watch put it, "It is clearly impossible that children placed through adoption represent more than a small fraction" of the country's abandoned children.[63]

In the past, we also assumed that those children who did not make it into the welfare system faired even worse than those in orphanages, probably suffering even higher mortality rates. However, the research reported here strongly suggests that, to a significant though unknown extent, adoptive parents have emerged spontaneously outside the orphanage system to handle the crisis of abandonment created by population control policies. Indeed, many Chinese parents defy law and policy to adopt, in part because the same policy creates a demand for girls among families who have filled, or overfilled, their quota of births with sons yet still long for a daughter. Couples who are infertile also want to adopt abandoned girls.

Children abandoned in rural areas who never enter the welfare system may be better off than those who spend months in an orphanage, where mortality rates may be high and where, until recently, severe restrictions limited the pool of potential adopters. Many children abandoned in rural areas are adopted within days, sometimes hours, and are simply reabsorbed within the local population, where they live normal lives as daughters in families that want them.

Undoubtedly, some children die as a result of abandonment. We heard stories of how fragile some of these otherwise healthy abandoned infants were when adoptive parents found them. Some required repeated hospitalizations, and others died in the first months after recovery. But the vast majority we learned about did extremely well in their new homes, where, for the most part, they appear to have been treated like birthchildren. Surely their fate was far preferable to being put into orphanage care.

We are not alone in noticing an increasing desire for daughters in adoption practices in central Chinese villages in the 1990s. An article in the journal of the Shanghai Civil Affairs Bureau states that the adoption of girls increased in the late 1980s and 1990s in the central China plain, despite stringent birth planning. The author's information appears to be based on an investigation by local civil affairs units of informal adoptions of abandoned children. According to the article, most of the families adopting girls have one or two sons but no daughters. The reasons for adopting a girl are similar to those in our findings: parents feel their family is "incomplete" without a daughter, and they desire the emotional closeness and attentive care that daughters are thought to provide. Mothers especially are said to desire the closeness of a daughter and miss the experience of raising a girl if they have only sons. Finally, the article notes what we have surmised indirectly from interviews: that because sons are seen as singularly responsible for continuing a family name and lineage, peasants regard the adoption of boys as more problematic.[64]

This positive outcome for the children who find adoptive homes testifies to a popular culture that supports the adoption of both unrelated children and girls. Even significant punishments and fines have failed to deter a considerable amount of adoption in violation of birth-planning regulations and the adoption law. This phenomenon sets China apart from other societies, such as Korea and India, where even concerted government efforts have been unable to secure enough adoptive families for all homeless children without turning to international adoption.

Simply stated, the biggest obstacle to finding more homes and protecting the interests of abandoned children in China is government policy. Easing restrictions on the adoption of *all* foundlings, coupled with an effort to publicize the availability of healthy children in orphanages, should make it possible to place many, if not all, healthy homeless children now in government hands. The government could then focus its efforts more effectively on the needs of the more difficult to place or "unadoptable" disabled children in its care. Many orphanages end up raising many more foundlings than necessary, and some babies who would thrive if placed quickly in the hands of new families suffer illness and may even die because of the risks that accompany institutionalized care.

Abandonment of healthy infants could be reduced significantly if the birth-planning policies were relaxed enough to allow some alternative for sonless couples desperate enough to abandon a daughter. Whatever benefits are presumed to derive from the relentless pursuit of these policies, the terrible consequences of harsh quota-based birth-planning policies for large numbers of children needs to weigh more heavily in the balance. Our interviews and opinion survey indicate that while some will do practically anything for a son, not everyone would proceed to higher-parity births just for the sake of a son. The desire for a son and a daughter is tempered by the well-established ideal of a small family. In a number of our interviews, those who had gotten away with having higher-parity births in order to have a son (or in some cases a daughter) felt that it was nevertheless a burden to have more than two children. Institutional and economic changes that lessen the need for sons for social security would likely make the perceived burden of more than two children loom even larger in the minds of peasants with daughters but no sons (see Chap. 1). And of course, pursuing a high-pressure birth-planning policy that creates a large population of "missing girls" and unregistered children does not lower population growth as much as it appears to, since many of these girls have been added to the actual population whether the government counts them or not.[65] Although a full discussion is beyond the scope of this chapter, there is much evidence that China's population is not a runaway train that morally justifies any means to stop it.[66] We must ask whether the resultant suffering, discrimination, and distortion of normal sex ratios is justified.

Recent Policy Changes

It is encouraging that some parts of the Chinese government, including the Ministry of Civil Affairs, have sought in recent years to provide greater funding for orphanages so that those foundlings who end up in state care have a better chance of survival and even good health (see Chap. 7). This funding has come not only from the fees paid for foreign adoptions, but also from increased government spending, solicitation of donations from the Chinese population, and charitable foundations within China and abroad, many of which are now active in various training and teaching programs as well. As a result, some of the largest orphanages have improved conditions considerably in the past five or six years. Many smaller orphanages in the system have also enjoyed increased funding.

It is also encouraging to find evidence of cracks in the rigid birth-planning consensus that led to such coercive, high-pressure practices in recent years. By the late 1990s a number of counties were designated as test sites for more "voluntary" birth-planning policies—that is, birth planning without quotas or harsh punishments aside from paying "fees" for overquota children.[67] Such policies, if they become widespread, could significantly lessen the full range of problems discussed here. Unfortunately, the changes in these experimental areas sometimes seem more apparent than real. There are also indications that birth planning tightened again in some rural areas in the period preceding the 2000 census.[68]

The most encouraging legal development is the 1999 revised adoption law, which lowers the minimum age to thirty and allows orphanages to arrange adoptions for foundlings in their care with adoptive parents who already have children.[69] If these changes are implemented effectively, they will help overburdened child welfare centers find more adoptive families inside China for the foundlings in their care. More domestic adoptions would indeed improve the prospects of abandoned children who fall into government hands and would represent at least a partial reorientation of the law to serve the interests of children rather than simply the demands of birth planning.

But aside from lowering the legal age to thirty for certifiably infertile couples, the 1999 revisions do not address the problems faced by the large numbers of abandoned children who join adoptive families without ever entering the orphanage or child welfare system. Such adoptions account for the vast majority of foundling adoptions. The revisions in the law clearly exclude those who find or adopt foundlings directly, even if the adoptions are processed through local governments. Such adoptions are considered lawful only if the adoptive parents are childless, infertile, and over thirty. Otherwise, the child may be deprived not only of all legal protection of her family rights, but of a legal household registration and all the social entitlements that come with it. Thus, while the 1999 revisions may help orphanage children, additional changes are necessary to remove the heavy burden and discriminatory treatment now experienced by the tens of thousands of families who have adopted foundlings outside of government institutions.

These parents have not only saved children's lives, but also saved the state from what would be a far greater financial burden were all these children suddenly dumped into the orphanage system. While the conditions in orphanages have improved a great deal since the beginning of the abandonment crisis in the early 1990s, it is inconceivable that the system could cope with the large numbers of abandoned children who are adopted directly by families. Forcing all of these children into orphanages to live for a minimum of two months prior to becoming available for adoption, as required by current implementation regulations, would be a nightmare not only for the welfare system, but especially for the children and the families who want to adopt them. These children need to have rights, protected by law, equal to those of birthchildren. They need nothing less than full legal status in their own birth country. The current law, even in its revised form, fails to accomplish any of this.

Obstacles to Further Change

After twenty years, powerful and entrenched birth-planning authorities are loath to give up control over adoption policy; loosening restrictions, they fear, would create a hole in the birth-planning dike. Proponents of "birth planning first" raised serious objections to the 1999 revisions when Premier Zhu Rongji and Civil Affairs Minister Dorji Cering brought those changes to the National People's Congress (NPC) in November 1998.[70] To appease birth-planning concerns, the NPC strictly limited the scope of the revisions to apply only to those who adopted children already living in an orphanage, thus covering only a small part of the widespread practice of adoption. The revisions were followed up with tough implementation regulations, including required certifications by local birth-planning authorities. Adoption policy is still held hostage to the needs of birth planning rather than serving the interests of homeless children.

In addition to opposition from birth-planning forces, the revisions have run into other obstacles, including less than wholehearted enthusiasm from some cadres in the welfare system. Despite brief initial publicity about the revised law, there has been no large-scale effort to publicize the availability of healthy orphanage children for legal adoption by families with or without birthchildren. The government and especially birth-planning authorities remain reluctant to acknowledge the large population of healthy children that they house in their orphanages for fear of reflecting negatively on the state's sacrosanct population policies. When they give publicity to orphanages, they often imply that only true orphans and disabled children live there—an impression that is clearly untrue. Most Chinese are completely unaware that they could legally and readily adopt a healthy infant from a welfare center.

In addition, some orphanage officials seem uninterested in promoting domestic adoption when a single foreign adoption can bring in twenty or thirty times the funds. Simply increasing the number of children adopted does not necessarily benefit the budgets of the welfare institutes, most of which charge an orphanage fee of between 500 yuan and a few thousand yuan for domestic adoption, depending on the income of the adopter. At the same time, some welfare institutes have set domestic adoption fees so high that they equal the US$3,000 paid by international adopters.[71] Fortunately, other orphanages have kept their domestic fees more reasonable, actively implemented the revisions, and increased domestic adoptions from orphanages in recent years.[72]

One can hope that in the future more thorough implementation of the 1999 revisions and more vigorous promotion of domestic adoption among the Chinese public will secure permanent loving homes for the healthy foundlings now in Chinese orphanages. Those institutions can then focus on the care and rehabilitation of disabled children who cannot live with their birthfamilies and cannot readily be placed in new adoptive families.

More fundamental changes in adoption policy are needed to provide respite and legal status for those adopted outside the orphanage welfare system as well, providing reasonable means to verify, register, and protect legitimate adoptions such as those we studied. Adoptive parents who have not wittingly abetted the abandonment of the child—who have taken in children of unknown parentage, as in the overwhelming majority of the cases of adoption we found—should not be punished for adopting and raising a foundling as if she were their birthchild, even if they have given birth to one or more children. Perhaps the revisions in the 1991 adoption law will eventually extend to those who adopt outside of state orphanages, though this change does not seem imminent. In the meantime, and in the breach created by recent state policies, we may at least rest assured that Chinese adoptive families have spontaneously emerged to provide many of the hundreds of thousands of healthy abandoned girls with new families and a new life as adopted daughters despite the obstacles they face in doing so.

CHAPTER FIVE

The Politics of International and Domestic Adoption in China, 2001

The relationship between international adoption and domestic adoption in sending countries has been a central concern of legal codes that regulate international adoption and seek to protect children's interests. The 1989 United Nations' Convention on the Rights of the Child and the 1993 Hague Conference's Convention on Protection of Children and Cooperation in Respect of Intercountry Adoption argue that an ethical adoption policy should privilege domestic adoption over international adoption whenever feasible within a reasonable period of time. Moving children across borders, which separates them from their country and culture of birth, is viewed as a last resort for adoptive placement, preferable to long-term in-country institutional care but less desirable than domestic adoption.

Scholars such as Barbara Yngvesson and Claudia Fonseca point out that some features of the Hague Convention and other international legal codes in fact mitigate against this prescription by valorizing a narrow definition of adoption and postulating a narrowly defined ideal adoptive family that in some cases (such as Brazil) lead social workers and lawyers to overlook local adopters and traditional forms of adoption in favor of international adopters. The latter offer not only wealthier homes than domestic placement but also a "stronger" form of adoption that places children permanently and exclusively in a nuclear family with sole legal custody, rights, and responsibility for the child.[1]

Nonetheless it is commonly understood that most sending countries participate in international adoption primarily because economic and cultural factors make it difficult to find enough homes for homeless children inside their country of birth. In such circumstances, institutional care may be the only alternative to international adoption. South Korea is seen as a prime example of this pattern. Tens of thousands of Korean children have been placed abroad in adoptive families rather than being raised in Korean orphanages or temporary foster care arrangements. Although annual numbers of children adopted from Korea declined in the 1980s and 1990s, over the past fifty years South Korea has been the largest single supplier of children to adoptive parents in the United States and elsewhere.

Poverty alone cannot explain the need to seek adoptive families abroad. While international adoption from Korea began in the midst of the devastation created by the Korean war, it continued well beyond the Korean economic recovery and subsequent "economic miracle," during which Korea witnessed some of the highest economic growth rates in the world. Today South Korea can no longer be considered a poor country, and yet it still sends between 1,500 and 2,000 children annually to the United States alone. Despite South Korea's political stability

and increasing wealth, many observers believe that the continuing grip of Confucianism, with its heavy emphasis on maintaining bloodlines together with a strong preference for sons,
has made it difficult to promote domestic adoption as a substitute for international placement despite the South Korean government's efforts to encourage domestic adoption over the past
fifteen to twenty years.

China, which surpassed Korea as a supplier of children to
the United States after 1994, is often presumed to be in the
same situation as Korea, with too many homeless children and
too few domestic adoptive homes. China, after all, is not only
poorer than South Korea, but also the birthplace of Confucius
and of the patriarchal family values that create fierce son preference and a devotion to male bloodlines as the central organ-
izing principle of kinship and community. Many commentators have assumed that the Chinese government, like the
Korean government, had to turn to international adoption to
find more permanent homes for the growing numbers of predominantly female foundlings living in overcrowded Chinese
orphanages in the 1990s.

This assumption is shared by Chinese and non-Chinese
alike. As the Chinese-born head of one of the largest U.S. adoption agencies told the *South China Morning Post* in 1999, "The
concept [of adoption] hardly exists in Chinese culture. Nobody
knows about it." By contrast, he goes on to say, "adoption has
a long tradition in the U.S. To a Chinese if a child is not of his
flesh and blood, he may not love the child as much as he loves
his own children. . . . Americans don't feel that way." Chinese
attitudes and culture are believed to make it harder for abandoned Chinese children to find loving adoptive homes in

China. "Every city in the mainland," the reporter concludes, "has a social welfare home which shelters abandoned children. But few mainlanders consider adoption."[2]

Similarly an article in the *Christian Science Monitor* on the improving conditions in Chinese orphanages quotes a U.S. official involved in adoption: "Would-be Chinese parents are beginning to adopt more and more, but almost all of the adoptions are of blood relatives. . . . Traditionally, Chinese have almost never adopted complete strangers." In the same article, China scholar Anne Thurston explains that in Chinese society abandoned children are "outcasts": "A child deserted by its family has no identity in China."[3]

Those involved in international adoption rarely question such portrayals of domestic adoption in China. As I launched a project in the mid 1990s to investigate contemporary Chinese adoption practices,[4] even some of my Chinese colleagues assumed that we would find domestic adoption to be rare today, confined largely to the adoption of relatives' children or the occasional unrelated boy.

Compounding cultural preferences and attitudes that are presumed to limit adoption as it is understood today, the Chinese government in 1950 banned the most common traditional form of adoption of infant girls. This practice was known as taking a *tongyangxi*, or "little daughter-in-law," whom the adoptive parents would raise to become the future wife of their son. With this practice prohibited, did any other common adoption practices today involve girls? Were people willing to adopt the children of strangers, including abandoned children? Or was conventional wisdom about Chinese adoption practices correct? Would we find that adoption today was rare, that when it occurred it involved primarily close relatives or boys, and that people generally shunned the adoption of strangers' children, especially abandoned girls?

Research Findings on Contemporary Adoption

Prior to our work in the mid to late 1990s, little research had been done on Chinese adoption practices after 1949. However, a demographic study in 1990 based on sample census data suggested that "informal adoptions" were numerous and increasing in the 1980s, although it was unclear from this demographic study what "informal adoptions" involved.[5] There was also evidence from this study and others that adoption might increasingly involve more girls than boys.[6] But the nature and purpose of adoption was still unknown. Was adoption usually permanent or temporary? Did it generally involve arrangements between close relatives and friends, perhaps for the purpose of hiding children from local birth-planning authorities, or were Chinese people adopting foundlings or the children of strangers? Our study suggested answers to these questions. Using information gathered from nearly 800 adoptive families between 1996 and 1999, we discovered that adoption—viewed as a permanent and complete transfer of children into the adoptive family—was common in many rural areas, that it involved girls far more than boys, and that only a minority of adoptions involved relatives or close friends. The largest single category of adopted children in our sample was abandoned children (56 percent of the sample), the vast majority of whom were girls (87 percent). In other words, many families were willing to adopt the abandoned female children of strangers.

Contemporary Adoption Practices

The historical and anthropological literature on the Chinese family indicates that adoption has been used to construct kinship in China for a very long time. Legal codes and lineage rules often stipulated that adoption must take place within bloodlines and should only be done for the purpose of obtaining a male heir of the same surname and patriline. Yet practice, supported by other culturally embedded ideas, often involved adoption outside bloodlines. The historian Ann Waltner argues in her study of Ming and Qing dynasty adoption practices that another adoption ideology competed with the dominant Confucian ideology and legal codes restricting adoption to bloodlines. This competing ideology was encoded in the term *mingling zi,* which literally means "mulberry insect children" but is commonly used to refer to an adopted person, especially to a child adopted outside the circle of patrilineal relatives.[7] Despite Confucian prohibitions against adoption except for securing a male heir, in practice Chinese people developed numerous traditional precedents both for adopting the children of strangers and for adopting girls. Overall, the diversity of customary practice created a popular culture of adoption that evolved over the decades since 1949 and adapted to new circumstances and new family aspirations. (See Chap. 4, pp. 97–99, for a detailed discussion of these traditions and their significance to contemporary Chinese adoption practices.)

While past practices shed light on the origins of popular adoption culture in China today, contemporary practices and attitudes do not merely reflect the past. Chinese family ideals have changed, and adoption reflects those changes. Our research confirms that the adoption of girls as "little daughters-in-law" is rare now. Today girls are adopted as daughters. Contemporary adoptive parents routinely insist that adopted children have the same status as birthchildren and are raised and treated "as if born to" the parents. The widespread adoption of girls as daughters fits in with modern popular ideals of a small but gender-balanced family. And while the felt need for at least one son remains prevalent, most people report that the ideal family has two children: one boy and one girl. While sons are said to be necessary for economic support in old age and to continue the family line, as only a male heir can do, girls are increasingly valued for their emotional care, loyalty, and closeness to parents.[8] Families that adopted girls often pointed to these particular strengths of daughters.

Although childless couples usually adopted girls because healthy girls were more readily available than healthy boys, many insisted that the gender of the child was not important. They just wanted a healthy baby they could raise "as their own." Some went further, pointing out the particular value of adopting a girl—that daughters are closer, more loving, and more loyal to their parents than boys are. Families with birth-sons but no daughters were particularly happy to adopt girls. These parents often commented that a boy and a girl made a family complete. So while sonless families, in the context of strictly enforced birth-planning policies, might sometimes abandon a higher-parity daughter in their quest for a son, daughterless families, also constrained by birth-planning policies, often welcome the opportunity to adopt abandoned girls as a way to "complete" their families through adoption.

In short, there exists in China today a popular culture of adoption that allows the use of adoption in the construction of the contemporary family and the approximation of popularly imagined family ideals. Had this culture of adoption not existed in the 1980s and 1990s, Chinese orphanages would surely have been far more crowded and stressed than they were. Though many Chinese adoptive parents suffered fines and penalties for violating the adoption regulations regarding childlessness or the minimum age requirements, they represented a social force that responded to the crisis of abandonment by taking in hundreds of thousands of foundlings over the past two decades and raising them "as if" they were birthchildren.

The Policy Context of International Adoption

Given these socially generated patterns of domestic adoption and a popular culture of adoption particularly in rural areas, why didn't the Chinese government and local civil affairs authorities vigorously promote domestic adoption as the first and primary means to find homes for the growing numbers of children in orphanages in the 1990s? The vast majority of Chinese adoptions occur outside of orphanages, but the patterns we found indicate that the domestic ground was fertile to promote more adoption through official channels, had the government chosen to do so. Why did it turn instead to international adoption to help deal with overcrowded orphanages?

In fact there was some domestic adoption from Chinese orphanages in the 1990s, although not a great deal. While precise official statistics are not available for this period, domestic adoptions from orphanages certainly exceeded international adoptions at the beginning of the decade. Some orphanage directors established their own networks to locate more Chinese adoptive families, but there was no coordinated systemwide effort to find adoptive families within China for the increasing number of orphanage foundlings. There was, however, a new nationwide system to facilitate the placement of children through international adoption and to regulate the exchange of documents, foreign currency, and the movement of children across international borders. To this day, no such organization facilitates the placement of children in domestic adoption.

While international adoptions increased rapidly—from fewer than 100 in 1991 to more than 6,000 by the end of the decade[9]—domestic adoption from orphanages seems to have increased little, stagnated, or even decreased in some places during the 1990s.[10] In the late 1990s, civil affairs officials reported that registered domestic adoptions during the decade ranged from 6,000 to 8,000 per year, without specifying what percentage were from orphanages or welfare institutes.[11] One can deduce from these low and stable figures for total registered adoptions that domestic adoption from state orphanages could not have exceeded a few thousand per year. By the end of the 1990s, international adoptions almost overtook domestic adoptions from government welfare institutes. Why didn't the government move just as vigorously to promote domestic adoption?

One answer, according to critics of China's human rights record, is that the Chinese government has used children as another export to make profits and earn foreign exchange for its growing capitalist economy. International adoption brings in US$3,000 per child in mandatory orphanage donations and an additional US$1,000–2,000 in other fees and expenses paid by adoptive parents in China. Yet any reasonable assessment of this charge would have to conclude that the amount brought in by international adoption is insignificant, indeed miniscule, in the broad context of the Chinese economy.[12] Fees alone cannot explain it, although orphanage donations have certainly bene-fited those welfare institutes that reap the lion's share of these funds for improvements and daily operations. From this per-spective, international adoption has been reasonably effective at bringing funds into the welfare system when it was sorely strapped and barely able to cope with the increasing numbers of children in care. Many outside observers, including myself, have noted significant improvements in the orphanages that participate in international adoption, including improved phys-ical plant, improved staffing, higher-quality medical care, and, in the best orphanages, improved attention to developmental and educational needs. Yet the utility of international adoption for meeting these important needs cannot explain why domes-tic adoption was ignored when it too could have provided addi-tional means to reduce the orphanage population, thus reduc-ing costs and allowing more focus on the disabled children who cannot be placed in adoptive families.

There were far more children in Chinese orphanages in the 1990s than international adoption could accommodate. Yet at the beginning of the decade, few Chinese people were aware of the location or even the existence of many orphanages. Some large urban orphanages disguised their true purpose by posting signs declaring that they were kindergartens or schools. Other orphanages were tucked away in inconspicuous spots and rarely drew public attention. This trend changed around 1993–94, when some local governments began efforts to raise donations for orphanages from citizens, as I discussed in Chapter 3. Still, few efforts were made to promote the domestic adoption of orphanage children.

Population Control and Adoption Policy

The greatest impediment to the promotion of domestic adoption has been the one-child policy. During the 1980s and 1990s, Chinese adoption policy became entangled with, and ultimately subordinate to, the state's top-priority population control policies. Observers have long understood the connection between the so-called one-child policy and female infant abandonment.[13] Less well known but equally clear on reflection is the way that birth-planning efforts quickly expanded into domestic adoption policy and fully took it over at the highest level of national legislation in 1991, when the first adoption law was passed (see Chap. 4). Not coincidentally, this legislation was formulated and passed in the midst of one of the harshest and most prolonged birth-planning campaigns that China has experienced.[14]

Heralded for paving the way to international adoption, the 1991 law also codified a highly restrictive policy that limited the adoption of foundlings to childless parents over the age of thirty-five. While there are many childless couples in China, as elsewhere, thirty-five is an unacceptably advanced age to become a first-time parent, according to Chinese social norms and practice, especially in the countryside where most Chinese live. Furthermore, by limiting the pool of adoptive parents to those who are childless, the law summarily eliminated a huge number of potential adoptive parents.

Clearly, finding adoptive homes for abandoned children within China was not a priority. Rather, the main purpose of the law was to shore up the "one-child" policy by eliminating adoption as a way to hide the birth of a child, typically a daughter, in order to try again for a son. As a result, adoption policy not only restricted legal adoption to a relatively small pool of older childless couples, but also indirectly contributed to rising infant abandonment. Birthparents who now found it more difficult to arrange an adoption for an unwanted or overquota child might decide to abandon the child instead. By the same token, while customary adoption practices in violation of the law continued outside the view of the government, legal adoptions from government orphanages and welfare institutes became more difficult.

At the same time, international adoption involved countries where potential adoptive parents tend to be older and the demand for healthy infants is high. This new source of adoptive families could at least partially compensate for the large number of Chinese families now disqualified from adopting. It could also help bring needed funds to improve care for the increasing numbers of children who would have to grow up in orphanages rather than in adoptive families. While this arrangement failed to serve the best interests of foundlings in orphanage care, it did provide financial assistance for caregiving institutions and homes abroad for a small but growing number of children. Foreigners adopted more than 35,000 children during the past decade, though many times that number of adoptable children remained behind in the orphanages.[15] While many of these children benefited from improved conditions, thanks in part to funding brought in by international adoption, the tradeoff was hardly a good one for those who had to spend their childhood in institutions.

Revisions to the Adoption Law

Because of some of the obvious contradictions created by the 1991 law, which restricted adoption at precisely the moment that more homes were needed for abandoned children, efforts began to revise the law to accommodate more domestic adoptions from orphanages. In the fall of 1998, a revised law was sent to the National People's Congress for approval. Enacted in 1999, it lowered the legal age for adopting parents to thirty and, most important, allowed families with children to adopt healthy foundlings. This seemed a major breakthrough in the way Beijing viewed adoption law, orienting it more toward the needs of children than those of birth planning.

Yet the results in the first couple of years were less sweeping than one might have hoped. In fact, birth-planning forces opposed the revisions at various stages and sought to restrict their scope.[16] When the law was finally approved and the regulations for its implementation issued, the scope of the revisions had been limited to the adoption of children "being raised in welfare institutions," and the most significant revision, allowing those with children to adopt healthy foundlings living in institutions, was buried deep in the fine print.[17] Aside from initial publicity trumpeting the passage of the new law, efforts to publicize the new possibilities for legal adoption were local and sporadic. Implementing regulations also stipulated that before parents could qualify to adopt a child, they required written approval from birth-planning authorities at various levels certifying that they had never violated birth-planning policies. In some places families with children found it very difficult to adopt from a welfare institute, while elsewhere orphanages reported a rapid increase in domestic adoptions.[18] The attitude of local orphanage authorities and their political relationships with other government officials affected the way the law was implemented.

Preliminary research on the impact of the 1999 law also indicates that those who adopted foundlings outside of welfare institutions have generally had a hard time using the new law to register their adoptions and obtain legal status for their adopted children.[19] Our sample of adoptive parents included a large number who had adopted abandoned children outside of government channels and without informing the government, either because they were underage or because they had other children. Explicitly excluded from the letter of the revised law, most of these families were still unable to legalize their adoptions. As a result, many of these children remain unregistered "black children" (*hei haizi*) lacking the papers necessary to gain access to good schools, or indeed to any schools beyond the primary level, and perhaps being deprived of other entitlements as well, such as mandated inoculations.

Birth-planning forces are not the only ones with interests that mitigate against a vigorous application of the revised law and the principle that domestic adoption should be expanded as fully as possible. Numerous vested interests and relationships have grown up around international adoption in the past decade, involving local orphanage and civil affairs officials, central adoption and welfare officials in the Ministry of Civil Affairs, and a host of international adoption agencies and charitable foundations that have become involved in care-giving programs within the Chinese child welfare system. While few could be accused of active efforts to block domestic adoption, many seem to see it as an afterthought, looking instead to the more institutionally routinized—and lucrative—sources of international adoption. Foreign agencies and Chinese organizations involved in international adoption are often barely aware of the great potential for domestic adoption and in any case have little motivation to explore those possibilities. Recall the comments at the beginning of this chapter from several officials, scholars, and heads of adoption agencies. At the extreme end of resistance to the new law are a few orphanage officials who worry about "the well running dry" for international adopters should domestic adoption become too popular. Some have set the fees for domestic adopters as high as those for foreigners: around 25,000 yuan, the equivalent of US$3,000. This sum is prohibitive for all but the wealthiest of Chinese and will surely keep domestic adoptions from such an orphanage to a bare minimum.[20]

Prospects for Change

Despite numerous obstacles, the revised law is a step in the right direction, bringing Chinese adoption policy more in line with accepted international adoption principles and the Hague Convention and giving a positive if limited boost to legal domestic adoption. Statistics published by the Ministry of Civil Affairs indicate that registered adoptions both inside and outside state welfare institutes increased significantly after 1998, compared to the early and mid 1990s. In 1992 the ministry reported only 2,900 officially registered adoptions.[21] There are no published figures available for domestic adoption from orphanages or from other avenues in the mid 1990s. However, as mentioned earlier, total registered adoptions during this period hovered around 6,000–8,000 per year, according to civil affairs officials interviewed in Beijing. Civil affairs statistics indicate that there were more than 38,000 registered adoptions in 1999 and 56,000 in 2000. Domestic adoptions from orphanages also increased to 6,700 in 1999, compared with 6,100 international adoptions, and 10,700 domestic adoptions from orphanages in 2000, compared with 6,700 international adoptions that year. There were also 24,400 registered domestic adoptions of foundlings outside welfare institutions in 1999 and 37,000 in 2000.[22] Since the actual number of foundlings adopted outside of orphanages each year is likely much higher than 37,000 and has been for many years, this figure does not necessarily indicate an increase in overall adoptions, but it does indicate a significant increase in the number of such adoptions that have been properly registered and legalized. That more parents are seeking legal status for their adopted children may be related to the way the revised law has affected adoption practices in some areas.[23] It may also result partly from greater efforts to legalize the status of "black children" who have, for one reason or another, fallen outside the "planned population" and been deprived of proper registration.[24] Whatever the reasons, the trend suggests that at least some officials are coming to grips with the unintended consequences of coercive population policies—consequences that have jeopardized the interests of thousands of children, deprived them of families, and often left them without basic legal rights.

Other positive efforts to find noninstitutional care for abandoned and orphaned children within China include new foster care systems connected to welfare institutes. Foster care has been promoted and funded by a coalition of Chinese welfare officials in the Ministry of Civil Affairs and charitable international donor organizations and adoption agencies involved in child welfare programs.[25] These arrangements are a positive development, especially when they accommodate children with special needs who are unlikely to be adopted.

Still, foster care is no substitute for permanent domestic adoption. Yet authorities seem more willing to promote and invest in foster care than to vigorously promote domestic adoption. Because foster care programs do not threaten birth-planning efforts or compete with international adoption, they don't face the opposition that confronts proponents of domestic adoption. Indeed, international adopters prefer foster care to orphanage care, since institutions are widely believed to create "damaged children." Thus the development of foster care dovetails well with the interests of both birth-planning forces and international adoption. That it does so is of course no reason to oppose foster care. But like international adoption, foster care should not be encouraged as a substitute for, or a means of avoiding, the active promotion of permanent legal domestic adoption whenever that is possible.

I have interviewed some foster families who are satisfied with their status even though they consider themselves to be adoptive families in every other way. As long as their position as the foster family is secure and permanent, it seems a decent tradeoff for the small financial benefits and the legal registration of the child. But the identity of the child as her parents' daughter is still confused by the foster care status, which consigns the child to an orphanage registration and carries negative social implications. Promoting legal permanent adoption rather than foster care would in most cases be far better for the child. Indeed, after 1999 many foster families who were caring for children on behalf of the government used the revised law to legally adopt their foster children.

Conclusion

It is still too soon to tell whether Chinese adoption policies are finally coming into line with the principles of the Hague Convention. The 1999 revisions still cater to birth-planning concerns by refusing to include the large number of legitimate adoptions of abandoned children that take place outside of orphanages under the new provision that allows those with children to adopt legally. The lack of promotion and implementation of the revision further constrains the impact of the legal change in many areas. International adoption has become deeply entrenched through central and local ties to international adoption agencies and to international nonprofit charitable foundations (some organized and funded by foreign adoptive parents) that have become widely involved in funding various orphanage and foster care programs. Many local orphanage officials have come to rely on the benefits of international adoption for improvements, and some seem less than eager to promote the domestic adoption of healthy children when they can place them internationally instead. Even where plenty of children are available for both international and domestic adoption, domestic adoption may get short shrift.

Advocates of domestic adoption have to fight not only against the entrenched power of the birth-planning establishment, but also against vested interests and institutional arrangements that have oriented significant parts of the child welfare system toward international adoption and the international donors it has generated. While there is a national ministry-level organization, the China Center for Adoption Affairs, to supervise, coordinate, and process international adoptions, there is no central organization to promote, coordinate, or represent the interests of domestic adoption. Domestic adoption from orphanages needs the support of a nationwide publicity campaign to find adoptive parents and convince them that their applications will be handled smoothly, with minimal bureaucratic problems and at minimal expense. Further legal change allowing legitimate adoptions of foundlings outside orphanages by those with children also needs to be pursued. One can only hope that more doors will open to the legal domestic adoption of foundlings, whether the children are living inside state welfare institutions or not. Promoting and legalizing all legitimate forms of domestic adoption would surely decrease the "hidden" population of children in China and enhance the rights of all China's children to a family and home in their country of birth.

For their part, international donors, to avoid inadvertently undermining the spirit of the United Nations' Convention on the Rights of the Child and the Hague Convention on Intercountry Adoption, must firmly base their commitment to support Chinese orphanage programs on the needs of the orphanage system and not be driven by the level of international adoption or the interest generated by it outside China. With fuller support for the promotion of domestic as well as international adoption, the need to care for large numbers of orphanage children should diminish over time, allowing the Chinese government, society, and international charitable organizations to focus on the needs of those disabled children unable to find homes either in China or abroad.

Birth-planning slogans appear prominently throughout China. The large characters to the left and right of the gate read: "Birth planning benefits the country and the people." Linquan, Anhui, 1996.

"Daughters are also descendants." Feidong, Anhui, 1995.

Left to be found: a baby girl abandoned on a hospital bench.
Anhui, 1993. Photo by Richard Tessler.

Box and blanket that held a foundling. Anhui, 2000.

Infants bundled up and placed close together for warmth. Changsha
Orphanage, January 1994. Photo by David Sutherland.

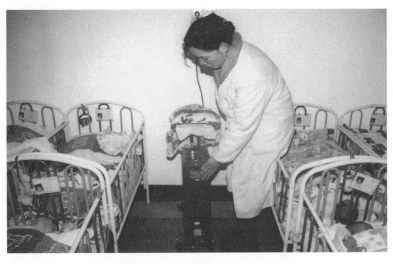

Adjusting the temperature in an infant room on the top floor of a
new government-funded building. Cribs, heaters, and air conditioners
donated by the Foundation for Chinese Orphanages. Changsha
Orphanage, December 2000. Photo by Terry M. Fry.

Front gate of the old Wuhan Orphanage a month before the author adopted her daughter. March 1991.

The New Wuhan Orphanage complex, built in 1997 with government funds and a large grant from a Taiwanese Buddhist organization. July 1998. The Chinese government at various levels rebuilt many orphanages in the late 1980s, thanks in part to the income from international adoptions.

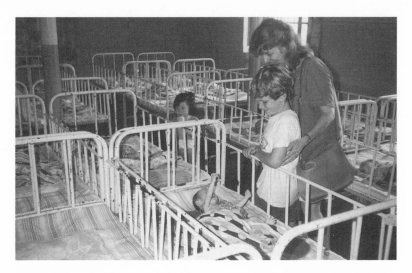

The author visiting the old Wuhan Orphanage with her son, Jesse, and daughter, LiLi (*center, standing*). June 1993. Photo by D. Gale Johnson.

Jesse in the infant room of the new Wuhan Orphanage. May 1998.

Recently abandoned child. Old Wuhan Orphanage, March 1991.

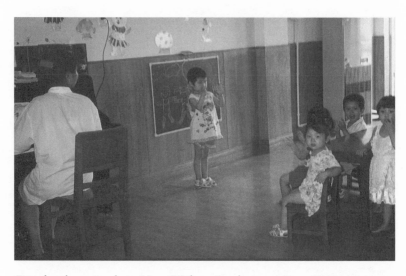

Preschool music class. New Wuhan Orphanage, June 2000.

Older orphanage girls posing in their dormitory with LiLi Johnson (*center right, in sleeveless dress*) and Yang West (*center left, in skirt and tank top*), both adopted to the United States from Wuhan as babies. New Wuhan Orphanage, June 2000.

Song and dance performance. New Wuhan Orphanage, June 2000.

Preschool funded by Half the Sky. Hefei Orphanage, June 2000.

Foster mother and child in Sunbeam Village, funded
by Alliance for Children. Hefei Orphanage, June 2002.

Classroom for disabled children in Oasis House, run by
International China Concern. Changsha Orphanage, December
2000. Photo by Terry M. Fry.

Amity Foundation caregiver with disabled baby. Changsha
Orphanage, December 2000. Photo by Brian Boyd.

Adoptive mother and daughter in their home. Anhui, November 2000.

Older adoptive mother with birthdaughter (*left*), adopted daughter, and birthson's toddler. Anhui, March 1996.

Adoptive parents and son. The parents have paid for several expensive surgeries to repair the boy's cleft lip and palate. They also have young adult birthchildren, a son and a daughter. Anhui, March 1996.

Adoptive parents and daughter. Anhui, March 1996.

Adoptive mother and daughter. Anhui, October 2000.

Adoptive parents with their teenage daughter. There are two older birthsons in the family as well. Anhui, June 2000.

Wang Liyao (*left*) interviewing an adoptive father at home. Anhui,
June 2000.

Huang Banghan on his way to interview a rural family. Anhui,
November 2000.

"A son and a daughter make a family complete." The author beams as her children, Jesse and LiLi, see each other for the first time. JFK International Airport, April 1991. Photo by William Grohmann.

The author visiting a foster family in their home. The parents have two birthchildren and a foster baby girl assigned to them by an orphanage. Anhui, June 2001. Photo by LiLi Johnson.

CHAPTER SIX

Chaobao

Overquota Adoption and the Plight of Chinese Adoptive Parents, 2002

As a China scholar and adoptive parent of a Chinese child, I am often asked to give talks to groups of American parents who have adopted children from China. I have found that, above all, these parents want to understand their children's birthparents and the circumstances surrounding the abandonment of children in China. Who are the biological parents of our children? Why did they abandon their birthchild? How did they feel about it? What consequences did they suffer?

Most American adoptive parents of Chinese children want to believe the best of their children's birthparents. Most want to put as positive a spin as possible on the story of abandonment. Indeed, many refuse to use the word *abandonment* and are surprised, if not offended, when I do. Many American parents prefer to frame the issues of abandonment as a type of "adoption plan" and speak of their children "being left somewhere to be found by others." They prefer to see birthparents as "forced" into the act of abandonment. Sometimes abandonment is even seen as a "brave act," undertaken at great risk to the birthparents, to save the child's life from abortion or infanticide. Whether the agent of force is government coercion, the iron grip of culture, poverty, or some combination, birthparents are portrayed as unwilling victims. A lot is at stake for adoptive parents. How should they tell their children about their early lives and explain how they lost their first families and came into their present families? How will they answer their children's questions about what happened to them in China?

The research I presented in Chapter 4 gives some support to the positive shaping of the story of abandonment, but it also undercuts it in many ways. Certainly most birthparents who abandon a second or third daughter are under great pressure from coercive government policies and actions. Yet birthparents are not *forced* in any literal way to abandon a child; indeed it is illegal and a violation of birth-planning policy to do so. Rather, a strongly felt need for a son in the face of severe birth-planning pressures drives some parents to abandon a daughter—a child they would probably have kept, regardless of the penalty, were it a boy. Many other Chinese parents in similar circumstances refuse to take this route out of a difficult situation, despite their desire for a son; to most, abandoning a birthchild is unthinkable. Nor is it accurate to construe abandonment as a brave act. Abandoning parents are not usually caught, and when they are, they are generally subject to the punishment they would suffer for having had the child in the first place—birth-planning fines and possible sterilization for an overquota child. In the vast majority of cases, abandonment does not serve the children's interests or needs but rather those of the parents and families who abandon them.

Similarly, the construction of abandonment as a type of "adoption plan" receives only mixed support from our findings. Some birthparents in our sample did indeed seem to have a well-thought-out adoption plan in mind. They carefully determined where they would leave the child to give her the best chance of gaining a new adoptive home, sometimes choosing the protected doorway of a childless or daughterless couple, maybe even setting off a firecracker to alert the potential adoptive parents inside that there was something waiting for them. But others simply left the child on the roadside or under a bridge, hoping for the best yet never knowing if the child would find a home or even whether she survived the ordeal. And, as in the United States, there were even a few who dumped the child recklessly in a garbage heap or hid her in an empty field, walking away without so much as a glance back. Those who traveled to a city—the site of abandonment for the majority of children who end up in the large state orphanages that do international adoptions— were particularly unlikely to know what happened to the child after abandonment. The city was seen not simply as a good place for the child to be found quickly and safely but also as a place of anonymity, far from the prying eyes or birth-planning concerns of local officials in the birthparents' hometown.

It is not surprising that American adoptive parents are most interested in the highly charged issue of their children's birthparents and the act of abandonment. My initial interest in doing research on the causes and patterns of abandonment in China in the 1990s was driven not only by my desire to understand a social phenomenon that was closely related to my previous research on

Chinese women and rural society, but also by a desire to learn more about my daughter's and her cohort's "story." Above all I imagined that the information gathered through this research would allow her to come to terms with her own abandonment and, I hoped, help her to understand the difficult circumstances that were likely to have surrounded her birthparents' act so that she could ultimately forgive them. Understanding, I hoped, would overcome the bitterness and lessen the sense of loss and rejection that must, at some level, accompany the knowledge that one was abandoned by one's birthparents.

Discovering Our Counterparts: Chinese Parents Who Adopt Abandoned Children

As my research progressed, the imaginative grip of the birthparents and their plight gradually gave way to an increasing appreciation of and interest in another group: Chinese parents who adopt the children abandoned by others. Here, as an adoptive mother of a Chinese foundling, I found my Chinese counterparts and the counterparts of the American adoptive parents to whom I often speak. I also learned about an important group of my daughter's cohort who remain in China, the abandoned children adopted by these Chinese parents. I was fascinated with the Chinese adoptive parents' stories and often strongly identified with them. Their motivations to adopt, the joy they expressed in their children, and their determination to raise them well—all seemed so familiar. Even more, I was in awe of the hardships that many of them endured to adopt and keep their children, hardships that far surpassed anything I confronted in adopting my daughter. The stress U.S. parents experience during the bureaucratic "paper chase" of international adoption or the endless wait for INS approval pales in comparison to the bureaucratic hurdles some of these Chinese parents face. Similarly, the verbal slights U.S. parents may hear at the grocery store, or the other subtle and sometimes not so subtle forms of social and cultural discrimination that they and their children experience in school and daily life, seem minor compared with the highly discriminatory legal and political obstacles that confront some Chinese adoptive parents and their children. While international adoption in the United States is considered extraordinarily expensive, open only to solidly middle- or upper-middle-class people, the expense relative to income is far less than what some adoptive Chinese peasants or townspeople of ordinary means must pay in fees and penalties to keep their children.

This side of my research has not gained as much attention from the American adoptive community as the few insights that I can offer into the motivations of abandoning birthparents and the consequences they suffer. Yet the experience of Chinese adoptive families is part of the larger story of abandonment and of the cohort of abandoned children, of whom only a small percentage are ultimately adopted abroad. Aside from the minority who are in orphanages, little is known of those who remain in China. Indeed, the very existence of a large group of adoptive Chinese parents of abandoned children flies in the face of deep and persistent stereotypes about Chinese attitudes, culture, and customs of adoption. It also undermines the common assumption that it is primarily international adopters who welcome these "unwanted girls," these so-called "lost daughters of China." These stereotypes create an imagined "other" to which American adoptive parents then compare themselves, concluding—inaccurately—that Chinese are generally unwilling to adopt children to raise "as their own" and are certainly far less willing to adopt than Americans and other Westerners. Chinese are often said to be especially unwilling to adopt the children of those who are not blood relatives, let alone the children of total strangers. Afflicted with strong son preference, Chinese parents are presumed to be particularly unlikely to adopt girls, who comprise most of the abandoned children languishing in Chinese orphanages. In contrast, American adopters are believed to be more likely to open their hearts to the children of strangers, regardless of gender or race, and to raise and love these children as if they were birthchildren.

In fact, our research found support for none of these stereotypes about adoption in China. On the contrary, nearly 60 percent of the roughly 800 adoptive families from whom we gathered information between 1995 and 2000 had adopted abandoned children, that is, children of unknown parentage found in public or semipublic places.[1] Only a handful of these 800 families had adopted from an orphanage; the rest adopted children who never entered the social welfare system. In the 1990s only a few thousand of the estimated hundreds of thousands of domestic Chinese adoptions each year involved orphanages.[2] The overwhelming majority of adopted abandoned children were girls. People who already had sons but no daughters were particularly eager to add a daughter to their family, reflecting a widespread desire among contemporary Chinese to have both a boy and a girl in the family.[3] These adoptions were generally permanent "strong" adoptions, and the children's status in their adoptive families was similar or identical to that of a birthchild. Although our fieldwork was primarily based in south-central China, all of these patterns have recently been confirmed by a field study conducted by Zhang Weiguo of more than four hundred adoptive families located in various parts of southeastern China, central China, and the north China plain.[4]

Even more gripping than the dismantling of false images were the stories of adoptive parents of abandoned children who suffered huge government penalties and long-term legal discrimination to keep and raise their adopted children. Not all adoptive families experienced such problems, and none of the small number who adopted from state orphanages did. But why did a large minority of those who adopted abandoned children outside the orphanages face official and legal obstacles instead of encouragement for adopting homeless children at a time when Chinese orphanages were increasingly overburdened and underfunded? Clearly these parents not only help the children they adopt, sometimes even saving their lives, but also save the government the expense of caring for these children in overcrowded and, in the 1990s, often grossly underequipped facilities.[5] Without this large group of adoptive families who were willing to put up with the problems they faced, state orphanages would have been totally overwhelmed with abandoned children in the 1990s. The answers to these questions illuminate another reason why Chinese adoptive parents have received relatively little attention and why so many of the adoptions we learned about took place outside official channels of adoption and outside the orphanage system, from which all international adoptions take place.

The One-Child Adoption Policy

Current adoption patterns are largely the product of population control policies that the Chinese government has pursued since 1979. In the mid 1980s, local officials throughout China, wielding the coercive power of fines and other penalties, began to enforce a number of restrictions on adoption to prevent people from using it as a way around the one-child policy. From the outset, many people tried to circumvent the birth-planning regulations, especially in the countryside, where there was more political, organizational, and physical "space" to resist.[6] One of the ways some peasants got around their birth quota was to adopt out a birthchild, usually a daughter, and then try again for a son. Sometimes these "adoptions" were temporary, intended merely to hide the child until the desired boy was born. But sometimes these were real adoptions in which the adoptive parents assumed permanent, full rights and obligations toward the child, and the child assumed the status of a birthchild in the adoptive home.

Birth-planning authorities quickly caught on to these schemes and brought adoption policy under their regulatory net. To tighten their grip on birth quotas, they not only regulated and punished birthparents who used adoption to avoid fines or to get the chance to have another child, but they also restricted the pool of potential adopters by allowing only older, childless, and presumably infertile people to adopt. All other adopters violated birth-planning regulations and were subject to penalties and fines. As I will discuss in greater detail below, those who already had birthchildren and adopted another child were particularly likely to encounter official pressure and penalties. Their adopted child was often treated exactly the same as an over-quota birth, or *chaosheng*. Hence this kind of adoption is sometimes referred to as an "overquota adoption," or *chaobao*. Meanwhile, restricting the pool of legally qualified adoptive parents to those who were childless and over a certain age made it less likely that birthparents could find adoptive families or use friends and relatives as a subterfuge for hiding children.

By the late 1980s, the interests of population planners, rather than the needs of parentless children, dictated local adoption regulations. As an unintended consequence, these restrictions led to more outright abandonments, and though they reduced "fake" adoptions and the use of fostering as subterfuge, they also pushed many real adoptions underground or at least away from official channels. Once codified into law, the restrictions also ensured that the numbers of people seeking to adopt from orphanages would remain small or even decline just as orphanages began to bulge with increasing numbers of abandoned children in the early 1990s.

Thus adoption policy in the 1980s evolved to mirror the one-child birth-planning policy,[7] with negative consequences for abandoned children and for the Chinese parents who sought to give them new homes. In fact, by the late 1980s adoption policy was even stricter than birth policy. By this time, in most rural areas the so-called one-child policy had become somewhat more lenient. Thanks to fierce resistance in the countryside—where, with no social security system, the felt need for a son was particularly strong and the ability to subvert birth-planning regulations much greater than in urban areas—most provinces allowed rural couples whose first child was a girl to give birth to a second child after a period of several years.[8] A few rural areas allowed two children, widely spaced, regardless of gender. Yet adoption policy continued to insist that only the childless could adopt and that they could adopt only one child. This restriction was true in rural as well as urban areas. Furthermore, adoptive parents had to meet high age requirements while rural birthparents were usually allowed to have children at a relatively young age, as befit rural social norms for childbearing.

In late 1991, in the midst of a massive birth-planning crackdown in large parts of the countryside, these adoption regulations were codified in the first national Adoption Law of the People's Republic of China, effective April 1992.[9] To international adopters and Western adoption agencies, this law heralded the "opening" of Chinese adoption to the world and hence the liberalization of adoption policy,[10] but from the perspective of domestic adoption it represented the legal codification of severe restrictions and the closing down of spontaneous and customary adoption practices that could have helped secure more homes for the increasing number of abandoned children. Instead of challenging the grip of birth-planning policies on adoption policy, and instead of carefully supervising rather than severely limiting domestic adoptions, the government turned to international adopters to help solve the growing problem of child abandonment.

The Impact of the One-Child Adoption Policy on Adoptive Families

In the Chinese countryside, practice often diverges from policy, and policy is always open to interpretation. Implementation in some areas, at some times, was strict while in other areas it was lax. Moreover, the national adoption law, like the local regulations before it, carefully exempted orphans from the restrictions. True orphans—that is, children whose parents were dead as opposed to children who were abandoned by living parents— could be adopted by relatives, friends, or others regardless of their age or the number of children in the adopting families. The relatively small percentage of families in our sample who adopted orphans (about 10 percent) encountered no difficulties from officials even if they had birthchildren or were young. Disabled children were also exempt from the restrictions. We found too few cases in this category to generalize, but their experience seemed to depend on how serious and irreversible the disability. In general it seemed that domestic adopters were subject to a much more stringent definition of *disability* than were international adopters.[11] The primary target of the restrictive adoption policy, like the birth-planning policy that dictates it, is healthy children whose birthparents choose not to keep them. Slightly less than 90 percent of our sample involved children whose adoptions were subject to the legal restrictions of childlessness and the minimum age requirement of thirty-five (reduced to thirty in 1999).

In practice we found that underage adoptive parents who were childless were rarely punished for adopting. Often their main difficulty was waiting until they reached the legal age before they could register the adoption and obtain a household registration (*hukou*) for the child. In other words, local officials did not seem to take the age requirement too seriously as long as the parents were childless and apparently infertile. Those who encountered the greatest difficulties were parents who already had one or more birthchildren, a group that comprised about half of our sample of adoptive families. These were the *chaobao,* or overquota adopters. They were, in effect, regarded by law as if they had had an overquota birth.

Not all overquota adopters in our sample were punished, just as not all birthparents who give birth to overquota children are punished. Many kept their adoptions secret from authorities; others lived in areas where the authorities ignored the violation or found it unreasonable to penalize them since they had, in fact, done a "good deed" by providing an abandoned child with a loving, permanent home. But about a third of these families were penalized in some way. As the 1990s progressed, it became increasingly difficult for *chaobao* to escape detection or penalties, and the percentage subject to penalties increased. In some areas by the late 1990s even underage childless adopters were sometimes fined. Apparently the impending 2000 census led to a tightening of all birth-planning restrictions, including those governing adoptions, in many rural areas.[12]

Chaobao adopters faced the full range of penalties suffered by those who gave birth to overquota children, the most common being stiff fines (sometimes equivalent to or greater than a family's yearly income) and, less often, mandatory sterilization of one of the parents. Wage earners, such as factory workers or state-employed teachers, might get a reduction in pay or lose their jobs. These are all typical birth-planning punishments. In most cases, birth-planning authorities—not civil affairs (the bureaucratic arm in charge of adoption and child welfare) or the courts—levied the penalties.

Yet *chaobao* parents also faced a penalty that overquota birthparents never faced: their child might be seized from them and placed in an orphanage or given to another legally qualified family, if one could be found. This threat was made even in areas where there were no orphanages or where orphanages were severely underfunded and overcrowded. Agreeing to fines and/or sterilization usually prevented the seizure of the child. But some adoptive parents simply could not afford the entire fine (which in extreme cases might be double their yearly income or more) and, despite their efforts to keep the child, might have her taken away. By contrast, some local officials listened to the angry protests of adoptive parents who could not afford the fines but refused to relinquish the child and let them off with only a token fine or none at all.

Unfortunately not all officials were so flexible or compassionate, nor could they be if birth-planning authorities were breathing down their necks. Some adoptive parents, afraid of being caught with an overquota adoption, might feel compelled to abandon their adopted child, submitting her to a second abandonment. To make matters worse for the child, even passersby who find abandoned children report that if they take a foundling to the police or to an orphanage, they may be suspected of violating birth planning themselves. To avoid being fined, they might have to prove that the child was not born to them, something that adopters who have avoided official scrutiny for some time cannot always do. They may be held accountable for the birth-planning fines in any case, even if they are not suspected of being the birthparents. As a result, the well-founded fear of punishment encourages some people to leave children by the roadside rather than deliver them safely to authorities. Hence the dynamics of this adoption policy lead to many more double abandonments than would otherwise be the case, subjecting some children to double jeopardy.

A Case of *Chaobao*

Wang Meiying's experience illustrates how tough things could get for a *chaobao* family in the 1990s. Wang lives in an area of southeastern China where birth-planning regulations, including the restrictive clauses of the adoption law, have been harshly implemented. She works in a shoe factory in a suburb of a medium-sized city, and her husband works as a laborer outside the area, returning home every few months. Shortly after they were married at age twenty-five in the mid 1980s, Wang gave birth to a son. Like other factory workers in her area, Wang was then required to insert an IUD and to sign a certificate pledging not to have another child. She had always wanted a daughter, but knew it would be impossible for her to give birth to another child; the penalties for doing so—a ruinously high fine, job loss, and sterilization—were prohibitive.

Several years later, Wang's mother found an abandoned baby near the steps of a hospital in her neighborhood. Her mother brought the baby home and took care of her while trying to decide what to do. A neighbor who had an only son very much wanted to adopt the baby girl and took her immediately to a doctor to see if the child needed treatment. Like most of the adoptive families we met, this woman felt that a child of each gender made a perfect family (see Chap. 4), and she had longed for a daughter after her son was born. Unfortunately, the doctor discovered that the infant girl was in extremely poor health and was unlikely to survive regardless of treatment. Reluctantly, the neighbor took the baby back to the hospital and left her on a bench in one of the wards, hoping the doctors would do whatever they could for the child.

When Wang heard about the baby, she rushed to the hospital, but the baby had already died. She was heartbroken. A few years later another baby girl was abandoned in the same area. No one dared take the child for fear of getting in trouble with the authorities, who were in the midst of a stringent birth control campaign. Although Wang feared legal consequences, she could not bear to leave the child, afraid it too would die.

Her in-laws were not pleased when Wang brought the baby home. They knew that it was illegal for her and her husband to adopt a second child and that the consequences could be severe. In response, Wang went immediately to the police station and asked permission to keep the girl at least until a childless family could be found. After gathering eye-witness accounts of when and where the baby was found, the police gave permission to register the child in Wang's household, that is, to give her a legal *hukou* for that area. The police were in fact grateful that the baby was being cared for, since it would be difficult and costly for them to provide the care. But when Wang took the police report and letter of permission to the local birth-planning committee, they refused to accept it. They said she could not register the child because she already had a child; she could, however, volunteer to care for the abandoned girl, at her own expense, while they looked for someone who was childless and over thirty-five to adopt her.

Two weeks later the committee had not found anyone to adopt the child. Yet after meeting to consider allowing Wang to adopt her, the birth-planning committee decided that the child had to be given up to the orphanage immediately. Wang was devastated. She had heard that conditions at the orphanage were very bad, and she had already fallen in love with the baby. "Everyday my love for this child doubled," she said.

She could not bear to do as she was told, so she left town with the baby and went to stay with a friend in a distant village. Her friend agreed to keep the child, and Wang went back and forth to visit. Gradually, Wang started to bring her adopted daughter home for long visits, telling people that she was caring for her friend's child. Yet during a campaign of renewed enforcement, birth-planning officials visited Wang's home and immediately suspected that this child was Wang's adopted daughter. Though Wang insisted that they were wrong, they threatened her with a fine of 20,000 yuan (several times Wang's yearly wages) and mandatory sterilization unless she sent the girl to the orphanage. Defiant, Wang again ran off with the child.

This cat-and-mouse game continued for years, during which Wang's relationship with her husband and in-laws deteriorated. Though her husband also loved the child, he worried about the negative impact of the situation on their older son. He also feared that eventually they would be caught and ruined financially by the fines. In the end the child would be seized from them regardless. While birthparents caught hiding an overquota child might be fined, sterilized, and fired from their jobs, in the end the child would still be theirs, even if they could not manage to pay in full. But Wang and her husband, as overquota adopters, had no such assurance.

Nonetheless, Wang remained determined to keep her daughter, causing great tension in the family. Meanwhile, the daughter, deprived of proper registration, could not enter school in her parents' area and had to be sent back once again to the village to attend a poor rural primary school that did not require a *hukou* to enroll. Adding insult to injury, Wang had to pay a tuition fee that was more than double what a legally registered child would pay to attend a far superior school in Wang's urban neighborhood. Wang's daughter also missed several of her inoculations because she lacked a legal identity. Wang was constantly afraid of being discovered with her "black child" and avoided situations where she might be asked to show the child's *hukou*.

Urban-Rural Differences and the Problem of *Hukou*

The story of Wang Meiying and her daughter has no happy ending. As far as I know, they struggled on with this barely tolerable situation hoping for some break that would allow a legal resolution of their status. While theirs is an extreme example both in the persistence of the adoptive parents and the relentlessness of birth-planning authorities to catch and punish them, it reflects a pattern familiar to many *chaobao* parents. While adoptive parents feel they are providing a loving family for a homeless child, saving not only the child but the government's money, birth-planning authorities see these parents as a threat to their control over the population's reproductive behavior. Neither the policy nor the letter of the law considers the interests of children, let alone those of adoptive parents.

Fortunately in practice the one-child adoption policy, like other government regulations, was implemented unevenly by local officials. In some areas, at least in the countryside, *chaobao* parents received lighter penalties or even no penalties at all. Often enforcement hinged on whether a birth-planning campaign was underway in the area. In the late 1990s, as the 2000 census approached, such campaigns intensified in many areas.[13] But in the mid 1990s, and wherever birth-planning enforcement was somewhat lax, there was greater flexibility in local enforcement.

In the countryside, *chaobao* families might go undetected or local cadres might look the other way for many years, allowing a more or less normal life for a family with an overquota adopted child. Locally, these parents were perceived as doing a "good deed," not committing a crime. While it became more and more difficult to get away with a *chaobao* adoption in the 1990s, the consequences were often less devastating in rural areas than in urban areas, such as the one where Wang Meiying lived. While urban birth-planning committees could threaten the loss of jobs as well as huge fines and sterilization, most peasants do not have wage-earning jobs to threaten, and fines, while high, were usually pegged to income.

Yet sometimes even in rural cases, birth-planning cadres demanded sterilization as the price for keeping an adopted child. We heard of one particularly egregious case in the mid 1990s. An older retired couple had found a sick abandoned child, paid for extensive medical treatment, and nursed her back to health. Unable to find her another family, they decided to adopt and raise her rather than deliver her into the hands of government officials who could not provide adequate care. When birth-planning officials discovered their "offense," they required the nearly sixty-year-old adoptive father to be sterilized and fined the couple 10,000 yuan, a huge sum for retired rural school teachers in 1996.

Extreme cases like this one were few. More often, when families were caught, they were fined and then usually, though not always, allowed to register the child. In one case, a poor family could not pay the fines and refused to hand over their child of many months, whom they feared might die in government hands. They stubbornly argued with the officials who came to their home several nights in a row, finally wearing them down and then, two years later, winning a *hukou* for their daughter. In the end, all agreed that this was the best result for everyone. Better-off families might pay their fines as they would take bitter medicine and then get on with their lives. One family named their adopted child Sanqian, meaning "three thousand," the amount of the birth-planning fine they had to pay for their overquota adoption. Whatever the fine or the extent of the struggle, we could not help but be impressed with adoptive parents' willingness to endure economic loss and sometimes extreme official harassment to honor their commitment to and love for these previously abandoned, mostly female children.

The Problem of *Hukou, Hei Haizi,* and the Rights of Citizenship

Despite dogged determination, many of these families had great difficulty gaining for their child the sine qua non of legal status as a citizen in China—the *hukou,* or household registration. While many eventually managed to buy or otherwise obtain a *hukou,* some lack a *hukou* throughout childhood. Thus many of the adopted children in China fall into the category of "illegal" children known as *hei haizi* (literally, "black children"). The consequences are not as serious as they were in the past, when *hukou* alone provided access to many goods and privileges, including the purchase of grain. Yet *hukou* are still needed to access basic childhood immunizations and schooling, especially beyond the primary level.

Urban *hukou* are both more valuable and more difficult to obtain than rural ones, since the entitlements of urban residents are closely guarded against the encroachment of outsiders, especially peasants. In large urban areas even primary-school enrollment requires a *hukou*. While some urban primary schools will take a child with a village *hukou* if the parents pay additional fees, a child with no *hukou* at all, like many *chaobao* children, may not be able to attend at any price.

There may also be psychological consequences to living as a "black child." Some parents report that their unregistered child senses she has a lower status than other children, not because she was adopted, but because she lacks legal status in her family and community. Sometimes children are teased for being "black children." When a child also knows she was abandoned and adopted, the effect on self-esteem must be even greater. One precocious girl cried when her kindergarten teacher told her she could not go on to primary school in the city where she lived with her family because she had no *hukou;* if she was to go to school at all, she would have to leave her family to attend a primary school in a distant village. "Why can't I go to school like my friends?" she cried. "Why can't I have a *hukou* like *gege* [elder brother]?" Her parents claimed that being adopted would not in itself be a source of discrimination or distress for this child, but the lack of legal status exacerbated her position as an outsider and created a gap between her and other children in the community who were entitled to attend the local school.

While many adoptive families struggle with these problems, finding ways around them through connections, money, or a sympathetic official, others fall apart. I have encountered quite a few cases of "double abandonment" where adoptive parents who raised an abandoned child for years ultimately gave up and took the child to an orphanage because they were unable to overcome the problems caused by their child's illegal status. In one instance, the adoptive parents hoped that they could re-adopt the child after the orphanage gave her a *hukou*. But the adoptive parents, lacking legal claim to the child and in viola-tion of birth-planning regulations for having adopted her in the first place, since they already had a birthson, were not allowed to readopt her. Instead they found out, after the fact, that the orphanage had allowed their seven-year-old daughter to be adopted by an American family and taken to the United States to live. The American adoptive parents were as shocked to learn the true situation as were their Chinese counterparts. For years, the child and both sets of adoptive parents have struggled with the painful consequences. Other Chinese adoptive families have also succumbed to pressure and handed their children over to the authorities, who—rather than grant the children *hukou* and legal adoptive status—put them into an orphanage at state expense and at great cost to the children's well-being. Even today children can lose a second family as a direct result of state adoption policy.

The Sunflower Organization

In response to these problems and a growing sense of injustice, a small group of adoptive parents in Beijing organized an infor-mal group in the mid 1990s to support each other and to pres-sure civil affairs to let them register their children by calling public attention to their plight. Their organization is in some ways like those that have sprung up in the United States, such as Families with Children from China, but the problems the Beijing adoptive parents faced were far more immediate and severe than those experienced by their U.S. counterparts. The Beijing group, organized by a single mother named Chang Lixin, called itself Sunflower, and for a brief time it attracted media attention, even from Chinese Central Television.

While traveling in Yunnan province in the early 1990s, Chang Lixin had found an abandoned baby. Though she obtained official documents from local police and birth-planning authorities testifying that the child was a foundling, the Beijing civil affairs authorities refused to allow her to register the child's adoption and denied the child a Beijing *hukou*. They said that Chang's single status made it impossible for her to adopt because she might some day marry and have a child. Even a signed statement guaranteeing that she would not do so failed to convince them to allow her to adopt her daughter. Since the adoption was illegal, the child was not entitled to a *hukou*. According to the authorities, Chang had brought the child from outside Beijing and should return her to the area where she was found.[14]

Several journalists who heard about the case and were sympathetic to Chang's plight reported her story (though they carefully downplayed some details that reflected poorly on local authorities and policies). Even China Central Television carried a human-interest story on how Chang, a single woman, found a frail abandoned infant in a poor minority area of southwestern China and saved her life. Chang was portrayed as a selfless person who had done a "good deed." She nursed the child back to health, paid to repair the child's cleft lip, and bore the burden of feeding, clothing, and raising the child all on her own. In the process she had sacrificed her marriage prospects, since it was assumed that few men would marry a woman who had already filled her one-child quota with an abandoned girl. Now Chang, like many other adoptive parents, was struggling to gain legal status for her daughter. Her story and the stories of other Beijing adoptive parents, most of them *chaobao,* were tearfully told.

The near universal inability of these adoptive parents to obtain *hukou* made a normal life and education for their children in Beijing extremely difficult. One of the goals of Sunflower was to raise money to start a private school for *chaobao* children. While some parents, like Chang Lixin, were able to get their children into schools as a result of favors, connections, or sympathy, doing so generally cost families a great deal in extra fees, and their children's position in the Beijing schools was tenuous at best. Some parents complained that their children were frequently teased and made to feel inferior by students and teachers. While Sunflower activists seemed to have a lot of energy and some public support in 1997–98, they failed to get permission to register as a legal organization. Chang Lixin herself seemed to weaken and emotionally collapse under the stress of her situation. In spite of public support for Sunflower, the children were often treated as pariahs. To be without *hukou* set one apart, on a lower social level than others. Even at a young age, some children felt the slights. Like other adopted "black children" that I have learned about, some Sunflower children "looked down on themselves" and sometimes had problems in school and in their neighborhoods. As someone commented about a particularly troubled abandoned, adopted, and unregistered child in Chengdu, "It was wrong that she was born."[15] A young adult woman who had been an overquota "black child" said she felt her entire childhood that she'd had to prove she "had a right to exist."

Recent Changes in Adoption Policy and the Limits of Change

In the late 1990s civil affairs authorities and reformers in the government sought to change adoption policy to allow more domestic adoption from overcrowded orphanages. In November 1998, Premier Zhu Rongji presented a revised adoption law to the National People's Congress for approval. The revisions would lower the legal adoption age to thirty and strike the childless requirement for those adopting abandoned children. There was considerable debate in the Congress about these changes, with staunch supporters of birth planning worrying that they would weaken population control efforts.[16] In the end the law passed, but with stipulations that carefully narrowed the childless exemption to those adopting children "living in state welfare institutions." Moreover, prospective adopters would have to gain certification from local birth-planning authorities that they had never violated any birth-planning regulations. Adoptions that took place outside of state welfare institutions—that is, the majority of domestic adoptions in China—were still supposed to be restricted to those who were childless and over thirty.

Nonetheless, some *chaobao* adoptive parents hoped that the new law would help them legalize their adoptions and obtain *hukou* for their children. In fact we met several adoptive parents who were able to do so after the revised law came into effect. One was a doctor in a county town in Anhui who had found a sick abandoned child during the floods of 1992. Because the local government had no one to adopt the child and had many flood victims to care for, they allowed the doctor to keep her in his family. But because he and his wife had three older birthchildren, they were not allowed to legally adopt the girl. When she turned six years old they found it impossible to send her to school in their town and had to send her away to a village school where fees were accepted in lieu of a *hukou*. The doctor said the girl often cried that year because she did not like being separated from her family, and she wanted to attend "the good school" in the town. When the revised adoption law was enacted in 1999, the doctor pursued the matter with county civil affairs authorities, who agreed to legalize the adoption and give their child a *hukou*.

This successful resolution of a *hukou* problem through the new adoption law was trumpeted in the local newspaper under the banner "Black *Hukou* Child Finally Sees the Sunlight."[17] Authorities in that county received a surge of adoption applications after the revised law was announced, as many parents sought to legalize previous adoptions. In some counties in Anhui and elsewhere, the first beneficiaries of the revisions were foster families who had been raising children with permission from the government, often at the government's behest, but who could not adopt them because they had birthchildren. Now many of these families applied to adopt their children, even though in some cases they would lose valuable subsidies. In 2000, the year after the revised law was passed, legally registered domestic adoptions increased significantly—from around 6,000 to 8,000 per year in the mid 1990s to over 56,000. About 10,700 of those children were adopted domestically from state orphanages; 37,000 were "foundlings adopted [directly] from society."[18]

Elsewhere in China the new law was interpreted differently, and *chaobao* adopters were still judged to have illegal adoptions that could not be set right by the law. In some areas a family who already had children might legally adopt an abandoned child, but only if they followed a strict procedure of reporting and applying to various civil, welfare, and judicial authorities at the time the child was found. Failure to follow the right steps in the right order in a timely manner could jeopardize one's chances. Those seeking to legalize the adoption of an abandoned child after the fact might find it impossible to do so.[19] In large cities like Beijing, Nanjing, and Shanghai, obtaining legal status and *hukou* for illegally adopted children remained particularly difficult.

Citizenship, Adoption Policy, and the Rights of Children

When I began this research, I was interested in investigating the extent to which social attitudes and cultural values today discriminated against adopted persons and their families. Had the social climate for adoptive families in China improved or worsened in recent years? Discriminatory attitudes and problems certainly continue, yet time and again such questions led adoptive parents to talk about the far more stark and debilitating political and legal discrimination that they and their children confront.

The greatest obstacles that Chinese adoptive families face in raising their children are government policies. The intended and unintended consequences of those policies withhold legal status from tens of thousands of adopted children, limiting their access to basic social entitlements such as "compulsory" education and health care, including mandated inoculations. We have found that many adoptive parents eventually manage to obtain a *hukou* for their adopted children, but success usually requires years of effort and often large sums of money. For children born outside the planned birth regime of the state, *hukou* and legally recognized family status—indeed, legally recognized existence—must often be "earned" or paid for.[20] Depriving children of basic rights, even the right to a family, has become a routine way of punishing birthparents and adoptive parents for violating birth-planning regulations. As a result, hundreds of thousands of children have been systematically denied citizenship in their country of birth.

Citizenship rights are problematic for many internationally adopted children as well. When children are moved across the borders of nation-states to be adopted into a new family and country, their legal status is often placed in limbo by competing claims and legal regimes. Until recently, children adopted into the United States were not automatically granted U.S. citizenship even after they became legally adopted children of U.S. citizens. Gaining citizenship required a separate and often time-consuming bureaucratic process. International adoptees whose parents failed to apply for their citizenship when they were minors entered adulthood with the legal status of resident aliens, deprived of the full protection and legal rights afforded U.S. citizens. They could even be subject to deportation under certain circumstances. To correct the legal inequality inherent in this situation, a new law, effective February 27, 2001, mandated automatic citizenship to all children adopted by U.S. citizens abroad as soon as they enter the United States. This change in U.S. policy was the product of hard lobbying by organized and vocal groups of U.S. families who had adopted internationally.

The Chinese government, in its negotiations with other countries, has championed the rights of Chinese children adopted abroad, including their right to full citizenship in their adoptive country and to equal treatment in their adoptive families. However, the same government has done far less to ensure the rights of most domestically adopted children to full legal status in China. Organizations such as Sunflower lack the clout and the minimal legal status that U.S. adoptive parents and their organizations use to demand redress for discrimination. We can only hope that in the future the Chinese government will move vigorously to eliminate these anomalies inside China as the authorities become more aware of the serious problems that their own population and adoption policies have created, so that adopted children too may benefit from the rights guaranteed by the Chinese constitution and various Chinese and international declarations on the rights of the child. Revising these policies with an eye to guaranteeing the rights of abandoned Chinese children to a family and full citizenship would make it possible for more children to secure homes in the country of their birth.

CHAPTER SEVEN

Chinese Orphanages Today, 2003

Twelve years ago this week, I left for China to adopt my daughter, Tang Li, then a three-month-old infant at the Wuhan Orphanage. As I reminisce about that March 1991 trip amid the drumbeats of a new war against Iraq, I recall ironically that twelve years ago I was waiting anxiously for adoption papers caught up in a U.S. bureaucracy preoccupied with the first U.S.-Iraq war. In mid February I had made a tearful call to my local Congressman's office, telling staffers that the orphanage had recently rushed my daughter-to-be to intensive care with a severe case of pneumonia, a life-threatening condition in an infant who was barely two months old at the time. I needed their help to get the FBI to clear my fingerprints, a routine task suddenly pushed aside as the FBI processed security checks of Arab Americans and Iraqis in the United States. A week later, a wonderful woman from the Immigration and Naturalization Service called to tell me she was processing my papers on an emergency basis and would send them out within a few days. I booked my flight and left at the beginning of March, spending the next five weeks nervously navigating and cajoling several Chinese bureaucracies and the U.S. Consulate in Guangzhou.

There was no well-worn path through this process, as there is today. The first week in April 1991, my father, lecturing in Beijing at the time, rushed to Wuhan with a letter from a former Central Committee member vouching that my family and I were "long-time friends of China." Such testimonials were sometimes required for non-Chinese adopters in the past, and it was suggested that I get one in case we ran into trouble. My stomach churned and my pulse raced every day until I passed the last U.S. immigration officer at JFK airport in New York on April 12, 1991, fearful at every turn that someone or something would wrest my wonderful daughter from my arms. I finally exhaled when I stepped out the door of the international arrival terminal, and my four–year-son, for whom my heart had ached for five weeks, ran into my arms, kissed me, and then turned to his new sister in my arms with a huge smile of welcome. My husband, camera at the ready, miraculously captured the moment.

That adoption trip was the most emotionally intense five weeks I had ever spent in China. Becoming the parent of a child from China not only changed my personal relationship to the country, long the focus of my professional energies, but shifted the focus of my intellectual interests as well. Having glimpsed the issue of infant abandonment and orphanage care in China at that time, I left with many more questions than answers and felt I had a great deal to learn about these problems. This aware-ness marked the beginning of twelve years of research to under-stand the conditions that surrounded my daughter's birth, her abandonment, and the abandonment and fate of tens of thousands of others like her.

This volume brings together the articles that grew out of that research. As I learned more, some of my initial ideas were challenged and shifted while others were confirmed. My focus also shifted from orphanage care and the causes and patterns of abandonment to adoption within China. Ironically, while pursuing the study of female infant abandonment—a profound manifestation of persistent son preference under pressures of the one-child policy—I learned about the increasing and in some ways equally profound desire for daughters. I began with the assumption that abandonment was all too often tantamount to female infanticide; that many, perhaps most, abandoned babies died on the roads and in the fields where they were left; and that only those children lucky enough to be found and taken to an orphanage were likely to survive. I learned that many, if not most, abandoned female infants were found and immediately adopted, often by families who were particularly happy to have the opportunity to bring a daughter into their lives. Such children not only survived, but also avoided the risks of orphanage life. Many more abandoned children were adopted in this way than through the orphanage system. I saw the desire for daughters in the heavy price that some parents were willing to pay for the privilege of raising an adopted daughter, the birthchild of strangers. As a parent I was moved and humbled by their devotion. This finding flew in the face of images of Chinese culture, especially patriarchal peasant culture, held by many Westerners (including my younger self) as well as urban Chinese.

Over these twelve years, not only did some of my ideas change, but some of the conditions I described in my earlier writings changed as well. Perhaps the most dramatic change over this period has been in the conditions of the orphanages that house some of China's abandoned children. This is where my adoption experience and my writing on abandonment began. The conditions of Chinese orphanages became the subject of an international human rights campaign during the mid 1990s, partly drawing on what I had written in the early 1990s. It is an issue that I wish to revisit here, bringing this book full circle.

The International Media Scandal

A few years after China opened a small number of orphanages to international adoption, Western human rights groups loudly criticized the inadequate care provided to the growing numbers of abandoned children in China's state-run social welfare institutions. A documentary called *The Dying Rooms: China's Darkest Secret* launched this campaign on Britain's Channel 4 in July 1995, followed in January 1996 by the publication of a report by Human Rights Watch (HRW) titled *Death by Default: Fatal Neglect in China's State Orphanages.* Many of the charges were correct: mortality rates were high, staffing was inadequate, and funding was too low to cover the minimal physical needs of the state's wards. HRW attributed this dire situation not to welfare system failures in a poor country but to an intentional government policy to weed out the weak within the orphanage system in order to keep the numbers down and expenses low at a time of escalating abandonment. HRW even suspected that some orphanages were set up to facilitate the speedy death of abandoned babies.[1]

HRW's accusation elevated the problems of Chinese orphanages to the highest level of state-directed human rights abuses, far above mere welfare failure and neglect. Failure and neglect in a state welfare system, although serious, is a charge one could level against all too many governments, including, for example, the United States for tolerating homelessness in the world's richest country.

HRW's politically sensational claim against the Chinese government was false. But China was indeed in the midst of a welfare crisis of huge proportions, one that was not well known even in China, even within parts of the government, because the root cause of increasing infant abandonment—the government's own sacrosanct one-child policy—was so politically sensitive that the true dimensions of the problem had to be hidden. Local civil affairs officials responsible for the care of abandoned children (a truly disenfranchised constituency) were fully aware of the problems they confronted, but were unable to call attention to the grossly inadequate conditions under which they labored and were forbidden to make public appeals for aid. The marginal status of welfare organizations, operating as part of a state monopoly, left this segment of the government bureaucracy almost as powerless and voiceless as its constituencies, without effective means to redress the state's inadequate funding of a collapsing system.[2] State monopoly and politically induced silence were disastrous for the orphanage system and the children who lived there.

The inevitable outcome of systemic neglect of heavily burdened orphanages—inadequate care and unnecessarily high mortality rates among abandoned children—warranted severe criticism. More open discussion and critical publicity might have helped draw official attention to the problems of politically weak welfare institutions and their wards. Yet even before Human Rights Watch launched its media campaign against the Chinese government, at least some government officials had begun to listen to the pleas of besieged local civil affairs officials, and efforts to improve the dire conditions within orphanages were beginning to emerge and spread. Opening to international adoption was part of the Ministry of Civil Affairs' growing acknowledgment that orphanages were overcrowded and needed help. Surely top officials realized that allowing international adoption inevitably meant that China's problem of infant abandonment would become more widely known to the outside world.

By 1993–94, a publicity campaign in a number of Chinese cities, spearheaded by Vice-minister of Civil Affairs Yan Mingfu, appealed for donations and volunteers to come to the aid of local orphanages. The ministry also solicited international funding for orphanage projects through overseas Chinese charities and other international nongovernmental organizations (NGOs). A new SOS children's village set up by the International SOS charity organization to house homeless children got favorable publicity, and a few private orphanages sprang up, seemingly with official approval, also amid favorable publicity.

These developments marked the beginning of a larger transformation of the Chinese welfare system from a total state monopoly accompanied by a high degree of secrecy to a somewhat more open, mixed system that, while dominated by the state, sought support from a variety of private and charitable sources and encouraged greater local initiative and community involvement. One scholar described this trend as an evolution from welfare statism to welfare pluralism.[3] If the financially strapped government could not or would not provide adequate funding, it would at least help solicit and institutionalize channels for outside support.[4]

The negative publicity of *The Dying Rooms* and the HRW campaign damaged these early efforts, even as they helped draw attention to the plight of orphanages. Because the producers of *The Dying Rooms* had lied their way into many Chinese orphanages, claiming to be social workers from America who hoped to better understand the problems of Chinese orphanages so as to provide help, the Ministry of Civil Affairs responded by closing orphanages to all outsiders, including most Chinese. While some early international adopters had been given open access to walk around and photograph inside orphanages, now many were not even allowed to drive by the outside. Some officials became suspicious of any offers of help. The Chinese government angrily denounced the report by Human Rights Watch, a relentless critic of Chinese policy, as groundless anti-China propaganda. The public discussion of problems of abandonment and orphanage care that had begun to filter into the Chinese media abruptly ceased amid official denials of culpability. Even worse, some international NGOs such as the Red Cross temporarily cut back some of their funding for fear of supporting a system accused of intentionally murdering children, and some private donations dried up as well.

Yet gradually efforts to improve orphanage conditions resumed and gathered steam. Throughout this time, international adoption increased, bringing in fees set at US$3,000 per adoption paid directly to the orphanage or its civil affairs welfare unit to support and improve orphanage operations. By the late 1990s some orphanages once again opened their doors to visitors, including foreign adoptive parents. International adoption agencies and charities, several of them funded by international adoptive parents of Chinese children, joined the Chinese government's ongoing efforts to improve orphanage care throughout the system.

There are, however, huge inequalities in this system, as there are in China as a whole. The distribution of funds contributes to the problem. Orphanages permitted to do international adoptions get to keep a significant portion of the fees that foreign adopters pay.[5] These same orphanages benefit disproportionately from the money donated by grateful foreign adoptive parents and the adoption agencies and charitable organizations they fund. Chinese central government organizations also favor areas that have well-run systems and that maintain good relations with the civil affairs bureaucracy. International organizations are steered in the same direction. Thus the most visible orphanages, generally located in major cities, have seen the greatest improvements. To be fair, these orphanages are also among the largest in the system and care for a significant number of abandoned children. And in some provinces a percentage of adoption revenues is set aside for poorer and more remote institutions within the child welfare system.[6]

While inequalities and problems remain great and rates of abandonment remain high (though perhaps now finally abating), it is clear that there have been dramatic improvements in the conditions of many orphanages since the early 1990s, when the economic boom that had swept China in the 1980s left the orphanages far behind, carrying a heavier burden with no increase in funding. By the turn of the twenty-first century, many orphanages had begun to benefit from the rising standard of living in China as a whole; several of them even appeared to have pulled ahead of what one might expect in a country that, while modernizing rapidly, is still poor, beset with budget deficits, and suffering from a variety of economic dislocations.

The orphanages that have improved the most are those best situated to take advantage of the government's new, more open and eclectic, approach to the organization and funding of the welfare system. The government is still squarely at the center of this system and has increased its per capita support for daily operations perhaps three- to fourfold. International adoption fees have brought well over one hundred million dollars into the system in the past decade, at a rate of around twenty-five million dollars per year in the past two to three years. While these fees add up to less than a drop in the bucket of the overall economy[7]—making charges that China is exporting babies to fuel its economic growth sheer nonsense—it is a significant amount for the child welfare institutions that receive these funds.

In addition to the fees collected from international adoption, the central government has established channels to bring in support, both money and expertise, from a growing number of international sources that have an interest in Chinese adoption and child welfare. While funding from these organizations is less than that derived from international adoption fees and far less than the government's funding of basic capital and operational expenses, it still amounts to several million dollars each year and contributes to strategically important off-budget improvements in the overall quality of life for children in the orphanages.

Cooperative interaction with various international NGOs and child welfare organizations has also led to the sharing of knowledge and experience from other countries, promoting improvements in childcare methods. One of the most important developments in this regard has been the recent spread of foster care programs, particularly for disabled children, a development that may be fundamentally altering civil affairs' long-standing preference for institutional care of abandoned and orphaned children. Only ten years ago, civil affairs saw foster care as a last resort, preferring instead to expand and improve institutional care facilities. International child welfare organizations and U.S adoption agencies have long believed that foster care was far better for children than institutional care, and this view is increasingly shared among experts in China as well. Some officials in the Ministry of Civil Affairs now hope to put up to half of the children under the ministry's care into some form of foster care within five years.[8]

My daughter and I have visited her orphanage four times in the past ten years. I have also visited several other orphanages during this time. Over the decade I have witnessed the resulting changes, particularly in two large state orphanages, Wuhan and Hefei. While these are by no means typical social welfare institutions, they illustrate the magnitude of change that has swept through the system since the mid 1990s.

The Wuhan Orphanage, 1991–2001

The first time I set foot in a Chinese orphanage was in March 1991 when I was adopting my daughter in Wuhan. I did not know what to expect. Although I had been to China many times in the 1970s and 1980s as a student and a China scholar, I knew little about orphanages in China or anywhere else and had only the vaguest understanding of the burgeoning problem of female infant abandonment or its relation to China's population control policies. The Wuhan Orphanage we visit today bears little resemblance to the orphanage that took in my daughter one cold night in January 1991.

At that time, the Wuhan Orphanage was housed in a nineteenth-century compound built by Italian Jesuits who ran a mission and a foundling home there until an American Catholic order took over in the early twentieth century. The buildings evoked the era in which they were built—solid, spacious, even grand, with an airy front portico, high ceilings, open balconies, and wide staircases, all set in an enclosed courtyard. Yet one could readily see that these grand architectural features did not adapt well to the needs of a late-twentieth-century orphanage. The high-ceilinged rooms with towering, loose-fitting windows and open balconies were hard to heat during the March winds and rains. A coal stove in the middle of the infant room barely warmed the babies, who lay in thirty cribs along the wall and in a double row down the center. While the outside temperature was around 45° F with a gray drizzle, the inside was perhaps 50° and nearly as damp. In January and February the outside temperature sometimes dipped below freezing, leaving the interior spaces in the forties. This cold, damp room housed about forty infants, some two to a crib, each infant wrapped at the opposite end of a single, thick, brightly colored cotton-padded blanket. Many babies were weak and needed attention. Several were tiny and appeared to be premature; six to eight of the children had shaved temples from recent treatment with intravenous antibiotics; many babies were coughing; some were crying. The two attendants in the room did their best to rush formula to a crying infant, standing and holding the bottle for a few minutes as the baby drank, then propping it if possible against the side of the crib before rushing to get a bottle to another waking baby.

Clearly the room was severely understaffed. When I asked what the most serious problem was for the orphanage, the answer was twofold: not enough hands and not enough money to pay for medical care. Since the orphanage had no medical facilities or trained medical staff at the time, sick children had to be taken to the hospital for treatment, which the orphanage then paid for out of its already tight budget. The highest goal of the institution was to meet basic needs within the limits of its scarce resources. Despite a dedicated staff, this was the best they could hope for as the numbers of children steadily increased and domestic adoption placements failed to keep pace, indeed even fell, owing to tighter restrictions on adoption imposed by birth-planning regulations, soon to be reinforced by the 1992 adoption law.[9]

This orphanage, like others in many parts of China, was under tremendous stress in the early 1990s. Understaffed and severely underfunded, orphanages had to struggle to provide barely adequate food and care to weak, often sick infant foundlings and other disabled children. Mortality rates were tragically high in these institutions, and orphanage staff was forced by circumstances to triage expensive medical care.

Improvements at the Wuhan Orphanage were evident as early as the summer of 1993. Funds from international adoption and private donations from international adoptive parents were used to increase medical care and to purchase air conditioners for the infant rooms to mitigate the killer heat waves of Wuhan summers. In 1993–94 a local campaign to aid orphans brought increased community support and medical volunteers to the orphanage. At the same time, the Ministry of Civil Affairs helped solicit funds from a private Buddhist charity in Taiwan to build a new orphanage next door, one that would be designed and equipped for air-conditioning in summer and heating in winter. The new orphanage, ready for occupancy in 1997, not only included improved living quarters, but was also designed and fully equipped to facilitate the children's education and recreation, with numerous classrooms, music and dance rooms, and outdoor play areas. The new facility also contained a medical clinic, which eventually acquired incubators and emergency medical equipment.

On my visits to the new orphanage in 1998, 2000, and 2001, I found a polished, well-functioning modern facility, reasonably well staffed, with well-equipped infant rooms and bright, spacious, nicely furnished dormitories for older children. Music and musical performances have become an important educational and therapeutic means to improve the emotional and cognitive development of the children. Older children, including several who are blind, learn to play *guzheng,* a traditional Chinese instrument, and piano, which is also used to accompany the orphanage children's acrobatic song and dance groups. The groups frequently perform for visitors, and the children obviously delight in these performances, beaming with pride when they do well and giggling playfully when they mess up. By 2000 the orphanage's excellent music and dance program had become well known, and members of the community began asking to pay tuition to send their children to the classes. Their tuition became an additional source of funding for the orphanage's music programs.

In the past two years, with help from the Amity Foundation, a Christian-affiliated Chinese NGO whose orphanage projects are funded primarily by Families with Children from China–New York (part of the FCC adoptive family network in the United States and Canada), the Wuhan Orphanage has also reestablished and expanded its foster care network. While the orphanage had some foster care in the early 1990s to handle overflow from the crowded orphanage, the foster program today is intended to provide stable, long-term home care for chronically ill, disabled, and developmentally delayed children who require special attention to physical and cognitive needs. Additional funding for foster care in Wuhan has come from special solicitations from Wuhan adoptive parents and from the Foundation for Chinese Orphanages (FCO), a nonprofit organization run by FCC–New England that has funded projects in seven provinces.[10]

While international adoption fees and international and domestic NGOs have brought in important resources to make it possible to move beyond basic operational necessities, it is up to provincial and orphanage officials to use those resources wisely. The two directors who ran the Wuhan Orphanage in 1991 and continued in their posts until 2002 led the orphanage through these dramatic changes and deserve much credit for the well-managed programs that became possible thanks to increased external support. Throughout this time they also did their best to facilitate the adoption of as many of their children as possible, both inside and outside China, including special efforts to place disabled children. Walking with them through the orphanage, I observed that they knew the children intimately— their personalities, their special needs, their dates of arrival.

Young children approached them to be picked up or to hide from me behind their skirts. Older children came over with requests or spoke freely with them as they passed by. The relationships between children and staff seemed friendly and relaxed.

Teachers, moreover, did not hesitate to put the interests of their children above the comfort of visitors. One day after walking up to the fifth-floor dance room, the director noticed that my daughter and I, along with several other guests, were hot and sweaty, so she turned on the air conditioner. The teacher immediately intervened, pointing out that the students had been exercising before we came in and that they should not cool down too quickly lest they "catch cold." When the children had cooled down, we could turn on the air-conditioning. This mundane exchange spoke volumes about staff relations and about the way children's interests took priority over others', even the comfort of honored guests.

The Hefei Orphanage, 2000–2002

During the 1990s, conditions at other major orphanages also improved, thanks to increased government funding, revenue from international adoption fees, and donations from domestic and international charitable organizations. While many have improved their physical plant and their ability to meet the children's basic needs, a small but growing number of orphanages, such as the one in Wuhan, have taken steps to improve the children's cognitive development and to enrich their lives. Another example is the Hefei Orphanage, located in the capital city of Anhui province, an area that has done a large number of international adoptions over the past decade.

As in the case of the Wuhan Orphanage, improvements at Hefei began in the early to mid 1990s, several years after the area experienced a surge in infant abandonment. By early 1996 a new building housed several hundred children. More than a hundred others were placed in a foster care village outside the city, and in the mid 1990s a medical clinic was established in the village for the foster children. The well-run orphanage now houses one of the first foreign-funded orphanage preschool programs, built and established with the help of Half the Sky Foundation (HTS), a charitable organization run by U.S. adoptive parents in partnership with a Chinese NGO, the Chinese Population Welfare Foundation. In 2001 the orphanage also set up Sunbeam Village, a new foster care facility on the grounds of the orphanage, housing sixty children in ten resident families. In this way the children who are raised in the institution benefit both from family-based foster care and a superior preschool program aimed at giving them an academic head start before they enter the neighborhood primary school at age seven or eight. Alliance for Children, a U.S. international adoption agency, financed the new, low-lying apartment complex that houses the foster families. The orphanage also benefits from a number of nurturing "grandmas" programs funded by Amity and HTS. The "grandmas"—some of whom are retired nurses, doctors, and teachers—give extra nurturing care to babies and special-needs children and sometimes train orphanage caregivers. The Foundation for Chinese Orphanages funds a library and resource center for school-age children to help them keep pace academically with their urban peers, and HTS recently added a "Big Sisters" program to provide tutoring and academic support for middle school children, some of whom are trying to prepare for the highly competitive national college entrance exams.

On several of my visits to the Hefei Orphanage, I observed the HTS preschool in operation and spent some time with the teachers and children. This program, with its child-centered curriculum, professionally trained teachers, and well-equipped classrooms, would be impressive in any setting in China. In fact preschools with similar philosophy and design are beginning to emerge in some cities as the best schools start to experiment with new teaching methods and ideas. But to find this new program up and running smoothly in a state-run orphanage is particularly impressive. I visited the preschool several times since its inception in 2000. The teachers and children were in bright, clean, carpeted rooms filled with children's art, potted seedlings, life-size cardboard constructions, and imaginative play areas. A number of special-needs and moderately disabled children joined the activities and seemed fully integrated with the other children in the room. The three professional teachers (working in a classroom with about twenty students) attended small groups of children, offering assistance when asked and gently urging exploration and cooperation. Outside the two main classrooms stood a bookcase filled with forty-some notebooks, each one detailing the activities and progress of an individual child. This is a preschool to which I would have been happy to send my own children. In March 1991 I could not have imagined that these impoverished welfare institutions could house such a well-equipped, child-centered educational program. Over the entrance of the Hefei Orphanage today hangs a huge banner declaring, "With your love and support, we grow to serve the children." And indeed they do.

In sharp contrast to the period immediately following *The Dying Rooms* and the HRW report, when the Chinese government closed the doors of most welfare institutes to outsiders, the atmosphere in the Hefei Orphanage today, like that in the Wuhan Orphanage, is open, relaxed, and friendly. Visitors come and go. Hampshire College students on an exchange program in Hefei sometimes come to the orphanage to tutor English to a couple of the older orphans, their schedule and freedom of movement unfettered. International adoptive parents, who arrive almost weekly, are also invited to visit the orphanage if they wish.

The buildings and grounds are kept in excellent condition. After frequenting the hallways of universities in Hefei, many of which are sorely in need of a good whitewash, I couldn't help but notice that the tiled walls of the orphanage were spotlessly clean, cleaner than any other public building I have seen in the city outside a four-star hotel. With a great deal of particulate matter in the polluted air of Hefei, it is not easy to keep large buildings clean. When I commented on this to the vice-director, Mr. Zhao, he nodded and pointed to his shoes, saying that because he spends his day inside the grounds of the orphanage they stay clean without the frequent dusting normally required by daily living in Hefei. The condition of the Hefei and Wuhan orphanages is obviously not the result of a quick scrub before visitors arrive, but the evidence of routine maintenance.

As in Wuhan, there is none of the dreariness of the older orphanages. Everywhere there is color, such as the bright handmade quilts and sweaters airing on the balconies or the cheerful prints on clothes worn by the generally clean and well-dressed children. Corridors throughout the main building are decorated in vividly painted three-dimensional pictures made from pieces of recycled Styrofoam arranged in the style of children's art. There is also a wall of photographs sent by parents of children adopted internationally from the orphanage. Anhui has one of the highest rates of international adoption in China, and there are Hefei children literally all over the world. I was surprised at how many faces I recognized just from my small corner of the northeastern United States.

The gregarious behavior of children cruising the balconies and hallways reinforces the positive impression. It is clear that the children are familiar with the director and vice-director. As we walked by the open door of a room of preschoolers one day, the children spontaneously rushed out and squealed for Vice-director Zhao to pick them up, one by one, and throw them gently into the air. It took him a long time to make his escape down the stairs to rejoin us. During another visit, when Director Zhang picked up a recently adopted three-year-old girl, the child, like many of the other children, called her "Nainai" (Grandma), wrapped her arms around her neck and, without prompting, kissed her cheek. The quality of the human relationships, as well as the physical surroundings, seems evident in these small interactions. This is a far cry from the orphanages that Western human rights groups portrayed so negatively in the mid 1990s.

On my most recent visit in June 2002 I saw Sunbeam Village, the new foster care facility financed by Alliance for Children and built on the premises of the orphanage. The compound contains two-story apartment buildings, each of which has ten spacious three-bedroom apartments. One apartment houses six children of various ages, from preschool through elementary school, cared for by foster parents whose own children are grown. The arrangement simulates family life, with parents and siblings sharing a home, meals, and daily activities. Depending on their age, the children attend the HTS-funded preschool in the buildings next door or a neighborhood primary school, returning home for lunch and again each afternoon by around three or four. Foster parents supervise homework for the older children, cook meals, and assume all the basic care for the younger children. The foster families function with the full support of orphanage services and educational facilities. It is hoped that this arrangement will improve the emotional and cognitive development of the children, providing them with more adult attention in a homelike setting. While the foster care village outside the city can provide family care for infants, it cannot provide the educational opportunities that are now available in the orphanage and the nearby urban schools. The orphanage has long had a policy of bringing back children from the village to the orphanage when they reach preschool or primary school age, a move that can be emotionally difficult. At least for some children, the new onsite foster care facility brings family-style care together with improved educational opportunities, including the urban schools.

Of course this orphanage, like most others, still has many problems and unmet needs. With roughly one caregiver for every twelve to fifteen children in the rooms where the infants and toddlers eat and sleep, the staff-child ratio is still far from ideal and must stretch the caregivers' attention thin, even though this orphanage has many younger children in foster care. We were told that a primary need is for more highly trained full-time staff and for facilities and programs to improve the children's cognitive development. In Hefei and Wuhan, as elsewhere, orphanage children are often at a huge disadvantage when they reach school age and leave the walls of the orphanage to attend local schools. From day one they are usually behind the other children in cognitive development and academic skills, reinforcing a tendency for others to look down on them. Without a good education—not just in the preschool years, but all the way through childhood and adolescence—children raised in the orphanage face a severely limited future in a rapidly changing economy and society. Maintaining the children's self-esteem and fostering a positive outlook become difficult, especially for those who are not fortunate enough to find adoptive homes before entering school.

The cohort of such children is large. Even though several hundred children are adopted internationally and domestically from the Hefei and Wuhan orphanages each year, the numbers of children raised by the orphanages steadily grew throughout the 1990s, when abandonment was high and the official rules of adoption were extremely restrictive. While those rules have loosened somewhat in recent years, allowing more domestic adoptions from orphanages in some areas, the barriers have not fallen as quickly or as fully as I had hoped. Regardless of what happens in the future, many children, especially those with special needs, will continue to grow up in the care of Chinese orphanages.

The Balance Sheet

There is reason to hope that the joint initiatives of the government at various levels, along with Chinese and international NGOs, will continue to improve the life chances of orphanage children. Channels of cooperation and new sources of funding are being institutionalized and are growing every year. Besides the adoption-related organizations mentioned here, many other foreign NGOs fund projects in Chinese orphanages. Some are American; others are based in Canada, the United Kingdom, Ireland, Australia, and other countries.[11] But there is still great need for these efforts to spread deeper into the system. Though some NGOs fund projects in small or remote orphanages, such as the UK-based Save the Children Fund, most are encouraged to help make the large urban orphanages even better, thereby increasing inequalities in the system.

According to Ministry of Civil Affairs statistics, in 2001 there were 41,098 children living in 1,550 state-run welfare institutions, almost half of whom (19,419) were housed in the 160 specialized child welfare institutes run by the state. An additional 9,492 children were scattered throughout thousands of small welfare organizations run locally by township and village governments or by private individuals.[12] Many of the institutions housing children, especially those outside the specialized child welfare system, probably have not benefited much from the new developments described here. But efforts are underway to reach more welfare institutions and homes. Greater efforts to expand foster care, especially for "unadoptable" children, are also needed throughout the system. Even well-provisioned orphanages are not good substitutes for a family. The Ministry of Civil Affairs intends to develop various foster care plans throughout the system in the next several years. Poorer areas may particularly benefit from this approach because foster care can be relatively inexpensive and fairly easy to manage in local communities.

Domestic adoption could reduce the burden throughout the system, yet it remains underutilized in many areas despite the formal loosening in 1999 of restrictions on adoptions of children living in orphanages. As we have seen, restrictive adoption regulations have long been a source of tension between birth-planning authorities and those working in child welfare. The need to balance these concerns continues to impede efforts to recruit local adoptive families despite the need for homes and the inability to provide adequate funding to all the orphanages in the system. Registered domestic adoptions inside and outside the orphanages have increased nonetheless.[13] Encouraging even more domestic adoptions through publicity campaigns and social networking requires merely the will and energy to do so.

Nevertheless, regulations governing the adoption of abandoned children outside the orphanage system remain as rigid and restrictive as before, both in the letter of the law and, with some exceptions, in practice. This issue deserves high-level attention and a policy change. With birth rates now extremely low in China and sex ratios worsening, it is hard to justify punishing legitimate adoptive parents for giving a permanent home to an abandoned girl simply because they already have a child.[14] The benefit to birth planning of maintaining this restriction cannot be worth the suffering caused to legitimate adoptive parents and, especially, to abandoned children, who sometimes end up losing a second family as a result.

The "one-child" policy remains at the center of this constellation of problems. Although abandonment resulting from illegitimacy is almost certainly increasing as a percentage of the whole, I have seen no convincing evidence to suggest that the one-child policy has been replaced as the primary cause of the abandonment of healthy children. My recent research on overquota and unregistered children indicates that some parents continue to struggle to avoid birth-planning penalties by hiding children and then trying again for a son. While the majority of these parents try to hide children by not registering them, by sending them to live temporarily with friends and relatives, or by arranging unregistered but permanent adoptions, a minority resort to abandonment, as many did throughout the 1990s. The fines are ruinously heavy today, amounting to two or three times a family's yearly income. Even worse, the continuing practice in many areas of sterilization after two children, or after the first overquota child, means that if a couple gets caught too soon after the birth of a second or third girl, they may forever lose the chance to try again for a son. Where abandonment rates are down, there is probably an increased use of ultrasound to identify female fetuses in second and third pregnancies and then abort them. Second and third daughters are becoming rarer and rarer as sex ratios increase sharply for each successive pregnancy.

In recent years there have been some indications of change. The style and methods of implementing the one-child policy have been changing in some areas, becoming less punitive, especially in urban environments where fertility desires are low. Mobilization campaigns have given way to routinized implementation of policy by trained personnel. Fines and threats of sterilization or other penalties have been replaced in some areas with fees and the assumption that the vast majority of people will voluntarily restrict births. A greater emphasis on delivering high-quality reproductive health services has also emerged in recent years. Along with these changes, a new emphasis on protecting certain individual rights under "the rule of law" is also evident. All these trends can be seen in the long-awaited Population and Family Planning Law passed at the end of 2001 and implemented in September 2002.[15] This legislation strengthens protections against extreme and illegal punishments, such as destruction of property or imprisonment. While many of the changes seem minor and semantic, the symbolic change from coercion and punishment to voluntary compliance and fees, and from political mobilization campaigns to the "rule of law," may become increasingly significant and lead to further positive changes.

Despite some encouraging trends in birth planning in recent years, intense monitoring of all fertile women, accompanied by severe penalties for failure to comply, increased in many rural areas at the end of the 1990s and 2000 as the national ten-year census approached and cadres scrambled to make their birth-planning records look acceptable. This pressure led at the turn of the millennium to new spikes of abandonment in some areas, as also happened around the 1990 census. More recently some orphanages have reported a drop in abandonments, particularly of healthy children without disabilities. Yet despite reports that abandonment is waning in some of the areas that experienced high rates in the past, by 2002 the total number of children in welfare institutions had not decreased; indeed it increased by about 3,500 in 2001, from around 46,500 in 2000 to just over 50,000, according to statistics from the Ministry of Civil Affairs.[16]

The abandonment of disabled children is reported to have increased as a proportion of abandoned children.[17] This trend certainly seems to be the case for some orphanages, although it is hard to know if it is true for abandoned children as a whole. The abandonment of disabled children arises from factors not directly related to the one-child policy, though some argue that the culture of "fewer but higher-quality children" that bolsters that policy has contributed to the devaluing of children born with physical or mental disabilities. Most important is the burden that raising a disabled child poses in China today. Poor rural families may find they are simply unable to take care of a seriously disabled child.

Outside a few cities and welfare institutions, there is little government support for families who wish to keep a disabled child at home or in an institution but still part of the family. If one is relatively poor, abandonment may be the only way to get a child into an institution. A few orphanage-affiliated programs now allow disabled children to enroll at low or no cost in rehabilitation programs as day students or as part-time boarders, instead of wards of the orphanage, and more such programs could help ease this serious problem. One foreign-funded example is the Peony Project at the Children's Institute of Luoyang, Henan province, run by the World Association of Children and Parents (WACAP) adoption agency with a $2.9 million grant from the Bill and Melinda Gates Foundation. Such programs need to be highly subsidized to make the price affordable or free to Chinese families with average or low incomes. Here is another welfare policy that needs greater attention.

Clearly on the negative side of the balance sheet at the turn of the millennium is the continuing rise of the reported sex ratio at birth, now among the highest in the world. In the national census of 2000, the average reported sex ratio at birth was 117 boys for every 100 girls, up from 111 reported in the 1990 census, with Guangdong and Hainan reaching an astounding 130 and 135 respectively. These soaring rates seem to have been achieved with the increasingly widespread use of ultrasound for prenatal sex selection. The ultrasound machine has become ubiquitous throughout the countryside, thanks in part to the government's efforts to monitor all fertile women for pregnancies several times a year. This widespread use of ultrasound may mitigate rates of abandonment. My own limited research, as well as the more extensive published work of other researchers,[18] indicates that ultrasound is commonly used in the countryside to select the sex of a second pregnancy when the first pregnancy produced a girl. While those living in one-son/two-child areas are usually happy to have a first-born daughter, most people want to ensure that their second and last permitted pregnancy is a son. The availability of ultrasound makes that perfect outcome possible. In some villages rumor has it that nearly every second pregnancy of mothers with a daughter is subjected to ultrasound, with abortion frequently resulting if the fetus is found to be another female. By 2001 some provincial governments were cracking down hard on this practice by levying fines for suspicious voluntary abortions not related to health concerns and denying permission for a second birth after such an abortion. Micromanaging the uteruses of hundreds of millions of women has led the state into a morass of intrusive and costly monitoring and proliferating punishments as women attempt to wrest from the state some modicum of control over their own fertility outcomes.

Hopes for the Future

It is my hope that over the next decade the need for a large-scale orphanage and child welfare system to care for abandoned children will diminish significantly and eventually disappear. When my daughter is a young woman, I hope she will return to "her" orphanage to find it transformed into a school of music and dance or a rehabilitation and training center for disabled children and young adults. The "unadoptable" disabled children, or disabled children who cannot be cared for at home, could then be the focus of state care, to be placed in stable foster care systems or well-run homes with trained personnel.

While I am confident that the government is on the path to providing better services to abandoned, orphaned, and disabled children, I am not confident that it will make the policy choices necessary to put an end to child abandonment itself any time soon. To do so, the Communist Party would have to abandon the politically entrenched hegemonic view that its one-child policy has been necessary to save the nation from starvation and environmental ruin and that it remains a prerequisite for continued economic growth if not survival. The Party has staked a great deal of its legitimacy and credibility on this view. Backing away from this position will be difficult, even though emerging political forces may increasingly seek to soften and modify the approach.

However, Chinese society is changing rapidly. Fertility desires have fallen and will continue to fall, as they have throughout Asia in the past two decades, notably without the highly coercive governmental birth-planning programs that have characterized China. Not only have the more economically developed countries in Asia, such as South Korea and Taiwan, attained fertility rates as low as China's, but the less prosperous Thailand and Sri Lanka have also reached low and stable rates during the past decade. Even a few relatively poor areas saw rapid fertility decline to below-replacement levels, the earliest and best known case being that of the Indian state of Kerala, later joined by Tamil Nadu and West Bengal.[19] The socioeconomic conditions that have contributed to this decline, such as increasing rates of female literacy and employment, have been important in China as well and will continue to advance there. Along with these changes the urgency of the felt need for a son will likely diminish and the value of daughters continue to increase among an ever larger segment of the population. Such trends should lessen the perverse consequences of entrenched birth-planning policy even if the state does not soon retreat from that unnecessary approach.

In the meantime, I am encouraged to see the Wuhan and Hefei orphanages as contemporary examples of how well-managed welfare institutes can take advantage of the new resources and "grow to serve the children." It is heartening to know that more and more orphanages, and the children they serve, are benefiting from similar improvements.

Notes

Introduction

1. "Immigrant Visas Issued to Orphans Coming to the United States: Top Countries of Origin," U.S. Department of State website, travel.state.gov/orphan_numbers.html.

2. Central Intelligence Agency, *The World Factbook, 1998.* By 2002, China's population growth rate had increased four percentage points over the 1998 estimate. It is unclear whether the growth rate itself increased or whether better reporting led to the upward revision. The current edition of *The World Factbook* is available online at www.odci.gov/cia/publications/factbook.

3. *World Factbook, 2002.*

1. A Chinese Orphanage, 1991–92

An earlier version of this chapter appeared as "Chinese Orphanages: Saving China's Abandoned Girls," *Australian Journal of Chinese Affairs,* no. 30 (July 1993): 61–87.

1. The Wuhan Orphanage has been known in English as the Wuhan Foundling Hospital, but this nineteenth-century term is

misleading today, for the orphanage is not a hospital and is no longer directly connected to one. The Chinese name posted over the gate of the main building in 1991—Yu you yuan, or Wuhan Kindergarten— deliberately obscured the function of the institution as an orphanage. The official name is Wuhan Children's Welfare Institute (Wuhan shi ertong fuli yuan).

2. Evidence here consists of interviews and statistics from the Wuhan Orphanage, Hubei province, gathered during visits between March 1991 and December 1992, and to a lesser extent on visitor reports and interviews at a similar orphanage in Changsha, Hunan province, during the same period. Information was also gathered from two smaller welfare houses, one in Xiangfan, a small city in western Hubei, and another near Shijiazhuang, the capital of Hebei province. For a brief report on the orphanage in Changsha, see Sheryl WuDunn, "China's Castaway Babies: Cruel Practice Lives On," *New York Times,* 26 Feb. 1991.

3. See, for example, Ho Ping-ti, *Studies on the Population of China, 1368–1953* (Cambridge: Harvard University Press, 1959), 60–61; John Henry Grey, *China: A History of the Laws, Manners and Customs of the People* (London: Macmillan, 1878), 2: 50; William Lockhart, *Medical Missionary in China* (London: Hurst & Blackett, 1861), 25–27.

4. Chinese culture, while extremely male dominated, supplies women with some powerful tools—such as norms of filial piety and parental control over children—that women regularly use to gain influence for their own purposes. The classic study of women's informal power in the family is Marjory Wolf, *Women and the Family in Rural Taiwan* (Stanford: Stanford University Press, 1972). Social historians such as Patricia Buckley Ebrey and Susan Mann have also illuminated sources of power, status, and influence for women within the traditions and practices of different historical eras; see, e.g., Ebrey's *The Inner Quarters: Marriage and the Lives of Chinese Women in the Sung Period* (Berkeley: University of California Press, 1993). Nonetheless, the recent emphasis in anthropological and social historical literature on

the ways women are active subjects of Chinese culture should not obscure the stark ways in which females continue to be disadvantaged.

5. The film's title, *Small Happiness,* comes from a common term for the birth of a girl. In contrast, the birth of a boy is a "big happiness."

6. Recent scholarship has stressed that customary practices are not as "pure" as the formal patrilineal kinship ideology suggests. See, for example, Ellen Judd, "Niangjia: Chinese Women and Their Natal Families," *Asian Survey* 48, no. 3 (Aug. 1989). Such practices nonetheless remain within a context of primary patrilineal relationships, which are, comparatively speaking, extremely dominant.

7. See, for example, John Lossing Buck, *Chinese Farm Economy* (Nanking: University of Nanking, 1930), 340–46; Arthur P. Wolf and Chieh-shan Huang, *Marriage and Adoption in China, 1845–1945* (Stanford: Stanford University Press, 1980), 230–33.

8. See, for example, Lionel Rose, *The Massacre of the Innocents: Infanticide in Britain, 1800–1939* (London: Routledge & Kegan Paul, 1986). A new study by Sherri Broder documents how widespread the problems were in late-nineteenth-century urban America. See Sherri Broder, "Infanticide, Abandonment, and Baby-Farming in Late Nineteenth-Century Philadelphia," draft in progress. AUTHOR'S NOTE, 2003: Broder later published her work as *Tramps, Unfit Mothers, and Neglected Children: Negotiating the Family in Nineteenth-Century Philadelphia* (Philadelphia: University of Pennsylvania Press, 2002).

9. Abortion, IUDs, and sterilization, which are heavily used in China's population control program, all carry risks under the best of circumstances. These risks are heightened by the coerced and often hasty way in which birth control is implemented, such as mass sterilization campaigns, which in 1983 alone resulted in over 20 million sterilizations. See Judith Banister, "China's Population Changes and the Economy," in *China's Economic Dilemmas in the 1990s: The Problems of Reforms, Modernization, and Interdependence,* Study Papers, Joint Economic Committee, Congress of the United States (Washington, D.C.: U.S. Government Printing Office, 1991), 1: 239.

10. On the importance of the "uterine family" as a traditional strategy of influence for women as well as a source of emotional comfort, see Wolf, *Women and the Family.*

11. After all, as a grandfather in the documentary film *Small Happiness* put it, "Giving birth to a girl is a 'small happiness'; you cannot say it is no happiness."

12. Sten Johansson and Ola Nygren, "The Missing Girls of China: A New Demographic Account," *Population and Development Review* 17, no. 1 (March 1991): 35–51; Sten Johansson, Zhao Xuan, and Ola Nygren, "On Intriguing Sex Ratios Among Live Births in China in the 1980s," *Journal of Official Statistics* (Stockholm) 7, no. 1 (1991): 25–43. Also see Nicholas Kristof, "A Mystery from China's Census: Where Have Young Girls Gone?" *New York Times,* 17 June 1991, p. 1. For a discussion of the problem of skewed sex ratios in Asia, see Amartya Sen, "100 Million Missing Females," *New York Review of Books* (December 1990); Ansley Coale, "Excess Female Mortality and the Balance of the Sexes in the Population: An Estimate of the Number of 'Missing Females,'" *Population and Development Review* 17, no. 3 (Sept. 1991): 517–23.

13. AUTHOR'S NOTE, 2003: The sex ratios at birth continued to climb throughout the 1990s, reaching about 117 boys per 100 girls by the 2000 national census.

14. For a more extended discussion of possible explanations for the skewed sex ratio in the 1990s, see Terence Hull, "Recent Trends in Sex Ratios at Birth in China," *Population and Development Review* 16, no. 1 (March 1990). AUTHOR'S NOTE, 2003: From the early 1990s on, prenatal sex selection through ultrasound became more widespread, skewing the sex ratio even further. For an early article on the role of ultrasound in the 1980s and early 1990s, see Zeng Yi et al., "Causes and Implications of the Recent Increase in the Reported Sex Ratio at Birth in China," *Population and Development Review* 19, no. 2 (June 1993): 283–302. A more recent study on prenatal sex selection is Chu Junhong, "Prenatal Sex-

Selective Abortion in Rural China," *Population and Development Review* 27, no. 2 (June 2001): 259–81.

15. Articles condemning female infanticide have periodically appeared in the Chinese press since the early 1980s, following the implementation of the one-child policy. See, for example, "Enhancing the Role of Women in Socialist Modernization," *Women of China* (March 1983): 2; "Female Infanticide Reported in Zhejiang," *Foreign Broadcast Information Service: China* (hereafter *FBIS-CHI*), U.S. Government, 5 June 1986, p. 2.

16. Johansson and Nygren, "Missing Girls of China." The Ministry of Justice recently stated that 184,691 adoptions were registered from 1980 through 1991. See Liang Chao, "New Centre Set Up as the Adoption Floodgate Opens," *China Daily,* 17 June 1992, p. 3.

17. See Johansson and Nygren, "Missing Girls of China."

18. See, for example, "Many Unplanned Births Discovered in Liaoning," *FBIS-CHI*-90-137, 17 July 1990. Also see Tyrene White, "Birth Planning Between Plan and Market: The Impact of Reform on China's One-Child Policy," in *China's Economic Dilemmas in the 1990s: The Problems of Reforms, Modernization, and Interdependence,* Study Papers, Joint Economic Committee, Congress of the United States (Washington, D.C.: U.S. Government Printing Office, 1991), 1: 267. Census data are not based on household registries. AUTHOR'S NOTE, 2003: The inaccuracy of household registration continued throughout the 1990s because there were so many "hidden" children, known as *hei haizi,* or "black children."

19. See Ann Waltner, *Getting an Heir: Adoption and Kinship in Late Imperial China* (Honolulu: University of Hawaii Press, 1990).

20. Wolf and Huang, *Marriage and Adoption,* 230–60.

21. Ibid., chaps. 9 and 26.

22. Ibid., 234–41.

23. White, "Birth Planning," 268.

24. "'Floating Population' Complicates Family Planning," *FBIS-CHI*-88-134, 13 July 1988.

25. In addition to the evidence from the Wuhan and Changsha orphanages and the three smaller welfare houses mentioned in note 2, there have been a number of articles in the Chinese press in recent years complaining about such increases. See, for example, "Discarding of Baby Girls 'Serious' in Fujian," *Zhongguo tongxun she* (22 March 1989), in *FBIS-CHI*-89-056, 24 March 1989, p. 61.

26. *Beijing Review* 34, no. 12 (25–31 March 1991): 33.

27. WuDunn, "China's Castaway Babies"; *Beijing Review* 34, no. 22 (3–9 June 1991).

28. A photo display of the old orphanage and its "crimes" still hangs in the orphanage, claiming that malice and neglect were responsible for the large numbers of deaths. It is clear from the mission's own records that the orphanage did indeed have very high mortality rates. Orphanage officials, clearly embarrassed by the old photo display, try to steer foreigners away from it and tell Chinese visitors they have little idea what the true situation was in the past.

29. See, for example, Lockhart, *Medical Missionary,* 25–27. On orphanages in the West, see Rose, *Massacre of the Innocents.*

30. Ho Ping-ti, *Studies on the Population of China,* 61. The expression "more than ten thousand" in Chinese is not necessarily intended to be taken literally, although it may have been in this case. Also see Hugh Baker, *Chinese Family and Kinship* (London: Macmillan, 1979), 7, 8–10.

31. The terms used are stark and unadorned: *yiqi* or *rengdiao*— to forsake, discard, abandon, throw away.

32. Wolf and Huang, *Marriage and Adoption,* 4.

33. See, for example, Edward Friedman, Mark Selden, and Paul Pickowicz, with Kay Johnson, *Chinese Village, Socialist State* (New Haven: Yale University Press, 1991), 5; Jerry Dennerline, *Qian Mu and the World of Seven Mansions* (New Haven: Yale University Press, 1986), 49.

34. A number of these orphanages, including the one at Wuchang, are mentioned in Sue Bradshaw, "Catholic Sisters in

China: An Effort to Raise the Status of Women," *Historical Reflections* (Canada) 8, no. 3 (1981): 201–13.

35. "Family Planning Regulations in Hubei Province," ratified by the Peoples' Representatives of Hubei Province, 19 Dec. 1987.

36. White, "Birth Planning," 258.

37. See, for example, Susan Greenhalgh, "Shifts in China's Population Policy, 1984–86: Views from the Central, Provincial, and Local Levels," *Population and Development Review* 12, no. 3 (Sept. 1986).

38. Susan Greenhalgh argues from her work in rural Shaanxi that the policy changes of the mid to late 1980s brought "state and society . . . closer together, and state policy itself was altered to reflect fundamental societal needs." See "The Peasantization of the One-Child Policy in Shaanxi," in *Chinese Families in the Post-Mao Era*, edited by Deborah Davis and Stevan Harrell (Berkeley: University of California Press, 1993), 250.

39. John S. Aird, *Slaughter of the Innocents: Coercive Birth Control in China* (Washington, D.C.: AEI Press, 1990), chap. 4, esp. 74–84. Also see White, "Birth Planning," 261; Judith Banister, "China's Population Changes and the Economy," 240–41; *FBIS-CHI*, 23 July 1990, p. 31.

40. White, "Birth Planning," 258–61.

41. These records are summarized in "Fulishiye" (Welfare activities), in *Wuhan shi zhi* (Wuhan municipal history) (Wuhan daxue chuban she, 1990), 66.

42. Although the reasons during this period for the relatively high percentage of boys, almost all of whom were disabled, are not entirely clear, the different ratio may have occurred because in the early years of the one-child policy, regulations did not clearly exempt disabled children from the quotas allotted to families. Thus disabled boys, along with healthy and disabled girls, were put at greater risk. In 1987 the exemption of disabled children from the quotas was clearly stated in the regulations, and the percentage of boys fell back below 10 percent by the late 1980s.

43. Wuhan Civil Affairs Bureau, "Welfare Activities."

44. Rubie Watson, "The Named and the Nameless: Gender and Personhood in Chinese Society," *American Ethnologist* 13, no. 4 (Nov. 1986).

45. AUTHOR'S NOTE, 2003: In 2000 the orphanage began to give all children who arrived without a name the surname Wu, for Wuhan.

46. Under the national adoption law, only childless couples were legally permitted to adopt an orphanage baby. However, as long as the couple had a five-year history of infertility prior to adopting a child, Hubei family planning regulations permitted them to give birth to another child should the mother subsequently become pregnant.

47. Jichuan Wang, "Women's Preference for Children in Shifang County, Sichuan, China," *Asian and Pacific Population Forum* 4, no. 3 (Fall 1990). For similar findings in Shaanxi, see Susan Greenhalgh, "The Peasantization of the One-Child Policy."

48. It is not clear why concentrations developed in these areas, other than that networks of information and connections between local welfare offices in these areas and the Wuhan Orphanage had developed over the years after several initial adoptions in the wake of the 1960–62 famine.

49. Wuhan Civil Affairs Bureau, "Welfare Activities."

50. John Henry Grey, *China,* 50–51; Lockhart, *Medical Missionary,* 26.

51. Under this provision, Yuan Hui was finally able to find a home in an American family who had several children.

52. See, for example, "The Abduction and Sale of Children in Shaanxi Has Caused Serious Concern in Society," *FBIS-CHI*-89-011, 18 Jan. 1989; Reuters, "Slavery Rises Again in Reformist China," *Daily Yomiuri,* 26 June 1991. AUTHOR'S NOTE, 2003: The practice of *tongyangxi* had died out in most places by the 1980s and 1990s. Our research from 1995 to 2000 found only a few cases among adoptions in the 1990s, and these arrangements were likely to be unsuccessful.

53. These cases differ from those where hospitals return babies the orphanage sent to them or send to the orphanage babies diagnosed as

terminally ill or beyond reasonable medical treatment. In such instances, the orphanage is expected to take the child back and provide basic care for it until it dies. Few hospitals in China have nursing staff to take care of the daily needs of patients, such as feeding, clothing, and bathing them. Families are expected to attend to such needs while the hospital staff provides medical care. Babies abandoned in the hospital are therefore a particular burden on hospital staff. When the orphanage sends babies to the hospital, it not only is expected to pay the bills but also to send one of its workers to provide basic care for the child.

54. According to the U.S. consulate in Guangzhou, which is responsible for issuing visas for children adopted in China by U.S. citizens, the number of adoptions to the United States from China was around twenty to thirty per year in the years before the first national adoption law. In 1992, the numbers grew significantly and reached around three hundred by the end of the year.

55. AUTHOR'S NOTE, 2003: By 1995 the orphanage had obtained a large donation from a Taiwan-based charity to build an entirely new orphanage next door to the old one. This new, fully equipped, modern facility opened in late 1997, totally transforming the physical conditions of this orphanage. See Chap. 7.

56. I do not mean that there has been no criticism, for there has been some, especially from various Women's Federation groups. Criticism was particularly evident around 1982–83, when severely coercive tactics were employed in many parts of China, with clearly disastrous consequences for many infants and pregnant women. But after the early 1980s, critical comment usually stopped short of implicating government policies, largely bemoaning the "remnant" backward ideology and ignorance of peasants. AUTHOR'S NOTE, 2003: In the late 1990s new critical voices could be heard from women activists concerning various aspects of population policy especially as they affect the treatment and health of women and girls. Female infant abandonment, however, has not been widely discussed in this context. See Susan Greenhalgh, "Fresh Winds in Beijing: Chinese

Feminists Speak Out on the One-Child Policy and Women's Lives," *Signs* 26, no. 3 (2001).

57. See, for example, Emily Honig and Gail Hershatter, *Personal Voices: Chinese Women in the 1980s* (Stanford: Stanford University Press, 1988), chap. 9.

58. For instance, Swedish demographer Sten Johansson (see n. 12 of this chapter) was invited by the Chinese government to help figure out what was happening to the "missing girls."

59. D. Gale Johnson, "Can There Be Too Much Human Capital? Is There a World Population Problem?" Office for Agricultural Economics Research, University of Chicago, paper no. 92 (Oct. 1992): 10.

60. Shanti Conley and Sharon Camp, *China's Family Planning Program: Challenging the Myths* (Washington, D.C.: Population Crisis Committee, 1992), 43.

61. AUTHOR'S NOTE, 2003: By the end of the 1990s orphanage conditions had improved dramatically in many places thanks to increased government funding, funds generated by international adoption, and increasing participation by international charitable organizations. See Chap. 7 for a discussion of these changes.

62. AUTHOR'S NOTE, 2003: Our research on abandonment and adoption carried out from 1995 to 2000 indicates that this belief may have been too pessimistic. In fact, we learned that many abandoned babies in the countryside are found and quickly adopted without ever entering government institutions. See Chap. 4 of this volume.

63. World Resources Institute, *World Resources, 1990–91* (New York: Oxford University Press, 1990), 259.

64. See, for example, Rose, *Massacre of the Innocents,* on the experience in England in reducing infant mortality by replacing institutional orphanage care with foster care.

65. For a critical appraisal of the failure of Western demographers to criticize and challenge the assumptions and methods of Chinese population policy, see Aird, *Slaughter of the Innocents,* chap. 1.

66. Susan Greenhalgh and John Bongaarts, "An Alternative to the One-Child Policy in China," *Population and Development Review* 11 (Dec. 1985); Jianguo Wang, "A Soft Population Control Policy: A Possible Solution to China's Population Crisis" (Ruanxing renkou zhengce sheji: jiejue Zhongguo renkou baozha wenti), Papers of the Center for Modern China (Princeton), no. 15 (Jan. 1992).

67. See Conley and Camp, *China's Family Planning Program.* Some have argued that this concession to attitudes that value males and devalue females (such as allowing a second birth if the first is a girl) condones and encourages such beliefs rather than working to change them. But the lives of hundreds of thousands of girls are too high a price to pay to hold the line on this issue. Change must be brought about, but in ways other than forcing an unwilling population to accept a one- or two-child policy.

68. Working Group on Population Growth and Economic Development, *Population Growth and Economic Development: Policy Questions* (Washington, D.C.: National Academy Press, 1986).

2. Orphanage Care, 1989–95

This chapter first appeared as "Abandoned Children and Orphanage Care in China: A Reaction to Human Rights Watch," *Families with Children from China–New York* (Winter 1996).

1. AUTHOR'S NOTE, 2003: In fact international adoption was not significantly affected by this negative publicity, although the government did close orphanage doors to almost all outsiders for several years thereafter. The openness that I experienced in 1991–93 disappeared as a result of the HRW report.

2. AUTHOR'S NOTE, 2003: All observers agree that conditions in many of China's orphanages have improved dramatically over the past decade. See Chap. 7.

3. Revival of Infant Abandonment, 1989-95

An earlier version of this chapter appeared as "The Politics of the Revival of Infant Abandonment, with Special Reference to Hunan," *Population and Development Review* (March 1996): 77–98.

1. See, for example, Sten Johansson, Zhao Xuan, and Ola Nygren, "On Intriguing Sex Ratios Among Live Births in China in the 1980s," *Journal of Official Statistics* 7, no. 1 (1991); also see Sten Johansson and Ola Nygren, "The Missing Girls of China: A New Demographic Account," *Population and Development Review* 17, no. 1 (March 1991): 35–51. AUTHOR'S NOTE, 2003: Sex ratios became increasingly skewed during the 1990s. Whereas the 1990 census recorded a sex ratio of 108.5 males to 100 females at birth, the 2000 census recorded 116.8 to 100. The increasing use of ultrasound for prenatal sex selection is widely believed to explain some of this increase. See Chu Junhong, "Prenatal Sex Determination and Sex-Selective Abortion in Rural Central China," *Population and Development Review* 27, no. 2 (June 2001): 259–81.

2. Zeng Yi et al., "Causes and Implications of the Recent Increase in the Reported Sex Ratio at Birth in China," *Population and Development Review* 19, no. 2 (June 1993): 283–302, esp. 295.

3. According to Tu Ping, data from the 1 percent sample of the 1990 census indicate that the sex ratio at birth climbed from 108.5 in 1981 to 114.7 in 1989. This ratio means that there were about 1 million missing female births in 1989. See Tu Ping, "Wo guo chusheng ying'er xingbiebi wenti tansuo" (An exploration of the sex ratio at birth in China today), *Renkou yanjiu* (Population research), no. 1 (1993): 6–13. Sample surveys in the early 1990s indicate that the number of missing births has continued to grow. See, for example, Nicholas Kristof, "China's Crackdown on Births: A Stunning, and Harsh, Success," *New York Times,* 25 April 1993, p. 1. AUTHOR'S NOTE, 2003: The reported sex ratio steadily worsened throughout the 1990s, reaching nearly 117 for the entire country in the 2000 census.

4. It is significant that most of the information on which this chapter is based comes from civil affairs publications and organizations under the Ministry of Civil Affairs.

5. Author's interviews with officials in Hunan and elsewhere.

6. The segment aired on the program *Eye to Eye,* 17 Aug. 1995.

7. This extremely damning and sensationalized documentary, titled *The Dying Rooms: China's Darkest Secret,* drew vigorous protests from the Chinese government and is discussed briefly later in this chapter. See also Chap. 2.

8. See, for example, Yi Xing, "Fuli jia jingyingde xiaoying—dui Wuhan shi sange fuliyuande diaocha" (Increasing the economic efficiency of welfare—an investigation of three Wuhan welfare centers), *Zhongguo minzheng* (China's civil affairs), no. 287 (Feb. 1992): 18–19.

9. Perhaps because of the severity of the foundling problem in Hunan or the greater openness of the Hunan provincial leadership, Hunan authorities were also the first to permit international adoptions on a significant scale in the late 1980s, followed shortly by Wuhan in neighboring Hubei and later by more than a dozen other orphanages around the country in the early 1990s. In April 1992 Beijing implemented an adoption law that applied to foreign (as well as domestic) adoption and established a national China Adoption Center to coordinate and control the process of international adoption. Prior to that time, only a few dozen international adoptions took place each year, aside from those where adoptive parents were of Chinese ancestry. In the early 1990s the numbers climbed to several hundreds per year to the United States and, according to the U.S. Embassy in Beijing, reached 2,130 for the fiscal year ending 1 Oct. 1995. AUTHOR'S NOTE, 2003: Through the rest of the 1990s, adoptions to the United States increased fairly steadily, reaching 5,053 in 2000. After dropping under 5,000 in 2001, the total again hit 5,053 in 2002, according to U.S. State Department statistics ("Immigrant Visas Issued to Orphans Coming to the U.S.," travel.state.gov/orphan_numbers.html).

10. See Kay Johnson, "Chinese Orphanages: Saving China's Abandoned Girls," *Australian Journal of Chinese Affairs,* no. 30 (July 1993): 61–87. A slightly revised version appears as Chap. 1 of this book.

11. See *Tianjin tongji nianjian, 1991* (Tianjin statistical yearbook, 1991) (Beijing: China Statistics Press, 1991), 594–97; *Shanghai tongji nianjian, 1993* (Shanghai statistical yearbook, 1993) (Beijing: China Statistics Press, 1993), 372–73. By contrast, the *Zhejiang Statistical Yearbook, 1993* indicated that the number of children brought into the major orphanages doubled between 1985 and 1992 (*Zhejiang tongji nianjian, 1993* [Beijing: China Statistics Press, 1993], 446). It may be that Tianjin and Shanghai, both special administrative units, are more insulated than cities like Changsha and Wuhan from welfare networks in surrounding rural areas. That is, special administrative status may protect municipal orphanages from influxes from rural areas. Orphanages in Changsha and Wuhan get most of their children from surrounding rural areas and not from permanent urban residents. Urban birth-planning efforts have been much more routine, stable, and closely monitored and are supported by numerous institutional arrangements and socioeconomic changes that have fostered a more "natural" fertility transition. See Martin King Whyte and William L. Parish, *Urban Life in Contemporary China* (Chicago: University of Chicago Press, 1984), 159–67.

12. There has been little study of the history of abandonment or of the welfare institutions that have dealt with the needs of children without families, so there is no clear picture of the regional distribution of the practice. One in-depth unpublished study of the history of welfare institutions in pre-1949 China that includes orphanages is Raymond Lum, "Philanthropy and Public Welfare in Late Imperial China," Ph.D. diss., Harvard University, 1985 (Ann Arbor: UMI Dissertation Services). Studies of Chinese adoption, limited primarily to the pre-1949 period, have dealt with family strategies for obtaining an heir or continuing the ancestral line and have not examined whether or how such practices intersect with the fate of abandoned children, most of whom are girls. See Arthur Wolf and Chieh-shan

Huang, *Marriage and Adoption in China, 1845–1945* (Stanford: Stanford University Press, 1980); Ann Waltner, *Getting an Heir: Adoption and Kinship in Late Imperial China* (Honolulu: University of Hawaii Press, 1990).

13. Information presented throughout this chapter on the history of abandonment in Hunan prior to 1949 is from *Hunan shengzhi* (Hunan provincial history), vol. 21: *Yiyao weisheng zhi* (Medicine and health history) (Changsha: Hunan renmin chuban she, 1988), 566–75.

14. The predominance of girls among abandoned infants is not necessarily the case everywhere in China, especially in some minority areas where abandonment also occurs. See, for example, Ren Xinlai, "Nan hang guer wentide diaocha yu jiejue" (Investigation and resolution of southern Xinjiang's orphan problem), *Zhongguo minzheng* (China's civil affairs), no. 225 (Dec. 1987): 24–25. Factors that motivate abandonment in many cultures, such as "illegitimacy," poverty, family disintegration, or disabilities, do not necessarily relate to or interact strongly with gender. While widespread abandonment was a problem in many parts of Europe in the nineteenth century, and in some places girls were abandoned more often than boys, it was by no means a single-sex practice. See David I. Kertzer, *Sacrificed for Honor: Italian Infant Abandonment and the Politics of Reproductive Control* (Boston: Beacon Press, 1993).

15. For a description of local efforts elsewhere in China during the Qing dynasty, see You Chi, "Infant Protection Society," in *Chinese Civilization and Society*, edited by Patricia Ebrey (New York: Free Press, 1981), 219–23.

16. In the early 1850s, these Hunanese-funded institutions were joined by an increasing number of foundling homes run by foreign missionaries. English, American, German, and Italian missionaries set up "several tens" of foundling homes in Hunan in the late nineteenth century, according to the compiled history.

17. It has been argued elsewhere that Confucian efforts to support orphanages were largely symbolic, meant to provide moral

example and a context for legitimizing the good deeds of the elite rather than to ameliorate suffering on a large scale. See Lum, "Philanthropy and Public Welfare," 197–211; and William T. Rowe, *Hankow: Conflict and Community in a Chinese City, 1796–1895* (Stanford: Stanford University Press, 1989), 105–6, 345–52. But the scale of operations of the Provincial City Foundling Institute alone suggests that these efforts, at least in some periods, were far more than symbolic and were indeed intended to have some demographic impact on an identified social problem: the abandonment and killing of girls.

18. An article by two Western demographers also finds that the incidence of infanticide in China generally declined precipitously during this period. See Ansley Coale and Judith Banister, "Five Decades of Missing Females in China," *Demography* 31, no. 3 (Aug. 1994).

19. Yueyang City Civil Affairs Department, "Qian tan qiying wenti" (A brief talk about the foundling problem), *Zhongguo minzheng* (China's civil affairs), no. 215 (Feb. 1987): 21–22.

20. Hunan Province Civil Affairs Bureau, Social Welfare Section, "Guanyu dangqian shehui qiying wentide diaocha" (Investigation concerning the current social problem of foundlings), *Zhongguo minzheng* (China's civil affairs), no. 274 (Jan. 1992): 34–35.

21. While it seems that there are larger proportions of disabled children in some of the major orphanages in the north, such as one in Tianjin visited in summer 1995 by the CBS film crew mentioned earlier, to my knowledge this apparent difference has not been investigated carefully.

22. "Fulishiye" (Welfare activities), in *Wuhan shi zhi* (Wuhan municipal history) (Wuhan: Wuhan daxue chuban she, 1990), 66. The Chinese term *canji,* variously translated as "handicapped," "disabled," or "special needs," is used to label children with a wide range of conditions from cosmetic imperfections, such as large birth marks, to congenital birth defects and life-threatening medical problems.

23. Johnson, "Chinese Orphanages," 69.

24. Discussed in John S. Aird, *Slaughter of the Innocents: Coercive Birth Control in China* (Washington, D.C.: AEI Press, 1990), 74.

25. Susan Greenhalgh, Zhu Chuzhu, and Li Nan, "Restraining Population Growth in Three Chinese Villages, 1988–93," *Population and Development Review* 20, no. 2 (June 1994): 365–95.

26. Susan Greenhalgh and Jiali Li, "Engendering Reproductive Policy and Practice in Peasant China: For a Feminist Demography of Reproduction," *Signs* 20, no. 3 (Spring 1995): 601–41.

27. See, for example, Nicholas Kristof and Sheryl WuDunn, *China Wakes: The Struggle for the Soul of a Rising Power* (New York: Random House, 1994), chap. 6, esp. 182–83.

28. While some rural areas adjacent to cities have begun to establish rudimentary social security schemes, and some have started to set up local funds and insurance schemes for families with no sons, these efforts fall far short of the guaranteed social security provided to state-sector workers since 1949. How credible they are in the minds of peasants who have seen policies come and go is also open to question. Most of the countryside remains without any social security programs. Figures from a 1987 survey showed that pensions represented less than 5 percent of the income of the elderly in rural areas. See Institute of Population Studies, Chinese Academy of Social Sciences, ed., *A Selection of Papers Presented at the International Symposium on Population Aging in China* (Beijing: New World Press, 1993), 128. The State Statistical Bureau's rural household survey of Sichuan for 1990 found that only 2.5 percent of the total income of households with an average age of 60 or more came from state-supported pensions. In Liaoning province the figure from the same survey was 1.1 percent. I am grateful to D. Gale Johnson for sharing these data with me.

29. Even in the face of continuing social security needs, the desire to have *many* sons has certainly diminished, and there is much evidence to indicate that many, probably most, peasants today would prefer a son and a daughter over two sons, suggesting that the value of daughters is increasing. For example, the data from a 1 percent sample fertility survey in Hebei in 1985 showed that the vast majority of rural and urban women who had one son but no daughters

wanted their next child (if they were permitted to have another) to be a girl. I thank Liming Liu for sharing these data with me. (Liming Liu, "Urban-Rural Differences Regarding Parents' Preference for a Son in China," master's thesis, University of Massachusetts, Amherst, 1995). Greenhalgh found similar views in her survey of Shaanxi villages in the late 1980s and early l990s; see Greenhalgh, Zhu, and Li, "Restraining Population Growth."

30. See Greenhalgh and Li, "Engendering Reproductive Policy," for a discussion of how contemporary fertility desires and behavior are not merely a "revival of tradition" but are shaped by new political and economic circumstances. The current obsession with sons in the culture of the reform era is the major theme of the movie *Women's Story*, made by a woman director, Peng Xiaolian. The film depicts several manifestations of this phenomenon in a rural area close to Beijing in the late 1980s. It shows the taunts and social humiliation suffered by the members of a sonless family as well as the desperate "guerrilla pregnancy" of a woman fleeing from birth-planning authorities, obsessed with the need to bear a son at any cost.

31. For a fascinating though brief account of one village cadre's experience in dealing with these difficulties, see Huang Shumin, *The Spiral Road: Change in a Chinese Village Through the Eyes of a Communist Party Leader* (Boulder: Westview, 1989), 175–86.

32. The average annual per capita rural income in Hunan in 1990 was probably around 400 yuan. The care of foundlings was relatively costly, partly because of the need to supply milk powder for infant formula.

33. This discussion refers only to domestic adoption in China, not to international adoption, which during the period discussed in this chapter accounted for only a tiny percentage of Chinese adoptions. In 1991 U.S. citizens adopted fewer than one hundred Chinese children; perhaps a few dozen came from Hunan, one of the first provinces to allow foreign adoptions.

34. These restrictive regulations, widely practiced with only slight regional variations in the 1980s, were incorporated into the

first national adoption law of the People's Republic passed in December 1991 and implemented in April 1992. The revised law of April 1999 removed the childless restriction for those adopting children living in welfare institutions and lowered the minimum age to thirty for all adopters.

35. According to interviews conducted in several locales, the enforcement of adoption regulations varied widely. Some adoptive parents with biological children suffered no penalty while others reported heavy fines. The Chinese media have reported cases of people who took in abandoned infants with the intention of adopting them, only to have the authorities fine them and take the children away. See, for example, *Xiandai jiating bao* (Modern family magazine) (Nanjing), 10 May 1995, p. 1.

36. Author's interviews.

37. Jiang Wandi, "Development of Women's Rights in China," *Beijing Review,* 15–21 Nov. 1993, p. 20.

38. The following discussion comes from a summary of the case and the public discussion it aroused (Jiang He, "Shei lai baohu Xiong Qi?" [Who will protect Xiong Qi?], *Zhongguo minzheng* [China's civil affairs], no. 295 [Oct. 1993]: 36–39), and from part of the original discussion that appeared in an article by Pi Xiaoming ("Xiao ku hai Xiong Qi fuyang an" [The adoption case of poor little Xiong Qi], *Nongjianü baishitong* [Rural women knowing all], no. 8 [1993]: 4–9).

39. Jiang He, "Shei lai baohu Xiong Qi?"

40. In commemoration of Children's Day (1 June) 1994, the China Charity Federation (Zhongguo cishan zonghui) published a pamphlet (n.p., n.d.) with the signed endorsement of twenty-five top leaders supporting, in their own words, a "plan to help orphans."

41. For example, "Yi dui Meiguo fufu fuzhu gu can shou dao Wuhan shi zhengfu biaozhang" (American couple supports orphans and disabled children, receives honor from the Wuhan government), *Renmin ribao* (People's daily), 1 June 1994.

42. See, for example, an advertisement in *Renmin ribao* (People's daily), 5 May 1994, p. 8, for a performance to raise charitable

donations to "save the orphans" *(jiu guer).* Also see He Yi, "You jiang mujuan yu fuli shiye" (Charitable donations and welfare affairs), *Renmin ribao* (People's daily), 11 June 1994, p. 8.

43. Author's interviews.

44. See, for example, Cui Lili, "Under the Flag of Humanitarianism," *Beijing Review,* 4–10 July 1994.

45. AUTHOR'S NOTE, 2003: The second national adoption law, effective April 1999, did ease restrictions on adopting orphanage children, allowing couples with a child in the family already to adopt another as long as both parents are at least thirty years old.

46. There has been no careful study of this issue, and estimates are rough at best. In general, these estimates are for infants (first year of life) and are given as annual percentages. Mortality rates among older children and among children resident for a longer period of time are usually much lower and are not included in these discussions. The most extensive statistics on mortality rates in Chinese orphanages appear in *Zhongguo minzheng tongji nianjian, 1990* (China civil affairs statistical yearbook, 1990) (Beijing: China Statistics Press, 1990), 100–103. These figures, which are difficult to assess precisely and are only for 1989, suggest that death rates for entering populations were in the range of 40–60 percent.

47. *Eye to Eye,* CBS, 17 Aug. 1995.

48. In 1992 a visitor to a welfare center not far from Shijiazhuang, the capital of Hebei province, was told that only around 20 percent of the abandoned infants they received survived the first year. As in other welfare centers investigated, most deaths occurred soon after arrival. However, the percentage of disabled infants was higher in this facility than that reported in Hunan and other southern areas; the relative prevalence of disabilities would make survival rates lower even if conditions in the welfare centers were comparable.

49. AUTHOR'S NOTE, 2003: Children who do not make it into the state welfare system may also fare better, as I later discovered in research conducted in the late 1990s; see Chap. 4 of this volume.

50. *The Dying Rooms: China's Darkest Secret,* Channel Four (UK), 14 June 1995. A Human Rights Watch report, *Death by Default: A Policy of Fatal Neglect in China's State Orphanages* (New York: Human Rights Watch, 1996), goes even further, asserting that China has a national policy to reduce the population of abandoned infants by the "routine murder of children through deliberate starvation." The report provides no direct evidence for this extreme accusation, basing its conclusions on evidence of intentional abuse in one institution coupled with evidence of high mortality rates throughout the orphanage system. As I argue in this chapter, the latter can more reasonably be explained by factors other than deliberate policy. For a response to the HRW report, see Chap. 2 of this volume.

51. Author's interviews with welfare workers. A pediatrician previously involved in the care of such children found that common, normally non-life-threatening viruses can be lethal among such a severely weakened infant population.

52. AUTHOR'S NOTE, 2003: Later research suggests that many infants abandoned in rural areas were actually recovered and adopted surreptitiously; see Chap. 4 of this volume.

53. Kertzer, *Sacrificed for Honor,* 138–44. Kertzer characterized nineteenth-century Italian foundling homes as "slaughter houses." In 1950, Communist Party authorities characterized a large Italian-run foundling home in Wuhan in precisely the same way. In fact, most foundling homes in China prior to 1949, whether run by foreigners or by Chinese, had horrific death rates, frequently over 90 percent.

54. If all abandoned girls become part of the "missing"—that is, remain uncounted because of death, because they are hidden by caregivers who find them and informally adopt them, or because they are unregistered or uncounted in welfare centers—then they might account for a significant percentage of the total in recent years. Many of the abandoned girls who are taken to welfare centers are eventually "returned" to census statistics by local public security and civil affairs offices, while bureaucratic obstacles leave many surviving foundlings in statistical limbo, as indicated in the section on problems of registration.

Those who die or are never recovered are, of course, permanently "missing." No effort has been made to relate female infant abandonment to the much-studied problem of the "missing girls."

55. Sheryl WuDunn, "China's Castaway Babies: Cruel Practice Lives On," *New York Times,* 26 Feb. 1991.

56. Lu Hui, "Children Without Parents," *China Today,* Sept. 1994.

57. See, for example, Liu Mingli, "Baba, Mama, bie diu diao wo . . . " (Papa, Mama, don't throw me away . . .), *Shehui gongzuo* (Social work) 1 (1993): 39.

58. There will also be some "accumulation," or holdovers from year to year. We simply do not know enough to be able to interpret these or any other publicly available figures of which I am aware. AUTHOR'S NOTE, 2003: There has been no improvement in the availability of statistics or estimates on abandonment. It remains unlikely that the government can accurately determine such numbers.

59. Stringent requirements that adoptive couples be childless have forced many parents to adopt without benefit of legal registration. See Chaps. 4 and 6.

60. Author's interview.

61. AUTHOR'S NOTE, 2003: In 2000 the number of registered domestic adoptions from orphanages did increase, as did the number of registered adoptions outside the welfare system. But vigorous efforts to promote domestic adoption have been lacking. Further, the liberalization of the adoption law that occurred in 1999 applies only to adoptions from welfare centers. For a fuller discussion of the revised regulations, see Chaps. 4 and 5.

62. AUTHOR'S NOTE, 2003: By the end of the decade, foster care programs were expanding and more funds were going to a growing number of welfare centers even outside the main cities.

63. The original text of these notes was provided to the author.

4. Abandonment and Adoption, 1996–2000

This chapter is based largely on data collected on adoptive families and abandoning families in China by a team of Chinese researchers and myself from 1996 to 1999. My co-researchers, headed by Senior Researcher Wang Liyao of the Anhui Academy of Social Sciences and Professor Huang Banghan of Anhui Agricultural University, have not participated in writing this article and may not agree with my analysis. Nevertheless, I am deeply indebted to them for their work on this project. Without them, collection of the rare data on which this article is based would have been impossible. Precise information on how these data were collected is not provided here. For the most part, people's names and place names are not used. An earlier version of this chapter was published as "Infant Abandonment and Adoption in China," *Population and Development Review* 24, no. 3 (Sept. 1998): 469–510.

1. *Zhongguo minzheng tongji nianjian, 1990* (China civil affairs statistical yearbook, 1990) (Beijing: China Statistics Press, 1990), 100–103; also see Chap. 1 of the present book. These high death rates were publicized in a sensationalized report issued by Human Rights Watch (HRW) in January 1996 titled *Death by Default: A Policy of Fatal Neglect in China's State Orphanages.* The report was based primarily on an account of institutionalized abuse in one large orphanage. Assuming that one institution accurately reflected conditions throughout China's vast orphanage system, HRW alleged a state policy of intentional neglect and starvation of infants aimed at keeping the orphanage population stable at a time of escalating admissions; this supposed policy, according to HRW, was the primary explanation for high death rates in state orphanages. The purpose of the report was to foster international condemnation of human rights abuses in China. While abuse within an institution is certainly possible, and in this case credible, there is no convincing evidence for the existence of such a state policy. There are many more plausible explanations for the high death rates that exist throughout the system.

2. Most rural areas moved from a simple one-child policy to a more lenient one-son-or-two-child policy around this time as a small concession to peasants' desire for sons and for more than one child. Under this policy, if the first child is a boy, no other births are permitted, but if the first child is a girl, a second birth is permitted. At the same time, the government launched efforts to enforce the policy more strictly in rural areas. See Susan Greenhalgh, Zhu Chuzhu, and Li Nan, "Restraining Population Growth in Three Chinese Villages, 1988–93," *Population and Development Review* 20, no. 2 (June 1994). As Greenhalgh points out elsewhere, this one-son/two-child policy, while formally more lenient than the one-child policy, institutionalized patriarchal attitudes toward girls as state policy. See Susan Greenhalgh and Jiali Li, "Engendering Reproductive Policy and Practice in Peasant China: For a Feminist Demography of Reproduction," *Signs* 20, no. 3 (Spring 1995): 601–41.

3. Institutionalized care for infants in many countries and time periods has been linked with high death rates and "failure to thrive"; see, e.g., Lionel Rose, *Massacre of the Innocents: Infanticide in Britain, 1800–1939* (London: Routledge & Kegan Paul, 1986). Orphanages are disadvantageous places for young children, even under the best of circumstances. Unfortunately, any objective effort to study the impact of improved conditions on mortality in Chinese orphanages has not been possible. Central Chinese political authorities closed the orphanages to outsiders in the wake of negative publicity by human rights groups in 1995–96 and kept access severely restricted for several years. While many orphanages have opened to visitors again since the late 1990s, authorities remain wary of revealing too much information about the orphanages. The government has not published mortality figures since 1990 and has not allowed researchers access to the relevant records.

4. "Fuli shiye" (Welfare activities), in *Wuhan shi zhi* (Wuhan municipal history) (Wuhan: Wuhan daxue chuban she, 1990), 59–97.

5. AUTHOR'S NOTE, 2003: The Chinese government allowed increasing numbers of international adoptions beginning in the early

1990s, mostly to adoptive parents in the United States and Canada. U.S. adoptions have increased from around 30 in 1990 to 3,597 in 1997 and 5,053 in 2002. Adoptions to other countries have also increased; U.S. consular officials estimated that in 1997 there were nearly 7,000 foreign adoptions from China. See Jeannette Chu, "How Many Orphanages Are There in China?" *China Connection* 4, no. 1 (Spring 1998): 5. According to *China Civil Affairs Statistical Yearbook, 2002,* there were 8,635 foreign adoptions in 2001 (*Zhongguo minzheng tongji nianjian, 2002* [Beijing: China Statistics Press, 2002]).

6. Nancy Riley, "American Adoptions of Chinese Girls: The Socio-Political Matrices of Individual Decisions," *Women's Studies International Forum* 20, no. 1 (1997): 90; Anne Thurston, "In a Chinese Orphanage," *Atlantic Monthly* 277, no. 4 (April 1996): 28–33. Also see Human Rights Watch, *Death by Default,* 110.

7. Sten Johansson, Zhao Xuan, and Ola Nygren, "On Intriguing Sex Ratios Among Live Births in China in the 1980s," *Journal of Official Statistics* 7, no. 1 (1991); Sten Johansson and Ola Nygren, "The Missing Girls of China: A New Demographic Account," *Population and Development Review* 17, no. 1 (March 1991): 35–51. A further analysis of the above data is in Sten Johansson, "Adoption in Contemporary China," in *Renkou yanjiu* (Population research) 19, no. 6 (Nov. 1995): 20–31.

8. Zeng Yi et al., "Causes and Implications in the Recent Increase in the Reported Sex Ratio at Birth in China," *Population and Development Review* 19, no. 2 (June 1993): 283–302.

9. See, for example, Liu Mingli, "Baba, Mama, bie diu diao wo . . ." (Papa, Mama, don't throw me away . . .), *Shehui gongzuo* (Social work) 1 (1993): 39. An editorial in *Renmin ribao* (People's daily) stated that China had 100,000 "orphans" (10 May 1995, p. 3).

10. Lu Hui, "Children Without Parents," *China Today* (Sept. 1994). Human Rights Watch also argues that there are many more abandoned children than those accounted for in state institutions (*Death by Default,* 107–10).

11. Bernice Lee, "Female Infanticide in China," in *Women in China,* edited by Richard Guisso and Stanley Johannesen (Youngstown, N.Y.: Philo Press, 1981), 163–77.

12. William Langer, "Infanticide: A Historical Survey," *History of Childhood Quarterly* 2 (1974): 129–34; also see Rose, *Massacre of the Innocents,* and David Kertzer, *Sacrificed for Honor: Italian Infant Abandonment and the Politics of Reproductive Control* (Boston: Beacon Press, 1993).

13. Lee, "Female Infanticide," 165–67; Hugh Baker, *Chinese Family and Kinship* (London: Macmillan, 1979), 6.

14. See Chap. 1 for a discussion of the Wuchang-Hankou-Hanyang area in Hubei. For a discussion of the development of foundling homes in Hunan, see *Hunan shengzhi* (Hunan provincial history), vol. 21: *Yiyao weisheng zhi* (Medicine and health history) (Changsha: Hunan renmin chuban she, 1988), 566–75. Also see Ho Ping-ti, *Studies on the Population of China, 1368–1953* (Cambridge: Harvard University Press, 1959), 60–61; You Chi, "Infant Protection Society," in *Chinese Civilization and Society,* edited by Patricia Ebrey (New York: Free Press, 1981), 219–23.

15. For demographic evidence of the decline in infanticide in these years, see Ansley Coale and Judith Banister, "Five Decades of Missing Females in China," *Demography* 31, no. 3 (Aug. 1994).

16. See Chap. 1, pp. 11–13.

17. For an excellent discussion of some of the ways policy implementation was tightened, see Greenhalgh, Zhu, and Li, "Restraining Population Growth."

18. See Chap. 2, pp. 43–44, and Chap. 3 in this volume. Although Greenhalgh and Li ("Engendering Reproductive Policy") do not find direct evidence of abandonment in their research in Shaanxi, they find a clear correlation between severely tightened birth planning after 1988, on the one hand, and increasingly skewed sex ratios and escalating numbers of missing girls, on the other. They find no satisfactory explanation for the rapid and drastic skewing.

19. For one such case and a discussion of why such cases are rarely prosecuted, see Jiang He, "Shei lai baohu Xiong Qi?" (Who will protect Xiong Qi?), *Zhongguo minzheng* (China's civil affairs), no. 295 (Oct. 1993): 36–39.

20. Everyone in China has an official *hukou* specifying place of residence and occupational category, primarily agricultural or nonagricultural. Until recently it was difficult to live outside the area of one's *hukou,* and if caught without permission, people would be sent back to their designated place. Today the system is not so rigid and is breaking down completely in places, but it still has important consequences. *Hukou* come in two main types: urban and rural. Generally, urban, which includes cities and towns, corresponds to nonagricultural employment status and rural to agricultural employment, but those who reside in towns may also have "agricultural" *hukou.* State employees have nonagricultural urban *hukou* regardless of where they live. An urban *hukou* is the most desirable because it gives one access to various subsidies that people with rural/agricultural *hukou* do not have, including, in the past, rationed subsidized grain. As I will discuss later in this chapter, current birth-planning policies place holders of urban *hukou* under the more rigid one-child policy, while holders of rural *hukou* in most places may have a second child if the first is a girl.

21. There are significant regional variations in the population of orphanages. Some orphanages in the north, such as those in Liaoning and Tianjin, reportedly have a high percentage of disabled children and more boys than orphanages elsewhere. In southern areas and central areas along the Yangzi, orphanage populations are predominantly female, with a larger proportion of healthy infants and young children. These areas appear to have been hardest hit by increasing abandonment in recent years, although other areas have not been spared.

22. Tyrene White, "Birth Planning Between Plan and Market: The Impact of Reform on China's One-Child Policy," in *China's Economic Dilemmas in the 1990s: The Problems of Reforms, Modernization, and Interdependence,* Study Papers, Joint Economic Committee, Congress

of the United States (Washington, D.C.: U.S. Government Printing Office, 1991), 1: 267.

23. Many people who live in towns in rural Anhui and many other provinces nonetheless have agricultural *hukou* and therefore also fall under the one-son/two-child policy.

24. Clear documentation of this pattern of escalating pressure and the risks for women comes from Greenhalgh, Zhu, and Li, "Restraining Population Growth." See also Susan Greenhalgh, "Controlling Births and Bodies in Village China," *American Ethnologist* 21, no. 1 (1994): 28.

25. Hunan Province Civil Affairs Bureau, Social Welfare Section, "Guanyu dangqian shehui qiying wentide diaocha" (Investigation concerning the current social problem of foundlings), *Zhongguo minzheng* (China's civil affairs), no. 274 (Jan. 1992): 34–35.

26. Li Xiaorong, "License to Coerce: Violence Against Women, State Responsibility, and Legal Failures in China's Family-Planning Program, *Yale Journal of Law and Feminism* 8, no. 1 (1996): 145–91; Hunan Province Civil Affairs Bureau, "Guanyu dangqian shehui qiying wentide diaocha," 34–35; Human Rights in China, *Caught Between Tradition and the State: Violations of the Human Rights of Chinese Women* (New York: Human Rights Watch, 1995).

27. For a discussion of how local cadres buffer themselves against the most contentious or unpopular features of birth planning, see Zhang Weiguo, "Implementation of State Family Planning Programs in a Northern Chinese Village," *China Quarterly*, no. 157 (1999): 202–30.

28. The age limit is an effort to ensure that the adoptive mother is unlikely to give birth at a later date. It assumes that by age thirty-five a childless couple have experienced a period of infertility. In the case of single parents, it assumes that any future marriage would take place too late to produce children.

29. Foundlings are presumed to have living parents who are legally responsible for raising them but have chosen to abandon them.

30. *Zhongguo minzheng tongji nianjian, 1992* (China civil affairs statistical yearbook, 1992) (Beijing: China Statistics Press, 1992).

31. Interviews, June 1996.

32. Liang Chao, "Law Helps Orphans Find Homes," *China Daily,* 20 June 1996.

33. Over half of these adoptions are by close relatives and step-parents. International adoptions to the U.S. grew from about 10,000 to 15,000 per year during the 1990s. U.S. adoption statistics can be found on the website of the National Adoption Clearinghouse (calib.com/naic).

34. Johansson and Nygren, "Missing Girls of China"; Tu Ping, "Wo guo chusheng ying'er xingbiebi wenti tansuo" (An exploration of the sex ration at birth in China today), *Renkou yanjiu* (Population research), no. 1 (1993): 6–13.

35. The government of India, with a high-priority (and, some would argue, a moderately coercive) population control program, has fostered various regulations and laws encouraging the domestic adoption of foundlings, most of whom are girls, as in China. The government of South Korea, long a major source of international adoptions, has tried to promote domestic adoptions to reduce international adoptions. China stands alone in turning to international adoptions instead of, or indeed as a means of avoiding, promoting more domestic adoptions.

36. The classic anthropological study of adoption in Chinese society is Arthur Wolf and Chieh-shan Huang, *Marriage and Adoption in China, 1845–1945* (Stanford: Stanford University Press, 1980). Another major study of adoption is by the historian Ann Waltner, *Getting an Heir: Adoption and the Construction of Kinship in Late Imperial China* (Honolulu: University of Hawaii Press, 1990). Also see James McGough, *Marriage and Adoption in Chinese Society, with Special Reference to Customary Law,* Ph.D. diss., Michigan State University, 1976 (Ann Arbor: UMI Dissertation Services, 1976).

37. Waltner, *Getting an Heir,* 144.

38. The folk story of the wasp is recounted in an essay by the twentieth-century writer Lu Xun (Lu Hsün), "Idle Thoughts at the End of Spring," *Selected Works of Lu Hsün* (Beijing: Foreign

Languages Press, 1957), 2: 124–25. Wolf and Huang report that the term *mingling zi* is also used in Taiwan (*Marriage and Adoption in China,* 110).

39. James Watson, "Agnates and Outsiders: Adoption in a Chinese Lineage," *Man* 10, no. 2 (June 1975): 298–99; Wolf and Huang, *Marriage and Adoption in China,* 209–11.

40. See Wolf and Huang, *Marriage and Adoption in China.*

41. Waltner, *Getting an Heir,* 122.

42. See Wolf and Huang, *Marriage and Adoption in China,* 82–93, 112–13. Here the term for *tongyangxi* is *sim-pua* in the local dialect.

43. Ibid., 131.

44. Greenhalgh and Li, "Engendering Reproductive Policy."

45. Johansson and Nygren, "Missing Girls of China."

46. Marjory Wolf, *Women and the Family in Rural Taiwan,* chap. 2.

47. Wolf and Huang, *Marriage and Adoption in China,* 238.

48. AUTHOR'S NOTE, 2003: Indeed, as a recent village study suggests, married daughters are more economically valuable to their parents than in the past because after marriage daughters are more mobile and have more control over their earnings and household financial decisions than before. Thus in addition to the emotional value of daughters to parents, married daughters may even help their own parents financially, not just their in-laws. See Zhang Weiguo, "Institutional Reforms, Population Policy, and Adoption of Children: Some Observations in a North China Village," *Journal of Comparative Family Studies* 32, no. 2 (Spring 2001): 308–18.

49. Riley, "American Adoptions of Chinese Girls," 90; interviews with civil affairs officials in Beijing, June 1996.

50. Many studies and opinion surveys since the 1980s show that the ideal family in contemporary China has two children: one boy and one girl. See, for example, Martin King Whyte and S. Z. Gu, "Popular Response to China's Fertility Transition," *Population and Development Review* 13, no. 3 (Sept. 1987): 471–93. Susan

Greenhalgh found a growing desire for daughters in the villages she studied in the 1980s and 1990s, even as problems such as abandonment increased as a result of birth-planning policies. See Susan Greenhalgh, "Fresh Winds in Beijing: Chinese Feminists Speak Out on the One-Child Policy and Women's Lives," *Signs* 26, no. 3 (2001). In our own survey on family ideals and attitudes toward adoption, over 70 percent of the 399 respondents said a family with two children, one boy and one girl, was ideal.

51. A traditional saying we heard in interviews (*Yangmu da ru tian*, or "the adoptive mother is greater than heaven") also stressed the greater importance, indeed the valor, of the adoptive parents who raise the child.

52. Childless couples who waited until age thirty-five to adopt tended to be better educated and were usually professionals. Several of the seven single women adopters, all of whom met or exceeded the minimum age requirement of thirty-five, were also better educated, including a university teacher, a rural middle school teacher, and a cadre. Twenty-two of the twenty-five single men adopters were over age thirty-five; most were rural bachelors who were quite poor, fitting a traditional pattern whereby poor men are sometimes unable to marry. The adoption law allows these men, as well as single women, to adopt children.

53. The average income for a rural worker in 2000 was about 3,400 yuan per year, according to *Zhongguo minzheng tongji nianjian, 2000* (China civil affairs statistical yearbook, 2000) (Beijing: China Statistics Press, 2000).

54. "Harbin Woman Challenges China's Adoption Law," UPI, Beijing, 6 April 1996, based on an article by the same name in *Zhongguo funü bao* (China women's news), 5 April 1996.

55. Various circumstances might lead to registration at a later time, including getting caught after several years and deciding to pay the fine. We talked to a number of parents who registered previously hidden overquota birthchildren and adopted children in 1994 because there was a major land redistribution at that time.

Some people calculated that it was worth paying the fine and obtaining legal registration so that the adopted child could get a land allotment, while others decided against it or were excluded by local practice. Many parents also chose to register a child and pay the resulting fine when the child reached primary or middle school age, when some rural and all urban schools require registration. Government encouragement and promises of partial amnesty just prior to the 2000 census induced many to register previously unregistered adoptions.

56. For an extended discussion of the legal and political discrimination fostered by population control policies, see Human Rights in China, *Caught Between Tradition and the State,* and Li Xiaorong, "License to Coerce."

57. Human Rights in China, *Caught Between Tradition and the State,* and Li Xiaorong, "License to Coerce."

58. That no families we interviewed had been forced to relinquish an adopted child may be partly an artifact of the bias of our research methods. We looked for adoptive families, not for failed efforts to adopt.

59. *Xiandai jiating bao* (Modern family magazine) (Nanjing), 10 May 1995, p. 1; "Harbin Woman Challenges China's Adoption Law."

60. Hunan Province Civil Affairs, "Guanyu dangqian shehui qiying wentide diaocha."

61. See Chap. 7, p. 204.

62. Lu, "Children Without Parents."

63. Human Rights Watch, *Death by Default,* 110.

64. Wang Zhengfeng, "Baoge nühai yangqilai" (Adopting and raising girls), *Shanghai minzheng* (Shanghai civil affairs), April 1995, p. 48.

65. The number of actual "missing girls" has also accelerated in recent years as prenatal sex selection has increased through the widespread availability of ultrasound B machines throughout the countryside. The 2000 census found a sex ratio of nearly 117, up 6 points from the 1990 census. Some of this increase is assumed to be caused by prenatal sex selection. See Chu Junhong, "Prenatal Sex

Determination and Sex Selective Abortion in Rural China," *Population and Development Review* 27, no. 2 (June 2001): 259–81.

66. For discussions of this debate, see Amartya Sen, "Population: Delusion and Reality," *New York Review,* 22 Sept. 1994; Roy Prosterman, Tim Hanstad, and Li Ping, "Can China Feed Itself?" *Scientific American,* Nov. 1996; D. Gale Johnson, "Effects of Institutions and Policies on Rural Population Growth with Application to China," *Population and Development Review* 20, no. 3 (Sept. 1994).

67. Interviews, May 1998. See Liz Sly, "China's Voluntary One-Child Policy Birthing New Revolution," *Chicago Tribune,* 24 May 1998, sec. 1, p. 1.

68. Author's interviews, June 2000. The importance of the 2000 census in explaining the current "cycle of tightening" was pointed out to me by Tyrene White, who is currently finalizing a manuscript on birth planning in China that highlights these cycles.

69. According to our findings, however, most rural childless couples turn to adoption before age thirty. And according to implementation regulations, adopters must certify that they have not violated birth-planning regulations—in other words, that they do not have "illegal" or "out-of-plan" children.

70. Daniel Kwan, "Dispute Flares on Adoption Changes," *South China Morning Post,* 28 Oct. 1998.

71. Although US$3,000 is reasonable by international standards and reasonably affordable for international adopters, it is an outrageously high fee for domestic adoption, amounting to 25,000 yuan—far beyond the means of the average Chinese. Individual orphanages can charge differently for domestic adoption because those fees are set locally.

72. Interviews, June 2000.

5. International and Domestic Adoption, 2001

An earlier version of this chapter appeared as "The Politics of International and Domestic Adoption in China," *Law and Society Review* 36, no. 2 (2002): 701–17.

1. See Barbara Yngvesson, "Un Niño de Cualquier Color: Race and Nation in Intercountry Adoption," in *Globalizing Institutions: Case Studies in Regulation and Innovation,* edited by J. Jensen and B. de Sousa Santos (Aldershot: Ashgate, 2000), 169–204; Claudia Fonseca, "The Circulation of Children in a Brazilian Working-Class Neighborhood: A Local Practice in a Global World," paper presented at the Conference on International Adoption, Hampshire College, 11–13 May 2001.

2. Vivian Chiu, "From China with Love," *South China Morning Post,* 15 Aug. 1999, agenda section, p. 1.

3. Kevin Platt, "Children of the Quake Thrive in China's Improved Orphanage Conditions," *Christian Science Monitor,* 29 Feb. 2000.

4. Kay Johnson, Huang Banghan, and Wang Liyao, "Infant Abandonment and Adoption in China," *Population and Development Review* 24, no. 3 (Sept. 1998): 469–510. A revised version of the article appears as Chap. 4 of this book.

5. Sten Johansson and Ola Nygren, "The Missing Girls of China: A New Demographic Account," *Population and Development Review* 17, no. 1 (March 1991): 35–51.

6. Ibid.; Susan Greenhalgh and Jiali Li, "Engendering Reproductive Policy and Practice in Peasant China: For a Feminist Demography of Reproduction," *Signs* 20, no. 3 (Spring 1995): 601–41.

7. Ann Waltner, *Getting an Heir: Adoption and the Construction of Kinship in Late Imperial China* (Honolulu: University of Hawaii Press, 1990), 144. Arthur Wolf and Chieh-shan Huang found the same term used in Taiwan; see their *Marriage and Adoption in China, 1845–1945* (Stanford: Stanford University Press, 1980), 110. The well-known twentieth-century writer Lu Xun recounts the folk story

of the wasp in his essay "Idle Thoughts at the End of Spring," *Selected Works of Lu Hsün* (Beijing: Foreign Languages Press, 1957), 2: 124–25.

8. The organizational and economic reforms of the post-Mao era have also made it possible for more daughters to remain close to and contribute to their parents after marriage. See Zhang Weiguo "Institutional Reforms, Population Policy, and Adoption of Children: Some Observations in a North China Village," *Journal of Comparative Family Studies* 32, no. 2 (Spring 2001): 303–18.

9. Adoptions to the United States, which comprised about 75–80 percent of international adoptions from China in the 1990s, grew from 61 in 1991 to 5,053 in 2000, according to U.S. State Department statistics based on visas issued to adopted "orphans." According to official Chinese statistics, foreigners adopted 6,678 orphanage children in 2000. But in 2001, the total number of foreign adoptions from orphanages increased to 8,638, while U.S. adoptions fell slightly to 4,681, about 55 percent of the total. See *Zhongguo minzheng tongji nianjian, 2001* (China civil affairs statistical yearbook, 2001) (Beijing: China Statistics Press, 2001); and *Zhongguo minzheng tongji nianjian, 2002* (China civil affairs statistical yearbook, 2002) (Beijing: China Statistics Press, 2002).

10. Interviews with local officials involved with adoption, 1991–2000.

11. The total number of adoptions in China is unknown, but it exceeds the number of registered adoptions by a great deal. The demographer Sten Johannson estimated that there were 562,000 unregistered "informal" adoptions per year in 1987 and that the number was growing (Johannson and Nygren, "Missing Girls of China," 44). Johannson estimated that there were a total of approximately six million children adopted from 1970 to 1987, far more than those officially registered ("Adoption in Contemporary China," in *Renkou yanjiu* [Population research] 19, no. 6 [Nov. 1995]: 19).

12. See Chap. 7, n. 7.

13. The term "one-child policy" is misleading. While the regulations in urban areas allow only one child per family, most rural areas have a slightly more lenient policy. Since the late 1980s, rural people have generally been permitted to have two children if the first is a girl; the policy in some areas allows two births, spaced four or five years apart, regardless of gender. "One-child policy," then, is shorthand for these more varied but still highly restrictive policies, and the government continues to refer to the whole range of birth-planning regulations by this term.

14. AUTHOR'S NOTE, 2003: Susan Greenhalgh suggested to me the possible significance of the timing of this legislation in making the law so restrictive and entrenching birth-planning policy so deeply within it.

15. In any given orphanage in China, usually 20 to 60 percent of the children are "disabled" (see Chap. 1). While some disabilities are minor, cosmetic, or correctable (such as prominent birthmarks or scars, cleft lip, and club feet), many are severe and incapacitating (such as congenital brain damage). Severely disabled children are not considered "adoptable," and most would not find adoptive homes regardless of the adoption policies set by the government.

16. See Daniel Kwan, "Dispute Flares on Adoption Changes," *South China Morning Post,* 28 Oct. 1998.

17. The China Center for Adoption Affairs' English translations of the 1991 adoption law (effective April 1992) and the revisions passed in November 1998 (effective April 1999) can be found on the website of Families with Children from China (fwcc.org/ccaalaws.htm). Mistranslations of the revisions have appeared in some other sources.

18. This discussion of the implementation of the 1999 adoption law draws on observations and interviews conducted in China after June 1999.

19. "The After Effects of an Unclear Certificate," *Hefei wanbao* (Hefei evening news), 8 Aug. 2000, p. 3; and author's interviews.

20. Because local civil affairs departments have the authority to set local fees for domestic adoption, it has been difficult for Beijing to

regulate those fees. International adoption fees are set by central authorities in Beijing.

21. *Zhongguo minzheng tongji nianjian, 2000* (China civil affairs statistical yearbook, 2000) (Beijing: China Statistics Press, 2000). *Zhongguo minzheng tongji nianjian, 2001;* John Gittings, "Lost and Found," *Guardian* (UK), 7 Aug. 2001.

22. *Zhongguo minzheng tongji nianjian, 1992* (China civil affairs statistical yearbook, 1992) (Beijing: China Statistics Press, 1992).

23. According to interviews conducted in 2001, regulations in some areas permit those who find abandoned children to legally adopt them as long as they report immediately to the police and then register with local civil affairs. In the past it was often difficult to adopt and register such children legally, especially if the adoptive parents already had children, so many parents did not report foundlings to officials.

24. Susan Greenhalgh, "Planned Births, Unplanned Persons: 'Population' in the Making of Chinese Modernity," *American Ethnologist* 30, no. 2 (May 2003): 1–20.

25. For an example of a UK charity working with the Chinese government on foster care, see Audrey Gillan, "Lost Babies, Found Babies," *Guardian* (UK), 12 Oct. 2002.

6. Chinese Adoptive Parents, 2002

1. The first half of this research was reported and analyzed in Kay Johnson, Huang Banghan, and Wang Liyao, "Infant Abandonment and Adoption in China," *Population and Development Review* 24, no. 3 (Sept. 1998): 469–510 (reprinted with some modifications as Chap. 4 of this book). The patterns found in the 397 adoptive families analyzed in that 1998 article are similar to those found in the entire sample of 771 adoptive families completed in 2000. Since 2000 I have continued studying Chinese adoptive families through interviews and other documentary research. The information and stories recounted in this article come from the large body of research that I have done since the early 1990s as well as the survey data gathered

from 1995–2000. In some of the cases discussed here, names and minor details have been changed to protect people's privacy.

2. Relatively few adoptions involved orphanage children partly because of legal restrictions that severely limited those qualified to adopt through official channels. These restrictions are discussed in earlier chapters and later in this chapter.

3. See Susan Greenhalgh and Jiali Li, "Engendering Reproductive Policy and Practice in Peasant China: For a Feminist Demography of Reproduction," *Signs* 20, no. 3 (Spring 1995): 601–41; Johnson, Huang, and Wang, "Infant Abandonment and Adoption."

4. Zhang Weiguo, "Child Adoption in Contemporary Rural China," MS, 2002, generously shared with me by the author. Zhang found similar patterns of adoption in a smaller published study of a Hebei village. See Zhang Weiguo, "Institutional Reforms, Population Policy, and Adoption of Children: Some Observations in a North China Village," *Journal of Comparative Family Studies* 32, no. 2 (Spring 2001): 303–18.

5. See Kay Johnson, "Chinese Orphanages: Saving China's Abandoned Girls," *Australian Journal of Chinese Affairs,* no. 30 (July 1993): 61–87, and Kay Johnson, "The Politics of the Revival of Infant Abandonment, with Special Reference to Hunan," *Population and Development Review* (March 1996): 77–98 (reprinted, with some modifications and updates, as Chaps. 1 and 3 of this volume).

6. Susan Greenhalgh, "Controlling Births and Bodies in Village China," *American Ethnologist* 21, no. 1 (1994): 3–30. For a discussion of the full range of strategies of resistance, see Tyrene White, "Domination, Resistance, and Accommodation in China's One-Child Campaign," in *Chinese Society: Change, Conflict, and Resistance,* edited by Elizabeth Perry and Mark Selden (London: Routledge, 2000), 102–19.

7. See Johnson, Huang, and Wang, "Infant Abandonment and Adoption."

8. See Susan Greenhalgh, "The Peasantization of the One-Child Policy in Shaanxi," in *Chinese Families in the Post-Mao Era,* edited by

Deborah Davis and Stevan Harrell (Berkeley: University of California Press, 1993), 219–50; and Tyrene White, "Birth Planning Between Plan and Market: The Impact of Reform on China's One-Child Policy," in *China's Economic Dilemmas in the 1990s: The Problems of Reforms, Modernization, and Interdependence,* Study Papers, Joint Economic Committee, Congress of the United States (Washington, D.C.: U.S. Government Printing Office, 1991), 1: 252–69.

9. The China Center for Adoption Affairs' English translations of the 1991 adoption law (effective April 1992) and the revisions passed in November 1998 (effective April 1999) can be found on the website of Families with Children from China (fwcc.org/ccaalaws.htm).

10. See, e.g., Laura Cecere, *The Children Can't Wait: China's Emerging Model of Intercountry Adoption* (self-published, 1999), 13, 213.

11. A twenty-five-year-old Beijing parent, discussed later in this chapter, who adopted an abandoned child with a cleft lip was not allowed to legalize the adoption on the basis of "special needs." Indeed, the adoptive mother seemed unaware that a cleft lip or palate might be considered a "disability," since it was a correctable problem. Yet during the same period when this Beijing parent was repeatedly denied registration for her adopted child, many foreign adopters who were underage or who had other children were allowed to adopt orphanage children with cleft lip or palate as "special needs" exemptions. Although the same law governed domestic and international adoption, it was implemented far more strictly for domestic adopters because the provisions of the adoption law were aimed above all at population control priorities in China.

12. I would like to thank Tyrene White for pointing out this pattern to me as I tried to understand why birth-planning implementation became so much tighter in rural Anhui in the late 1990s, despite pronouncements from Beijing that the policies were being implemented in a more reasonable, less coercive manner. Professor White said that she had found similar tightening leading up to the 1990 census as local cadres tried to improve their birth-planning record.

Caregivers at an orphanage in Hunan and another in Anhui cited the combined effects of census workers and population-planning enforcement campaigns to explain why the infant populations in their welfare centers increased dramatically between 1999 and 2000 (Amy Klatzkin, personal communication; and author's interviews).

13. See n. 11 in this chapter.

14. This account is pieced together from numerous articles and interviews published in China about Chang Lixin's story and her efforts to organize Sunflower. One account—"Sunflower's Embrace of Love," by He Ping—appeared in the international edition of *People's Daily,* 17 Jan. 1997. For an English translation, see He Ping, "China's Sunflower Children: In China, Parents Who Have Adopted Orphans Organize to Give Their Children a Better Life," trans. Shixian Sheng, in *A Passage to the Heart: Writings from Families with Children from China,* edited by Amy Klatzkin (St. Paul: Yeong & Yeong, 1999), 216–17.

15. The child was a twelve-year-old truant *hei haizi,* emotionally buffeted by abandonment, adoption, the death of her adoptive mother, and the birth of a brother, all the while lacking a legal status of her own. Ching-ching Ni, "Two Families but No Place to Call Home," *Los Angeles Times,* 29 March 2000.

16. Daniel Kwan, "Dispute Flares on Adoption Changes," *South China Morning Post,* 28 Oct. 1998.

17. *New Anhui Evening News,* 21 May 1999.

18. John Gittings, "Lost and Found," *Guardian* (UK), 7 Aug. 2001; Kay Johnson, "The Politics of International and Domestic Adoption in China," *Law and Society Review* 36, no. 2 (2000): 701–17 (reprinted with some modifications as Chap. 5 of this volume).

19. Another Anhui newspaper covered a local story about the problems involved in trying to legalize a foundling adoption after the fact ("The After Effects of an Unclear Certificate," *Hefei wanbao* [Hefei evening news], 8 Aug. 2000).

20. For a general discussion of "unplanned persons," see Susan Greenhalgh, "Planned Births, Unplanned Persons: 'Population' in

the Making of Chinese Modernity," *American Ethnologist* 30, no. 2 (May 2003): 1–20.

7. Chinese Orphanages Today, 2003

1. Human Rights Watch, *Death by Default: A Policy of Fatal Neglect in China's State Orphanages* (New York: Human Rights Watch, 1996), 112.

2. For an excellent discussion of social welfare organizations and their marginalized status in post-1949 China, see Linda Wong, *Marginalization and Social Welfare in China* (New York: Routledge, 1998). A brief but cogent discussion of how these problems affected the care of institutionalized children in this era can be found in Xiaoyuan Shang, "Looking for a Better Way to Care for Children: Cooperation Between the State and Civil Society," *Social Service Review* 76, no. 2 (June 2002): 203–28, esp. 205–6.

3. Shang, "Looking for a Better Way."

4. As the Chinese economy grew under the economic reforms of the 1980s and 1990s, the percentage of gross domestic product (GDP) controlled by the central government actually declined dramatically because of decentralization and the growth of nonstate sectors of the economy. At the same time that the state ceded much of its central control over the economy, it also reduced its responsibility for funding local social institutions.

5. Domestic adoption fees, unlike international fees, vary from place to place and sometimes by income of the adopter, but generally are equivalent to a few hundred dollars or less—a small fraction of the international fees. Therefore domestic adoption does not provide much funding for the orphanages.

6. Beijing has granted the provinces a degree of autonomy in allocating the money that comes in from international adoptions, although regulations state it must be spent on orphanage care. In Anhui province, for example, a number of county-level orphanages have benefited from the wide distribution of international adoptions and funds.

By contrast, in Hunan in 2003, where international adoptions take place in twenty-four out of eighty-five orphanages in the provincial social welfare system, a civil affairs official stated that 5 percent of international adoption fees are redistributed—a tiny amount relative to provincial orphanages' overall expenses. Visits to several rural orphanages in Hubei province as early as 1998 revealed substantial investments in new buildings and equipment even in some social welfare institutions that did not do international adoptions. Yet throughout China there is no question that the orphanages that do international adoptions benefit most from the practice and have a stake in its continuance, often allocating resources within the institution in favor of those children most likely to be adopted internationally.

7. In 2001, China's total export earnings amounted to US$133 billion, according to *China Statistical Yearbook, 2002* (*Zhongguo tongji nianjian, 2002*) (China Statistics Press, 2002). International adoption fees thus account for less than two ten-thousandths of annual export earnings.

8. Shang, "Looking for a Better Way."

9. See Chap. 4 of this volume for a discussion of the restrictions in the 1992 adoption law.

10. In 2001 the New York and New England chapters of Families with Children from China established a joint fundraising effort for their respective orphanage assistance projects, Amity and FCO. More than thirty chapters nationwide participated in the combined FCC National Appeal of 2002.

11. The mix of NGOs funding a particular orphanage varies greatly. For example, the Changsha First Social Welfare Institute receives funding from the FCC National Appeal (both Amity and FCO) for school fees, equipment, surgeries, and baby-floor renovations; an Irish foundation has renovated a building for disabled children; and International China Concern runs well-equipped living and rehabilitation facilities, including special-education classrooms, for one hundred disabled babies and children at the orphanage.

12. *China Civil Affairs Statistical Yearbook, 2002.* Child welfare institutes (*ertong fuliyuan*) are able to focus all their resources on children, whereas regular social welfare institutes (*shehui fuliyuan*) also care for disabled adults and/or elderly people.

13. See Chaps. 5 and 6 of this volume.

14. See Chap. 6 of this volume.

15. For an excellent discussion of these trends and their significance, see Edwin Winckler, "Chinese Reproductive Policy at the Turn of the Millennium," *Population and Development Review* 28, no. 3 (Sept. 2002): 379–418.

16. *China Civil Affairs Statistical Yearbook, 2001* and *2002.* Of course this increase may or may not indicate an overall increase in abandonment because most abandoned children never enter government hands.

17. Xiaoyuan Shang, "Moving Toward a Multi-level and Multi-pillar System: Institutional Care in Two Chinese Cities," *Journal of Social Policy* 30, no. 2 (2001): 259–81.

18. See, e.g., Chu Junhong, "Prenatal Sex Determination and Sex-Selective Abortion in Rural Central China," *Population and Development Review* 27, no. 2 (June 2001): 259–81.

19. The well-known economist Amartya Sen, among others, has long argued that rapid fertility decline can occur without coercion even in relatively poor developing economies when female employment and literacy are high and infant mortality rates low. This was the experience of the above-mentioned states in India in the 1990s. See Amartya Sen, "Challenge of the Twenty-first Century: The Completion of Democracy," *The Hindu,* 26 Dec. 1999. For a recent analysis of the rapid decline of fertility in most of the "developing countries" of the world during the second half of the twentieth century (with the oft-noted exception of areas of sub-Saharan Africa), see Chris Wilson, "On the Scale of Global Demographic Convergences, 1950–2000," *Population and Development Review* 27, no. 1 (March 2001): 155–71.

Index

abandoned children. *See* abandonment; female infant abandonment; foundlings; orphanage children

abandoning families. *See* birthparents

abandonment, 218n31; as adoption plan, 89–91, 109–10, 155–57; of disabled children, 2, 17–18, 27, 46, 83, 85, 87, 207–8, 219n42; double, 124, 167, 168, 174–75; as infanticide, 8, 38, 43–44, 185; of older children, 14, 31, 39; "organized," 60, 63; other reasons for, xxi, 1, 81, 86, 104–5; regional differences in, 10–11, 36, 50, 52–53, 76, 81, 84, 226n12, 227n14, 239n21; of sick children, 21, 31–32, 44, 71, 103; sites of, 18–19, 21, 31, 38, 44, 46, 90; of sons, 21, 87; statistics on, 49–50, 52, 54, 79, 125–26, 207, 234n58, 255n16; "traveling," 60, 89–90, 157; by unwed parents, xv–xvi, 82, 85,

87, 104, 205–6; in Western countries, 4–5, 157. *See also* birthparents; birth-planning policies, and abandonment; female infant abandonment; fines and punishments

abortion: as birth control, 56, 87–88, 215n9; sex-selective, xvii, 57, 206, 209, 216n14, 224n1, 244n65

adopted children: denial of rights to, 118–24, 131, 168–71, 173–77, 180–82, 252n15; returned to birthparents, 117, 118; seized by state, 124, 166–67, 169, 170, 175, 231n35; status of, 102, 113–18, 141–42, 160–62, 174, 177, 243n51. *See also* domestic adoptions; international adoptions; overquota adoptions

adoption. *See* adopted children; Adoption Law of the People's Republic of China, first and

Respect to Intercountry
Adoption (Hague Convention),
135–36, 149, 152–54, 182
Convention on the Rights of the
Child, UN, 135–36, 153–54, 182

daughters: changing role of, 24, 47,
106–7, 127, 141, 242n48,
247n8; conventional wisdom on,
xvii, 185; desire for, xviii,
xxi–xxii, 5, 22, 23–24, 47, 58, 65,
89, 107, 116, 126–29, 141, 160,
185, 229–30n29, 242–43n50;
first-born, xxii, 16, 88–89, 209;
foster, 151–52; to "lead in" sons,
7, 24, 100, 117; in patrilineal
family, 3–4, 7, 11, 36, 53, 84,
99, 116, 215n6; second and
higher-parity, 16, 18, 58, 84–88,
109, 141, 156, 206, 209; as victims of government policies, xxii,
35, 221n56. See also daughters-
in-law; domestic adoptions;
female infant abandonment; hidden children; international adoptions; "missing girls"; tongyangxi
daughters-in-law, 4, 36, 102. See
also tongyangxi
Death by Default. See Human
Rights Watch report
Deng Xiaoping, xix
disabilities, range of, 17, 28, 45,
228n22, 248n15. See also disabled children
disabled children, 208; abandonment of, 46, 83, 85, 87; adoption
of, 21, 26–30, 45, 47, 69, 77, 95,
103, 118–19, 165, 176, 196,
203, 207–8, 219n42, 228n21,
232n48, 239n21, 248n15,

251n11; boys among, 21, 87,
103; in foster care, 192, 196; in
orphanages, 2, 17–18, 19, 43, 52,
68, 77, 83, 128, 132, 144, 154,
194, 195; "unadoptable," 46,
128, 133, 154, 248n15. See also
disabilities, range of
domestic adoptions: to circumvent
birth planning, 54, 64, 110, 118,
139, 146, 162, 163; cost of, 133,
149, 159, 245n71, 248–49n20,
253n5; of daughters, xxii, 6, 7,
22, 23–24, 65, 79, 89, 97–101,
102–4, 106–10, 116, 126, 127,
134, 139–42, 160–62, 185; of
disabled children, 21, 26–28, 30,
45, 69, 77, 103, 118–19, 165,
176, 251n11; Hague Convention
on, 135–36, 149, 152–54, 182;
illegal/informal/unregistered,
xxii, 6–8, 54, 59, 64–65, 72,
78–79, 95–96, 101, 111–13,
118–25, 126–28, 130–31,
133–34, 139, 149–50, 152,
160–82, 185, 206, 222n62,
234n59, 247n11; international
adoptions favored over, 125,
133, 142–47, 152–54, 164; of
kin, 97–98, 102–4, 108, 113,
118, 139, 165; to "lead in" sons,
7, 24, 100, 117; to make family
complete, 107–8, 117, 127–29,
140–42, 160, 168, 229–30n29,
242–43n50; myths about,
xvii–xviii, 107, 126, 137–39,
159–60, 185, 222n62; of nonkin,
xviii, 97–99, 102–4, 108–13,
114, 124, 139–42, 158–59, 185;
obstacles to, xix, 28–29, 39, 69,
77–78, 94, 123, 132, 145–49,